Outdoor Learning in the Early Years

Now in its third edition, *Outdoor Learning in the Early Years* is the complete guide to creating effective outdoor environments for young children's learning. Comprehensively revised and updated throughout, this book covers every aspect of working outdoors in the early years and fully explains the importance of outdoor play to children's development.

Key topics covered include:

- How to manage and set up the outdoor area
- What children gain from being outside
- How to allow children to take managed risks
- Making sense of work and play
- How outdoor provision helps children become self-regulatory
- Providing for both boys and girls in the outdoor environment
- Research supporting the outdoor approach.

A book for practitioners at every level of their career, each chapter includes discussions and questions for continuing development that can easily be incorporated into INSET as well as training within further or higher education.

Outdoor Learning in the Early Years contains a multitude of ideas and activities for working outdoors in the early years and provides a framework within which professionals can analyse and develop their outdoor provision and environment. This book is essential reading for all EYFS and Key Stage 1 practitioners, and for trainee teachers, their tutors and mentors.

Helen Bilton is the Director of the PGCE Primary and Early Years Programme at the University of Reading where she lectures in Early Years Education.

D0217980

Outdoor Learning in the Early Years

Management and innovation

Third Edition

Helen Bilton

Routledge
Taylor & Francis Group

LONDON AND NEW YORK

First edition published 1998
by David Fulton Publishers
with the title *Outdoor Play in the Early Years*

Second edition published 2002
by David Fulton Publishers
with the title *Outdoor Play in the Early Years*

This edition published 2010
by Routledge
2 Park Square, Milton Park, Abingdon, Oxon, OX14 4RN

Simultaneously published in the USA and Canada
by Routledge
270 Madison Avenue, New York, NY 10016

Routledge is an imprint of the Taylor & Francis Group, an informa business

Typeset in Optima by Glyph International Ltd
Printed and bound in Great Britain by
TJ International Ltd, Padstow, Cornwall

British Library Cataloguing in Publication Data
A catalogue record for this book is available from the British Library

Library of Congress Cataloging-in-Publication Data
Bilton, Helen.
  Outdoor learning in the early years : management and innovation / Third Edition
Helen Bilton. – 3rd ed.
      p. cm.
  Includes bibliographical references and index.
  1. Outdoor education. 2. Outdoor recreation for children. 3. Education, Preschool. I. Title.
  LB1047.B498 2010
372.13'84–dc22   2009030356

ISBN10 : 0-415-56759-9 (hbk)
ISBN10 : 0-415-45477-8 (pbk)
ISBN10 : 0-203-86013-6 (ebk)

ISBN13 : 978-0-415-56759-6 (hbk)
ISBN13 : 978-0-415-45477-3 (pbk)
ISBN13 : 978-0-203-86013-7 (ebk)

Contents

List of figures

Acknowledgements

I would like to thank the following people for their assistance in too many ways to list: Kriss Turner, University of Reading; Georgina Lovett, University of Reading; Helen Porter, Furze Platt Infant School, Maidenhead; Emma Milligan, PGCE Primary Programme 2007–8; Mia Taylor, PGCE Primary Programme 2008–9; Frances Taylor, PGCE Primary Programme 2008–9; Sue Booth and the children at Caversham Park Primary School, Reading; Prue Walsh, Playconsulting, Queensland; Sue Humphries, Coombes School; Coombes School and the children; Chrissie Brooks, Hawthorns School, Woosehill; Community Playthings and the children; Ruth Moore, Early Years Strategy Manager; Carla Coward; Sue Coffey; Dave Bilton; Esther Bilton; Rachel Bilton; Josh Bilton.

Particular thanks have to go to Anna Ephgrave, the inspirational teacher at De Bohun Primary School and the staff and children of the school who provided me with so many wonderful images of outdoor learning and teaching in action.

Introduction

Children and outside

Children playing outside has been happening across the globe, for a very long time. In early years educational establishments, outside has been seen as the raison d'être and nursery schools and classes have always possessed this secure outdoor space. The outdoor area is a complete learning environment, which caters for all children's needs – cognitive, linguistic, emotional, social and physical. It should be available every day alongside the indoor class and throughout the year. Outdoors, children have space, freedom, fresh air and time to work at their current interests.

Anyone who has spent time observing young children will be aware of, in most cases, their lack of concern for the prevailing weather conditions. Rain or shine, young children want to play outside. Even with a poorly equipped outdoor area, which may have no resources, children will 'champ at the bit' to get outside: they seem naturally drawn to the area. Either young children are perverse, or in fact they instinctively know something: namely that the outdoors is a natural learning and teaching environment for young children and is one in which most children feel settled and capable. At training sessions I ask participants to share their own childhood outdoor play experiences, whether it be at the local park, in their own garden, street or fields, and Figure 0.1 is a list of the activities shared at the most recent training. What is significant about this list or any list that is generated by a group is that some are dangerous and some of the participants did get hurt but no one died. All the people involved love talking about their experiences and there is always a lot of laughter and fun discussing it. The activities mostly involved using whatever resources were available at the time, so if nothing was available then the children just used leaves, twigs and so on. The inventiveness of those involved is inspiring, some of the games are universal and they all involve so many aspects of development. Outdoor play in the early years does not need to be much more than this, but to get this type of environment in a 'controlled' place, rather than a completely free one, takes a good deal of role modelling and explaining on the part of the adults so children understand what is wanted and what is okay. Unless the adults make this very conscious effort, children assume outside play is simply that which happens at primary playtime, a lot of running around and survival of the fittest. And in itself this is interesting as many of the young children, if they have no older siblings, will not have ever seen a primary playground in action.

Digging
Den building
Lighting fires
Collecting catkins in yoghurt pots
Curby – throwing balls at the side of the curb
Making mud pies
Jacks
Burning holes in plastic shoes
Fighting
Making beer from water and washing-up liquid
Wheelbarrow rides
Building traps
Closing road and washing it
High jump
Sledging on an old car bumper
Planting up weeds in pots and selling them
Picking leaves for pretend food
Picking petals, soaking in water to make into perfume
Hopscotch
Jingle jangle
Threading petals
Saturating the ground to find worms
Skipping
Ball games
Climbing in trees and hanging ropes from them
Playing house and army games
Making villages and road systems in sand/mud
Recording bird songs
Sitting

Figure 0.1 Games and activities played by adults when children

Increased interest in outdoor play

There has been an increasing appreciation in the importance of outdoor play (DfEE 1996). Organisations such as *Learning Through Landscapes* have been given a higher profile, and the government has shown a greater interest in outdoor play through such documents as *Learning Outside the Classroom Manifesto* (DfES 2006) and *Play England* (Shackell *et al.* 2008). Although commendable, I strongly debate the level of understanding demonstrated through documents such as these. For example, the *Play England* document has only two images which actually show children playing with loose materials. In every other photograph children have to interact with what is on offer, with what adults have created for them, having no opportunity to change and adapt their environment. These examples are of poor practice! There are also a growing number of quangos who pontificate on subjects such as play; again I strongly question what they really know and understand when all the images are of fixed climbing apparatus. So there is a renewed interest in play and the outdoors but we have to be very wary that these opportunists know what they are talking about and watch they do not hijack these concepts for their own self-development.

The importance of the nursery outdoor area has now been formalised by the Early Years Foundation Stage guidance, introduced in September 2000 and reconfirmed in the *Early Years Foundation Stage Framework* (May 2008). The Framework firmly places outdoor provision and outdoor play at the heart of under-fives educational provision. Throughout the document there are references to outdoor play, including '[t]he rich and varied environment supports children's learning and development. It gives them the confidence to explore and learn in secure and safe yet challenging, indoor and outdoor spaces' (DfCSF 2008 Cards: 3.3) and 'Play underpins the delivery of all the EYFS. Children must have opportunities to play indoors and outdoors' (DfCSF 2008 Practice Guidance: 07). So it is not a case of if you fancy going outside; it is a must. This also means there should be no excuses as to why a quality outdoor area cannot be provided. I always say: 'compensate for the constraints and exploit the opportunities' or 'where there is a will there is a way'.

Types of outdoor provision

There are many examples of outdoor provision, but not all represent quality outdoor provision. So it is relevant to unpick what these types are to ensure we do actually offer quality. There seems to me to be six types of outdoor provision, only one of which constitutes real outdoor play and provision:

1   Primary playtime – this is when children go out into a playground area for a set period of time, either fifteen to twenty minutes or longer after lunch. Children have minimal supervision by unqualified adults, and often little to occupy them. This is rarely a place the staff concern themselves with and is not seen as a learning or teaching environment. However, in contrast children see it as a place for social and physical activity and where they can get away from adults – a time that may have more significance to them than any other time of the school day. This is an important place for children and where the very important social interplay occurs. But it is a space dominated by some groups and the needs of others are subservient. What happens at playtime can impact greatly on how things progress after break as poorly behaved children are 'dealt' with by teachers and issues of unresolved conflict spill into the lessons. Children can often get needlessly hurt, in an atmosphere of 'chaos, confusion, disorder, wildness' (descriptions from Year 6, 7 and 9 children). This is not what is hoped for in a quality outdoor environment.

2   The outdoor classroom – some use this to describe outdoor activity per se; however, I tend to use this term to describe an area outside which has been created to house a whole class of children or groups for adult-led activities such as stories, singing or a science lesson, or that children can use on their own. This could be a tree house, Wendy house, circle of logs, seating area with pergola and boundary, or playground markings.

3

It is something which has a clear boundary to it. This may be within a quality outdoor area but would not be the totality of it.

3 Using outdoor features – this describes the process of going out to discover, experiment and discuss the features unique to it, such as the weather, mini-beasts and plant life. The whole class, groups or individuals could use this provision and the session might be adult led and have specific outcomes or might be child led. This would be a feature of any good outdoor area, but just because a setting had a pond or garden area would not make it a candidate for the best early years outdoor area.

4 Recently, 'learning outside the classroom', a phrase coined by the government in their *Learning Outside the Classroom Manifesto* has been created. This defines 'learning outside the classroom' as: 'the use of places other than the classroom for teaching and learning' (DfES 2006: 1). So this is when an activity/lesson can be taken outside, not necessarily to use the outdoor features but simply to be outside, such as doing a piece of maths or reading a story. It could be where a visit is made to the school by outsiders or where children make a visit elsewhere. Although it is commendable that the government is now acknowledging outdoor learning as a significant part of a child's education, they miss the point if they think that is all outdoor provision is about. The early years outdoor environment is half of a whole, not an add-on as implied in this manifesto. So quality outdoor provision would incorporate this type of practice, but merely taking indoor equipment outside does not constitute quality outdoor provision.

5 In addition, there is poorly planned timetabled outdoor provision. This is where outdoor play is available at a set point in the day, it is announced, and where everyone is expected to go out. What then happens is bike fever. This is where particular bikes are sought after and kept at any costs. The space is ruled by the children on bikes and staff simply react to children's calls for a turn on a bike or complains about other children's behaviour. Staff see this as their break time, so do not plan for the space or for learning and at the end of the 20-minute slot throw lots of tricycles back into the shed, pleased they are not on outdoor duty until Thursday week.

6 'The outdoor teaching and learning environment' describes one half of the combined teaching and learning environment of in and out, which involves careful planning and assessment. The outdoor area hopefully has grass and tarmac, hideaways and open spaces, low and high ground, resources and activities. Children are able to control and modify this environment to help in their learning, and interested, well-informed adults work alongside them. There is no division between work and play or a hierarchical division between work inside and play outside. Both the outdoor classroom and using outdoor features will come into the work of this provision, but do not, on their own, make the totality of it. Primary playtime has nothing to do with quality Early Years Foundation Stage outdoor provision.

A description of what good outdoor provision might look like

When I wrote the first edition of this book I was advised that the title 'nursery garden' was unworkable. I think this is a shame because when you describe it as a garden you have an image of beauty, various smells, fresh air, relaxing or working in the vegetable plot. If I look out at a good outdoor area I see children involved in what they are doing, confident to pursue their interests, keen to make more of what they are doing, oblivious of the adults until they need one, inventive and exploratory. I would see complicated creations whether they be a road system created from material and pieces of wood, bits of Lego blocks, lollipop sticks or a house created under the canopy of a tree, with material and pegs and crates for the cooker and washing machine, canes for the walls. The activity would be sustained and the ideas would be never ending. There would be other children busy digging, watering, sweeping up, pruning, completely engrossed in the job at hand. Children would need the adult to be a play-mate, a helper or the instigator. Children and staff would talk to each other as equals about the current interest, from a discussion about where to plant the carrot seed, to whose turn it is to weed or how to attach the log to the pulley. And this would be whether talking with an 18-month-old or a 15-year-old. Figure 0.2 is an example of such a place.

This edition

This, the third edition of a book first published in 1998, retains much of the information from that publication albeit in different places. For example this edition still emphasises the centrality of organisation and management and that unless the outdoor space is organised correctly it will not be effective, but this is more integrated into the book than in the previous editions. There is a greater discussion about the terms 'teaching', 'learning' and 'play'. The book's title has changed to reflect the understanding that the outdoor environment is a learning and teaching space as the indoors is, with play being a part of the teaching approach. Each chapter contains photographs, case studies and discussion, questions and activities for follow up. The information is centred on children aged 2 to 6 years of age, in an educational setting but totally relevant to those working with younger and older children whether in a school setting, home or other setting. A 15-year-old may still want to play make-believe but a World War I soldier in the Trenches, not the milkman. Eighteen-month-olds can still climb on the equipment but with adult assistance and a very watchful eye. I have tried to synthesise the research so that it is manageable and useful.

The book is about what children need, not what government documentation tells us or how to achieve the best Early Years Foundation Stage (EYFS) profile. It starts with children and then discusses how to ensure those needs are met. The reading list has been added to and I have included older references where I feel the material is still relevant and all that is available. Some reading I have looked at in greater detail, for example Whitebread, Gallahue and Katz, as I consider the research of deep importance.

Figure 0.2 Quality outdoor play

Chapter summaries

The book is divided into four sections, the first setting the scene, the second putting the ideas into practice, the third looking at the variety of spaces and the fourth detailing contacts and references.

Chapter 1 looks at what children need and gain from being outside. We have to be convinced that it is worth making all this effort outside, why not just educate them inside? This then begs the question what do we mean by outside play? Definitions and agreements have to be made so there is a shared understanding of what constitutes outside play. Chapter 2 looks at the environment for teaching and learning and the significant terminology and meaning of various crucial concepts, such as time, space, play and work. Chapter 3 looks at the roots of nursery education to understand why early years education is as it is and why in particular it has outdoor experiences. It includes a discussion about childhood and the international perspective.

Chapter 4 looks at the ten guiding principles for outdoors which ensure the environment is organised and managed in such a way as to make it an effective space. Chapter 5 describes the learning bays or zones or experiences which could be included. Chapter 6 looks at children playing and working generally and outside, picking out some significant research. Key skills and attitudes are suggested. Chapter 7 focuses on the adult's role outside and discusses adult behaviour and the problems associated with poor behaviour.

Chapter 8 focuses on improving practice and some of the key issues to be addressed. It also includes a discussion about primary playtime and taking the curriculum outside in the primary school.

How to use this book

This book is designed to be dipped into. It is aimed at those working with any age of child in any setting, even the garden of the home for the Year 9 child. The principles and aims remain whatever the age and place, although the research is mostly, but not exclusively, from the early years and primary age children. It is more particularly aimed at those working with children aged 2 to 6 but lends itself easily to children aged 2 to 8.

The book is for those who are knowledgeable and for those who are novices. The inclusion of subheadings in the Contents enables the reader to be quite specific about what they wish to focus on. Each chapter has a discussion and questions which can easily be a part of INSET training or training within further or higher education. It is intended that this book is a framework within which professionals can analyse their practice and develop their outdoor provision. It is also intended to celebrate outdoor play and strengthen the arguments for providing this outdoor learning space.

Terminology

There is a plethora of terms used to describe the area: 'outdoors', 'the garden', 'outside', 'outdoor class', 'outdoor area', 'the playground', 'the yard'. The pioneers of nursery education referred to it as 'the garden' because it was seen as a child's garden, different from a suburban garden, park or the playground of the elementary school. Over time this changed to 'playground' as a result of the influence of elementary and primary education. I will mostly use the terms 'outdoor play area', 'outdoor space', 'outdoor area', 'outdoor environment' and sometimes 'garden'.

The Early Years Foundation Stage (EYFS) is simply a term used to describe the period from age 0 to when a child becomes five. The Early Years Foundation Stage guidance offers principles for early years education, what might be expected of children at different stages from nought to five, and what staff could do to put the principles into action. Throughout this book therefore, I will use the term 'Early Years Foundation Stage' to describe this period of time in a child's educational life. I will also use the term 'nursery' which has two meanings. One describes establishments run by the LA, offering education and care of children, mostly in purpose-built buildings, employing nursery teachers and nursery nurses. However, this term since 1997 has also been used to describe any establishment catering for under-fives, such as playgroups and settings run for profit. These are not 'true' nurseries as envisaged by the founders of nursery education (see Chapter 3 for a more detailed discussion).

For outdoor play to be effective and instrumental in children's learning it has to be organised in a particular way, and there are a number of guiding principles which need to be adhered to. The driving force has to be the will to want it to work, a belief in its value and an enjoyment of working outside. Without this the principles cannot work.

Discussion

I love outdoor play! But it has to be right. If I look into my mind's eye this is what I would experience:

What I would see – children active in their pursuits, playing alone, with others (children and adults) content in imaginative play, climbing, building, drawing, gardening, finding out. Not flitting but engrossed for long periods of time, whether 2 or 16 years of age. Lots of natural materials and absolutely no brightly coloured plastic.

What I would hear – squeals of delight, laughter (from the pit of your stomach laughter), sometimes no sounds except for traffic, aircraft, birds, sometimes shouting and talking in play, conversations: people (children and adults) really talking and listening to one another.

What I would smell – fresh air, sweaty bodies, sometimes wet ground, ground heat, scents, exhaust fumes.

What I would feel (emotionally and physically) – a sense of freedom, happiness, absolutely-mind-blowing-knocked-dead-hands (children's hands are so beautiful, they have to be the eighth wonder of the world), sometimes cold, sometimes hot, breath on my face (as I talk to a child at their level), plants, earth, sand, water, tired from activity.

What I would taste – edible plants, food, drink.

If you are outside and see, hear, feel, taste and smell these things for you and the children then you are doing a good job, if not, it is time to improve children's lives.

Section 1 Putting the outside into perspective

The benefits of outdoor learning

1

Summary

Working outside can be harder than inside, one may be physically more active, regularly battling against the elements and often more alert – watchful for potential dangers. Being involved in play and constantly mindful of play possibilities can be mentally exhausting. There can then be the added pressure of the head demanding 'results'. Overall education out of doors is physically and mentally taxing. We have to be convinced all the effort is for a good reason.

Children have to be outside because there are things they need – for example fresh air, sun and daylight. They need to learn not to be frightened of outside but to simply see it as part of life, just as water is. They can be physically more active than inside, and so can become and stay healthy. They are able to learn in an environment that is comfortable and non-threatening and learn through play and movement – both easy vehicles for learning for young children. One parent in the Brent Project, in which outdoor practice was improved, summed it up beautifully, saying: 'my child comes home refreshed not frustrated' (Bilton *et al.* 2005). 'Frustrated' was how the child was when the nursery ran poorly timetabled outdoor play and 'refreshed' was how she described him when he experienced quality outdoor play.

Children will do many things that we bid – stick tissue paper on card, complete worksheets, run around outside like headless chickens – but just because children do them does not mean they are appropriate. Children love junk food and TV, but this does not make them right for children. As Katz and Chard argue: 'When both the normative and dynamic dimensions of development are taken into account, it seems reasonable to suggest that just because children *can* do something when they are young does not mean they *should* do it' (1989: 18–19). We need to protect children and make sure they do what is age and stage appropriate, not that which will damage them, possibly for life. Being outside and being outside engaged in meaningful activities is appropriate for children and particularly the young child. It is not a case of needing to prove that outside is better than inside; both environments have benefits. It is a case of being aware that outside is a part of our life and benefits us physiologically, psychologically, physically, socially and so on. It is of mind and body benefit.

Discussing playtime, Pellegrini said:

> A long standing criticism of school is that children's social-affective needs have been ignored while aspects of children's cognitive needs have been stressed ... it seems to me that the role of schools is to educate good citizens. Good citizens should be friendly and cooperative as well as literate and numerate. Indeed, would school be considered successful if we had uniform literacy and numeracy but high levels of juvenile delinquency?

(1991: 234)

Outside is both an educational and a social experience. If you look back in the Introduction (Figure 0.1) at the games people played as children there was a lot of conversation and negotiation going on as well as learning. Aasen and Waters (2006) argue that learning involves both formal and informal components but the younger the child the more informal is has to be. Young children learn through 'play, social interaction and in day-to-day activities and care situations' (127). This can so easily be provided outside (see Figure 1.1).

It is to the benefits of being outside and being outside engaged in meaningful activities that we now look.

Figure 1.1 Easy outdoor play, Community Playthings

Children being outside

There is clear evidence that children play and exist outside less than they used to. In 1985/6, 21 per cent of 5- to10-year-olds travelled alone to school; in 2005 this figure had dropped to 6 per cent (Department for Transport 2002, 2006). In England in 1971, 80 per cent of 7- to 8-year-olds were allowed to go to school without an adult; in 1990 this figure had dropped to 9 per cent (Hillman *et al.* 1990). They also looked at other unaccompanied activity outside, including crossing the road, using buses, cycling on roads and going out in the dark; the data for 1990 showed children had less freedom than in 1971. Interestingly the researchers found children in Germany had more freedom in 1990 than English children.

The fear of injury or death from vehicles means parents limit children's play outside when they are not at school. Parental fears of child abductions or harm give them another reason not to let their children out. The additive nature of technologies, such as computer games and electronic gadgets, mean unless parents actually push children out they can be stuck indoors all day. Suburban garden pride can ensure some children are denied the use of their garden, as they must not spoil it, and other children may have no access to their own private outdoor space. Ironically the car has given freedom to adults but less to children. Reliance on the car ensures children do not experience outside, with some parents dropping their child off at school without even having dressed them in a coat. Children are taken to organised activities – football, ballet, gymnastics – where previously they would have organised their own games or taken themselves. For others, particularly teenagers, coats are seen as 'uncool' and they learn to dislike outside because they get cold very quickly. Some children are forced inside by being banned from using outside by intolerant adults arguing children are noisy or a nuisance (Children's Play Council 2003). Some children can become so anxious about all the dangers adults have suggested are out there that they choose not to play out as it is associated with danger (Thomas and Thompson 2004, Dillon *et al.* 2006). What all this evidence tells us is that children are existing less outside than they used to and that some children are building up an antithesis to outside.

A thorough research programme which gathered data using diaries, questionnaires, activity monitors and GPS monitors looked into children's (8- to 11-year-olds) independent movement in the local area (Mackett *et al.* 2007). The research found that:

- boys were allowed to participate more in travel activities than girls, except going to organised activities
- those who were allowed out without an adult actually visited more places than those who were not allowed out
- of those allowed out without an adult two-thirds spent more than 3 hours outdoors at the weekend and slightly under half spent this amount of time outdoors during the week
- those allowed out without an adult were more active

- those allowed out without an adult were more likely to go to a friend's house
- when walking without an adult children moved slower than when with an adult, but boys used more calories even though walking more slowly because they made random, angular and sometimes rapid movements, that is they walked this way and that, messing about play fighting, etc.
- girls moved the slowest when walking with other children and without an adult, possibly because they tend to chat more than boys.

Activities such as walking to school without an adult have benefits, some of which we may never have considered, including socialisation, higher levels of activity and visiting a greater range of places and people. The walking to school research indicates the importance of close study of children. We could assume children just walk to and from school and there is nothing in it. But the research suggests that 'children do behave differently at a microscale' (Mackett et al. 2007: 11), that children walk differently to and from school and that boys and girls walk differently from each other. Children make more turning movements when going to school than when coming home, probably because they are more tired at night and boys dance around more than girls, possibly because they tend to be more active and interested in play fighting. The upshot of less walking without an adult to school is that children are being less active and have fewer opportunities to be with friends, fewer chances to socialise and fewer opportunities to widen their horizons visiting various new places. Although we are dealing with younger children, the implications of this research are that children do behave differently and in very specific ways dependent on the environment and we have to watch and not assume. It also suggests we need to ensure children do get outside as much as possible as they are having fewer opportunities when away from adults.

Environmental influence

The 'environment' in which we find ourselves can impact on us differently. Environment means any space-room, corridor, forest, field, street, etc. For example going underground on the London underground is experiencing a different environment, but some of us like it, some of us do not. Ask any group and there will be some who enjoy the brilliance of the underground system of getting you from point a to point b, the hustle and bustle, the variety of people. Others will describe the fear it instills, the hatred of being cooped up, of being in close proximity to others. This is one environment, but it impacts on people differently. Likewise being in the outdoor area can impact on children differently, they can behave differently and do different things and sometimes an environment can have a greater impact on some children more than others.

We could say that children do not need to go out, but if we look to the research of Blakemore and Frith (2005) in their addictive book *The Learning Brain, Lessons for Education,* their evidence strongly suggests that you cannot deny an environment to children. This book looks at how and when the brain learns and considers the implications of this scientific research for educational policy and practice. They argue that:

- there is both nurture and nature and both contribute to the making of the person
- 'deprived' environments are never good for the brain
- there is 'no evidence that hothousing is beneficial to brain development' (35)
- there are sensitive periods of learning, although 'missed opportunities can to some extent be reversed' (36).

What this indicates in terms of activity out of doors is that children need a full range of experiences and out of doors is a part of being human and should be a part of their experience; if we deny children experience outside then we are offering a 'deprived' environment. Allowing children to play does not mean they are going to fail and in fact stuffing them with facts and skills at a young age is not going to help them. There are periods when children need particular approaches, as Trevarthen (1994) indicates, curiosity is something which needs to be stimulated at around age 4. We need to ensure we are approaching children in a way that is developmentally appropriate. Finally, outside offers another place to observe children and pick up on possible difficulties, particularly visual and auditory; as the authors indicate, the sooner we pick up on problems children face the quicker remedial action can be put into place and recovery can occur.

As can be seen in Chapter 3, outside has always been viewed as a restorative environment. 'Monasteries once had healing gardens,' (Bird 2009: 22), rich people had fabulous gardens to walk in, horses to ride. The seaside became a place of rejuvenation; a 1930s railway poster advertised 'Skegness, it's so bracing'. In late Victorian times the availability of mass cheap transport and the increase in free time enabled the better-off working classes and lower middle classes to spend a day at the seaside to get away from the unhealthy conditions of the city. Parks were created to become the lungs of the cities:

> Victoria Park in the East End of London was created not for environmental reasons, but after the Registrar for Births, Marriages and Deaths noted the death rate in Bethnal Green was much higher than elsewhere due to overcrowding, unsanitary conditions and polluted air.
>
> (Bird 2009: 22)

Victoria Park was built in 1850. A walk on Hampstead Heath was a place Londoners escaped to from the factories and slums (Martin 1974: 62). The sea, springs and spas attracted people and still attract people for their restorative features. Outside is good for us. Bird (2009: 22) discusses the powerful effect of the natural environments:

> Children become less hyperactive, can concentrate better and play more independently with greater balance. They develop lifelong ability to connect with nature but only if they are allowed to play freely in streams and woods before the age of 12. After this the effect rapidly diminishes.

OUTSIDE	INSIDE
'Look at me'	'Look at what I have made'
Environment of change	Stable environment
Freer and less controlled	Controlled
Interaction different	
Open	Encompassing

Figure 1.2 Differences between inside and outside
Source: Stephenson (2002)

Stephenson (2002), looking into the relationship between indoors and out in one setting in New Zealand, describes four major differences as listed in Figure 1.2. Looking to the detail of the differences, they may not be the same as seen in this country, but what is significant is that children and adults saw there were differences and behaved differently in each space. So outside, children required something different from the adult, to inside. Outside children drew adults' attention to what they were physically doing, but inside children wanted adults to look at what they made. Outside children were more involved in longer-term projects such as building in the sand, they were more physically active and involved in physical play. Stephenson also noted an age difference with younger children using more fixed equipment and older children more on the move. Outside was a space of change in terms of 'temperature, light, movement, colour, smell, texture' (2002: 31) and so children were more exposed. She found there was more change occurring outside than in, but staff felt this was the right balance, with inside being a more constant environment for children. Inside had more routines than outside, and rules were more relaxed outside than in, loud noise was acceptable out but not in. Inside was seen as a space where there were specific outcomes such as in a puzzle, but outside there was less structure with unknown outcomes and an acceptance of the open-ended nature of play. Transporting materials occurred outside but little inside and was seen as significant in supporting children's trans-porting schema. There was considered a difference in the styles of teaching in each space, outside was actually seen as the place more directed teaching occurred, because there were more physical skills to be taught. This was not seen as a role so much inside, where staff nurtured but did not necessarily demonstrate a skill such as kicking a ball. Outside was the place where bigger groups of children and a mix of older and younger children tended to work together, but this was not so inside. Overall the differences are summed as outside being 'open' and inside being 'encompassing'. Outside is:

> an environment that could be described as 'open'; open in the sense of accepting and less controlled, of incorporating change and unpredictability, but open also in the sense of lacking the security of enclosure and surrounding walls. They com-bined to form an environment that could be experienced both as dynamic and open-ended, and yet simultaneously as unpredictable and even threatening.
>
> (Stephenson 2002: 37)

So the benefits are quite clearly many and varied.

Grahn *et al.* looking at Danish early years education 'compared children in nurseries with little or no outdoor provision to those that had provision and where children were outside for a significant time each day'. The children with the greater outdoor experience showed greater skills in: 'concentration, play, creativity, motor ability and control' and there were fewer children with infections and allergies' (cited in Williams-Siegfredsen 2005: 5). Although the methodology has not been looked at, the authors seem convinced by this evidence and there were differences. Significant with the Danish experience is that most have some form of nature or forest experience, this contact with the natural world is central.

The environment for learning then has to be a stimulating space not a 'deprived' environment.

Fresh air

We all need oxygen to live. In any room with people in it there is a build up of CO_2 which is produced when we breathe out. There is also a build up of heat. Staying in a stuffy room does not help anyone to function, to think or to stay well. We all need to get out to stay healthy and alert.

Professor Derek Clements-Croome at the University of Reading has made the link between CO_2 and heat in the classroom and children's performance and shown that many classrooms are very unhealthy. The classrooms studied had up to 3.5 times the recommended average levels of 1500 parts per million of CO_2 (Building Bulletin 101 2006) and were simply too hot. The study was conducted in eight primary schools, and looked at reaction times and pupil memory: 'When CO_2 was very high, the reaction times would slow and memory would be affected. The kids would also get drowsier' (Clements-Croome 2008). Where tasks which required complex skills were performed the negative impact of poor air was even more marked. Other health issues associated with high levels of CO_2 made apparent in the study included headaches, dizziness, lethargy and difficulty with breathing. From my experience of classrooms I can only concur with these findings, as I regularly find myself stuck in hot and smoggy rooms with red-faced and agitated children. I can only describe it as disgusting – to have to exist in this very smelly, stale and sweaty atmosphere. Professor Clements-Croome and colleagues argue that:

- air quality in classrooms needs to be high on the list of priorities
- adequate fresh air in all classrooms is needed at all times
- some way of continually monitoring the CO_2 and heat levels in classrooms is needed.

He argues that a ventilation rate of 8 litres per person is recommended (Bako-Biro *et al.* 2008): 'An examination of over 300 peer reviewed articles of indoor air quality (IAQ), ventilation and building-related health problems in schools has shown that ventilation is inadequate in many classrooms and was considered to be the main cause of health symptoms' (Clements-Croome *et al.* 2008: 362). In classrooms the density of bodies is high particularly when compared to adult work conditions: 1.8–2.4m²/person in class-rooms compared to 10m²/person in offices (Clements-Croome *et al.* 2008). Finally the research indicates that it does not take long, even just 15 minutes, for the quantity of CO_2 to be at an unhealthy level. Just before the lunch break the level of CO_2 was found to be at its highest. Unsurprisingly, the authors suggest that if classes are ventilated and air quality improved, people do a better job and likewise children in a classroom are found to be more able. What this tells us about practice is that:

- classrooms need to be ventilated so they do not end up like a sauna, and without correct levels of oxygen
- a system which monitors the air and heat quality is needed, because staff often seem oblivious to the problem
- children need to feel secure to mention if they find themselves too hot and to be able to move so they can cool down or to open a window
- throughout the day windows and doors need to be opened and closed a number of times to ventilate the room, and that a through draft needs to be created so the air can move and circulate
- children and staff need to get out regularly throughout the day or session, par-ticularly as some class windows do not give the ventilation needed.

Following on from air quality within a room, we need to look at illness and fresh air. Some parents will ask for their child not to go out at nursery because they have a cold or so they do not catch a cold! Cold viruses do not live in fresh air, they live in us. So fresh air is not going to cause a child to become ill, getting chilled might but not being outside per se.

A study at the Common Cold Centre in Cardiff in 2005, which took 90 students and chilled their feet in cold water for 20 minutes, showed that the chilled group had twice as many colds over the next five days as a control group of 90 students whose feet were not chilled. It proposed that when colds are circulating in the community some people carry the virus without symptoms, but if they get chilled the cold symptoms come out. It found that chilling the feet causes a constriction of blood vessels in the nose and this inhibits the immune response and defences in the nose and allows the virus to replicate and cause cold symptoms. The chilled person believes they have caught a cold but in fact the virus was already present in the nose but not causing symptoms (Eccles 2008).

The study further argues that colds are seasonal and more people have colds in the winter. One theory suggests the reasoning for this is that the nose gets cold in the winter months and lowers our resistance to infection (Eccles 2002). There is also evidence that the cold virus tends to go from person to person via contaminated surfaces – an infected person touches their nose and then touches door handles, other people and so on (Gwaltney *et al.* 1980). Finally, it is argued that the longer you are exposed to the infection the more chance you have of catching it. This is why many people end up with a cold after having travelled on a long-haul flight. The close proximity of everyone on a plane for a long time enables the viruses to take hold of some passengers.

So what does all this evidence tell us about practice?

- Children shouldn't get chilled, they need to be wrapped up, ensuring feet, hands and head, in particular, are warm.
- Children need to keep their noses warm in cold weather, so the wearing of scarves or balaclavas is a good idea.
- Children and staff must wash their hands regularly.
- Equipment, furniture and resources must be cleaned very regularly.
- Children must not be stuck in hot and stuffy rooms.
- Children and staff must go out every day for long periods of time so germs cannot take hold.

Margaret McMillan, the founder of the English nursery school movement in 1914, made it clear that children would be more healthy and less likely to get ill if they were outside. Chapter 3 describes her success. This belief was taken up by many local authorities during the First World War and then in the 1930s and 1940s. Open air schools were set up to help children who were poorly. It was argued that if these children were given nutritious food, rest, exercise and fresh air, their health and strength would be restored. These sick children were outside for a good deal of the time, or at least in spaces where fresh air was in abundance. They even went to rest outside. One such school was the Hull Open Air School, conceived in the First World War. The city council sought a loan from the government to buy a piece of land, but it wasn't until 1931 that the school was opened for 270 day pupils. Children suffering with malnutrition, asthma, as well as tuberculosis and anaemia were sent to the school. Children often had their lessons outside dressed in coats and gloves. Much of the time was spent being active outside – doing gardening, PE or playing (Booth 2008). Today it still holds that if children are given nutritious food, sufficient rest, exercise and fresh air they will be healthy. One school in the Brent Project (Bilton *et al.* 2005) confirmed this belief, finding that the instances of coughs and colds reduced as more outdoor play occurred. Even a child with severe asthma did not have as many bouts of illness.

We cannot allow parents to dictate whether a child goes out or not. If children are well wrapped up and in an atmosphere that is cool and oxygenated, they will be able to concentrate and learn effectively and will not get ill. It is not a case of maybe we can go out, it is a case of children must get outside everyday.

Sunlight and daylight

Another important reason for being outside is that we experience light. We do not do well as a species without sunlight and particularly in the winter months when there are only eight hours of daylight. Vitamin D regulates the amount of calcium and phosphate in the body and is vital for healthy bones. However, the vitamin is activated under the skin in reaction to sunlight; therefore we need to be exposed to sunlight for it to be activated. Although the research was looking at older people, Dr Harald Dobnig from the Medical University of Graz found that low levels of Vitamin D were associated with a higher risk of early death; the study argues that Vitamin D is important for general health, including healthy bones, and that low Vitamin D levels are linked to an increased risk of death due to heart disease as well as death from any cause (Endocrine Society 2008).

In times gone past children suffered with rickets caused by a lack of Vitamin D, not helped by a lack of exposure to sunlight to activate that vitamin. In terms of children today we need to get them out as much as possible, so that Vitamin D can be activated, just 10–15 minutes a day without sun cream is sufficient. This can help ensure a healthy body in childhood and in adulthood, strengthening bones, protecting against osteoporosis and cutting the risk of cancer, of clogged arteries and of heart disease (Fletcher 2008). Mohr *et al.* (2008) found that a lack of sunlight may increase the risk of lung cancer. Vitamin D stimulates the release of chemicals which, in combination with calcium, form a glue-like substance that binds cancerous cells tightly together, and puts a brake on their division and thus on their infection of the body. In the research there was evidence that Vitamin D may slow the progress of cancer once it develops.

Heschong *et al.* (2002), in their study of elementary (primary age) children in schools in two districts in America, found that 'overall, elementary school students in classrooms with the most daylight showed a 21 per cent improvement in learning rates compared to students in classrooms with the least daylight'. This research indicates that daylight has a positive effect on pupils in terms of learning.

It does not take much exposure to the sun to ensure the Vitamin D is activated, so again children need to be outside in the sun or at least in the daylight to stay healthy now and into the future. This means that every day, not just in the summer, unless the weather is appalling, children need to be out.

Peace and quiet

Classrooms can be quite noisy places and so, too, can playgrounds, but does it matter to children? Research by Shield and Dockrell (2008) found that excessive noise has a harmful impact on children whether the child is inside or outside. The effect on children with special educational needs (SEN) is even greater. The background noise level in a room affects children the most, and individual events have the most impact outside. What this means is that the background noise inside and outside needs to be lessened. Having many noisy children charging around on bikes does not help in enabling children to learn. But also outside the siting of classrooms has to be considered much more carefully than it is now.

Dockrell (2009) suggests to lessen the noise level there can be acoustic treatment (such as tiles on the ceiling) and amplification within the space. She found that these improvements did impact on the children positively in terms of spelling, comprehension and speed. She also found that with amplification, fewer hands were raised, suggesting that children raise their hand not necessarily because they do not understand but because they cannot hear.

Physical development, motor development, exercise and rest

Physical development is not simply about children getting bigger but about children growing, developing and maturing. As Bilton (2004a: 6) discusses, growth, development and maturity are as follows:

Growth – the body getting bigger over time.
Development – the body changing over time so that all parts work more effectively together.
Maturity – the body getting closer to adulthood.

Growth, development and maturity, although to some extent are going to happen whatever, benefit from happening in a supportive environment, one that is outside. By being active, children learn to refine and improve motor skills, and develop their coordination, balance and body awareness. Physical exercise helps strengthen muscles, improve muscular endurance, increase bone density and flexibility and improve the cardio-respiratory functions. Bird argues that by being active most of the time 'helps keep blood pressure down, generate good cholesterol, allow more oxygen to the heart and muscles and keep our joints healthy and free of pain' (2009: 21). The Allied Dunbar National Fitness Survey (Sports Council 1992) established how little activity is being undertaken by different age groups and that there is a clear association between past participation in sport and physical recreation and the prevalence of breathlessness, angina and heart disease. This research found that activity levels varied according to social and economic status, with those in the lower groups tending to exercise less. A study of 10- to 16-year-olds found that British children rarely take part in vigorous sustained activity sufficient to optimise their aerobic fitness (Armstrong and Bray 1991). The National Osteoporosis Society found, for young children in particular, that exercise and good calcium intake are two keys to preventing osteoporosis in later life. However, they also noted that this is not happening (Edwards 1992). More recently the Welsh Assembly's policy on exercise and sport was published in 2005. This document reiterates the findings of the Allied Dunbar publication thirteen years previously that as a result of inactivity 'too many people are unfit or unwell, and too many people die too soon' (Pugh 2005: 14). It stipulates a number of priorities for sport and physical activity including the need for Wales 'to maximize the synergy between sport, physical activity and the natural environment', to ensure it has 'healthy citizens to deliver long-term prosperity', to have people who are 'more physically literate' and its 'communities to be more physically active' (Pugh 2005: 5–6). It argues that exercise reduces stress and ensures people feel happy and are more confident. The actions to be taken to achieve its aims include 'building physical activity back into daily life', 'encouraging play as an essential component for healthy development' and to see as part of 'personal development, the acquisition of physical literacy is as important as the development of literacy and numeracy skills' (Pugh 2005: 18).

Research from Blakemore and Frith links adult activity with mental well-being and an absence of ill-health and suggests exercise: 'may boost brain function, improve mood, and increase learning' (2005: 134). The authors indicate that exercise can actually affect chemicals in the brain which alter the mood of the person and thereby be a treatment for depression and mental health problems. The Chief Medical Officer argues 'that being active has the same antidepressant effect as taking tablets' (Bird 2009: 21). Mental illness is on the increase with the World Health Organisation suggesting that depression will be the second biggest cause of ill-health across the world. Likewise, for healthy elderly people and those suffering stroke and head injury 'daily physical activity improves learning and overall mental capacity' (Blakemore and Frith 2005: 136). Exercise can raise the mood of a person, lessen anxiety and raise self-esteem (Gruber 1986, Calfas and Taylor 1994, Fox 1996). By offering a structured PE programme to children with coordination problems, who also lacked confidence, had poor behaviour and poor handwriting, it was found that not only did the children's motor skills and stamina improve but so too did their self-esteem, both in PE and in general class activities (Stewart 1989: 32).

Exercise is the normal state of affairs – we should be doing it! It also makes the brain more efficient at learning: 'through increasing the ability of blood cells to absorb oxygen, exercise does not just improve muscle, lung and heart function: it also improves brain function' (Blakemore and Frith 2005: 136). These findings were referring to a study in England which found that when the children exercised before the required academic task they were more motivated and able to complete it than when they did not exercise. Ploughman, reviewing various pieces of research looking at the link between cognitive function and exercise in children with disabilities, concludes that children with disabilities may not benefit from improved cognitive function because often they are less active. Looking at animals he argues that learning and memory are improved through activity. 'In clinical studies, exercise increases brain volume in areas implicated in executive processing, improves cognition in children with cerebral palsy and enhances phonemic skill in school children with reading difficulty' (2008: 236). Goddard-Blyth (2000) argues that those children who do not go out and for long periods of time are connected to electronic gadgets will be building up many problems:

> These children run the risk of later specific le2ring difficulties, behavioural and social problems not because they lack intelligence, but because the basic systems fundamental to academic learning are not fully in place when they begin school. Attention, Balance and Co-ordination are the primary ABC on which all later learning depends.
>
> (Goddard-Blyth 2000: 23)

We have to ensure they have these basic systems in place.

Interestingly, Goddard-Blyth argues that moderate exercise not intense is most beneficial, with the latter actually potentially causing stress. 'Clearly, moderate physical activity is important for youth whose brains are highly plastic and perhaps even more critical for young people with physical disability' (2000: 237). Jago (referring to Blair and Connelly 1996 and the Health Education Authority 1998) looking at how much physical activity children should do, states that 'recent scientific evidence and "expert opinion" … now accepts that repeated bouts of moderately intense exercise can confer health benefits to children' (Jago 2002: 43). Vogele (2005), reviewing various research evidence, also makes the conclusion that moderate activity as opposed to intense is acceptable to keep healthy. Mostofsky and Zaichkowsky (2006) researched into how exercise and sport can help with chronic disorders and how people can be positively responsive to a well-planned programme of exercise to help improve their condition. So the message is this: activity and exercise are crucial to us all whether children or adults.

However, we have to make sure we view exercise as part of life, not something which happens in a designated place, such as the gym. Bird (2009) argues that we were not meant to go to gyms and go on walking machines. When you watch people playing, whether children in streams or adults walking outside, they are not doing it to stay healthy, they are doing it because it is fun and enjoyable. Exercise should just happen in our daily lives, not because we have to do it as part of our regime! In the past we were fit because we had to walk to school – there was no option, we had to mow the lawn using a manual lawn mower, we had to wring the clothes by hand. Labour-saving devices have meant we throw the clothes in the machine and have no exercise from it; we use the electric mower and simply exercise a bit of an arm-muscle group! Alongside this there has been a change in approach to fitness and exercise with a boom in health clubs, with the emphasis changing from exercise to fitness as a lifestyle choice. To some extent this has been mirrored in schools, with a desire for children to take part in exercise sessions. But in itself these exercise classes do not make children fit, children need to be physically active per se, 'whole body activity' (Jones 1996: 52) needs to be fostered, and regular vigorous activity is needed. Separating PE from the rest of the activities in school has made sure that the development of body and mind are separate, as though the mind is developed in the classroom and the body through a PE lesson. Boorman argues that '[C]ognitive, physical and emotional growth need to develop alongside one another – each contributing to the other' (1988: 232). Physical activity needs to pervade all tasks and involve the whole body, not just parts of it. So the benefit of children being outside is they have the freedom to be physically active, whether pulling a truck or digging the ground. It also denies them the opportunity to partake of sedentary activities such as watching the TV or playing computer games. 'Children deserve to be given back the freedom to play and exercise in safety enjoyed by previous generations' (IOTF 2002: 28). They can be active and be exercised at the same time, without any sense of strain.

'Obesity is rising at an alarming rate throughout Europe. It forms a pan-European epidemic that presents a major barrier to the prevention of chronic non-communicable diseases' (IOTF 2002: 3). 'Worldwide, over 22 million children under the age of 5 are severely overweight, as are 155 million school-age children. There are 14 million overweight school-age children in the European Union (EU), of whom three million are obese. The number of overweight children in the EU is rising by around 400,000 per annum, of whom 85,000 are obese' (BMA 2005: 8). In 1997, 9.6 per cent of children under 10 were obese; by 2003 it had risen to 13.7 per cent, that is 1 out of every 7 children. Nine out of every ten children are set to become 'couch potatoes' (Cunningham 2006: 242).

Finally, child participation in physical activity is mirrored in adult participation; if children do not get involved in physical activity, it is unlikely they will as adults:

> There is strong evidence to suggest that it is the quality of physical activity that has a lasting impact: when students leave school with positive attitudes towards sport and their own ability, they are more likely to be physically active as adults.
>
> (BMA 2005: 23)

The message is that children need to take part in whole body activity. This does not necessarily mean sport but activities such as walking and moving when playing. Jago (2002), looking into exercise at primary school, argues that through activity at playtime children could be ensuring that they make a significant contribution to fulfilling the Health Education Authority's (1998) recommendation that children need an hour per day physical activity. Jago found that by increasing the knowledge of all involved, involving all adults and making sure there was enough time and space, children could and did increase the amount of time they were physically active, although it would appear boys were more active than girls. All children need opportunities for vigorous and moderately intense activity which gives psychological benefit that will carry on into adulthood. Children leading a healthy lifestyle hopefully will mean healthy adults. The European Network of Health Promoting Schools, a research development project, is involving a number of schools in the country in following a health curriculum and so contributing to the health of their community.

As much as exercise children need rest, not only do they need enough sleep at night they also need periods of rest during the day. Exercise, well-being, ability and sleep are all inter-related. On average adults need seven and a half hours sleep per night, children need longer (see Figure 1.3). Young children on average need a lot more sleep than we think. Most importantly through research on humans and animals it has been shown that sleep does play an important role in learning, so what has happened to you during the day in terms of learning can be laid down in the long-term memory. Sleeping increases energy levels, and 'may improve learning, decision making, and innovation' (Blakemore and Frith 2005: 173). With the National Curriculum came the demise of the afternoon rest, particularly for children aged 3 to 5. The afternoon rest or nap needs to be reintroduced into all early years settings. It should not be the case of the needs of parents coming first to have worn-out children who sleep immediately they are picked up from a hard day at nursery but the needs of the child to be reinvigorated at the time they need it. 'The brain reactivations during sleep may reflect the reinforcement of connections between neurons that are important for the task. In this way, they allow the new skill to be incorporated into long-term memory' (Blakemore and Frith 2005: 175). In the study the authors cite that the researchers found that people's ability to complete tasks deteriorated as time went on but improved significantly after a proper nap. There is evidence that not having enough sleep triggers the hormone involved with hunger. In an adult sample the hormone responsible was found to be 15 per cent higher in those who had only 5 hours' sleep than those who had had 8 hours' sleep. Less sleep means you feel more hungry and eat more. Sleep is also related to exercise in that if you are tired

---

Here are some approximate numbers based on age, as recommended by the Millpond Children's Sleep Clinic:

One week
- Daytime: 8 hours
- Night-time: 8.5 hours

Four weeks
- Daytime: 6.75 hours
- Night-time: 8.75 hours

Three months
- Daytime: 5 hours
- Night-time: 10 hours

Six months
- Daytime: 4 hours
- Night-time: 10 hours

Nine months
- Daytime: 2.75 hours
- Night-time: 11.25 hours

Twelve months
- Daytime: 2.5 hours
- Night-time: 11.5 hours

Two years
- Daytime: 1.25 hours
- Night-time: 11.75 hours

Three years
- Daytime: 1 hour
- Night-time: 11 hours

Four years
- Night-time: 11.5 hours

Five years
- Night-time: 11 hours

Six years
- Night-time: 10.75 hours

Seven years
- Night-time: 10.5 hours

Eight years
- Night-time: 10.25 hours

Nine years
- Night-time: 10 hours

10 years
- Night-time: 9.75 hours

11 years
- Night-time: 9.5 hours

12 years
- Night-time: 9.25 hours

13 years
- Night-time: 9.25 hours

14 years
- Night-time: 9 hours

15 years
- Night-time: 8.75 hours

16 years
- Night-time: 8.5 hours

Figure 1.3 Amount of sleep
Source: Millpond Children's Sleep Clinic
(www.nhs.uk/Livewell/Childrenssleep/Pages/Howmuchsleep.aspx)

when you wake or during the day you are likely less inclined to be active and want to take part in physical exercise. All aspects of our being are related.

In terms of health education:

> the World Health Organization (WHO 1981) defines health education as all those planned activities that contribute to people wanting to be healthy (health motivation), to knowing how to achieve health (health knowledge), and to helping people to translate this knowledge into action (health behaviour), alone or with the assistance of other people or organizations.
>
> (Vogele 2005: 272)

So it is not a case of doing a bit of aerobics as part of a theme one term and periodically going outside, it is about health education and health promotion which establish protective behaviours for the long term. It will often be necessary to help parents and carers appreciate the impact of being outside and being active outside and to demonstrate the benefits – this may take the form of:

- enabling the parents to join in and for staff to unpick what children are learning
- booklets accessible to parents
- workshops for all to attend
- daily conversations about the health implications of working outside.

For change to occur people have got to see a benefit to it and that they can achieve it. Whatever children do whether it be playing or competitive sport, they need to enjoy the activity and find that it is attainable – it is not so vigorous as to put children off (Vogele 2005: 283). Childhood obesity is on the increase and where physical activity and nutritional education are combined improvements are made. Children need to be active outside so physical activity is seen as part of life and so they can become and stay healthy.

Freedom

Outside is a natural place for children to be and play and there is a freedom associated with it. However good and inclusive the school or class is, when asked, children will always say the classroom is controlled or owned by the teacher. When asked it will be the parent, most often the mother, who controls the home. But outside, no one owns it or controls it. No one owns it therefore there is no accountability. Children feel free outside, they do not need to explain themselves, they do not need to prove anything, they can just be themselves. This means children are likely to achieve more and more easily and we can view their true selves. Dillon *et al.* (2006), citing other research, talks in terms of outside being 'the world of our physical surroundings' and indoor activities 'the world of school' (108), suggesting a clear distinction between the two and a more academic perspective for inside and a more natural perspective for outside. Research by Wikeley 'found that it was not the content of extracurricular activities that was important, but the interpersonal and practical skills learned from them' (Lepkowska 2008: 1). The impact of not being 'institutionalised' and feeling free, even doing academic subjects, meant children did not feel there was the pressure to succeed and could take risks when they were partaking of clubs and activity outside school. It could be this is why children outside in the garden feel freer, it simply is not school.

Generally, all children feel this sense of freedom outside, but there are also some children who visibly change once outside. They have two personalities – one for inside and one out. The inside persona is quiet and compliant, keen not to be noticed, playing with the resources which receive little adult attention. Outside the child becomes vocal, bouncy, keen to play with other children and adults. It is as though a pressure has been taken away from them and they can just get on. I can remember one child who first thing Monday morning would walk into the class and straight out to the garden. He would not look at anyone or communicate. Once outside he would find something to sit on up high and then just look into the middle distance. He had a lot of pressures put on him at home and our outside space was somewhere he needed to go to simply be himself without a care in the world. When we first knew this child and he did not go outside straight away he was very difficult to be with; once this cathartic process was allowed he was a different child. The example in Chapter 8 shows a challenging Year 6 child working outside who simply changes and is more compliant and able in that space compared to being inside when he demonstrates quite difficult behaviour. Children need to get outside to feel that freedom and to relax into being capable.

Risk and challenge

In Chapter 3 there is a discussion about childhood today. It suggests that children are on the one hand expected to be like mini adults and on the other in need of constant protection, so they are not able to either enjoy or benefit from their childhood and are unable to become independent. Gill argues that 'childhood is becoming undermined by risk aversion' (2007: 10) and echoes a sentiment expressed by Cunningham (2006) that adults are interfering too much with childhood. There is excessive containment to the child's life now – containment in a car, at the controlled after-school activity, in the classroom where children need even more adults than in times gone by, in the bedroom while on the internet. It has to be appreciated that children need challenges to help them become self-regulatory in their safety. If they cannot regulate themselves they cannot find out what is safe and what is not. The Royal Society for the Prevention of Accidents (RoSPA) argues that children need challenges: 'It is essential to their healthy growth and development. Children need to learn about risk, about their own capabilities and to develop the mechanism for judging it in controlled settings' (Cook and Heseltine 1999: 4). Children do not need to be faced with hazard and danger, but they do need to experience risk and challenge. There are challenges in all aspects of life – whether it be the challenge and potential risk of reading a new word or of climbing up a plank. Our role is to help children to take risks and rise to challenges. Outdoors, more often than indoors, provides the opportunities to take risks and be successful.

The wheels seem to be turning with a more sensible approach emerging to risk. The Better Regulation Commission recently produced a report entitled: 'Risk, Responsibility and Regulation: Whose risk is it anyway?' arguing that risk can be beneficial and that managing risk is a shared responsibility. The Health and Safety Executive (HSE) in 2006 campaigned under the title: 'Get a Life' and was critical of petty health and safety concerns. In the informative book by Guldberg (2009) there is a list of different influential and knowledgeable institutions who are concerned we are overprotecting children (see Figure 1.4). So I think the message is 'get real': if the Health and Safety Executive are saying it is okay for children to take risks then this seems a pretty solid backing to my mind. Guldberg cites Louis Pasteur: 'When I approach a child, he inspires in me two sentiments: tenderness for what he is, and respect for what he may become. But childhood prolonged cannot remain a fairyland. It becomes a hell' (2009: 72).

There will always be accidents and these are awful, but it is important to think how we respond to accidents. Guldberg (2009) shares the story of the death of a five-year-old in Norway in 1994. The child was beaten by three five-year-olds, who ran away, and she died. It transpired that her injuries were minor, but the boys did not tell anyone and so she died of hypothermia. Although there was a national debate, the Norwegians did not react by banning children playing outside. It was considered children need a healthy and rich childhood including playing outside unsupervised and so it was not banned. Things happen, they do not stop happening because we ban them. Banning can cause more problems than we had before. Esther Ranzen with her 'That's Life' programme campaigned to have safety surfaces installed under all equipment. Safety surfaces may be safer than other surfaces but they are not 100 per cent safe as the media led the general public to believe. Children can get a false sense of security and as Gill writes, 'A growing number of experts think that the rubber safety surfacing most often used in the UK may lead to more broken arms than other types of surface' (2007: 29).

We need to learn to step back and allow children to resolve issues with other children. If we constantly jump in when children are having 'boisterous banter or everyday playground disputes' (Guldberg 2009: 94) then we are not enabling them to sort these disputes out, we are actually setting them up to always be reliant on others. Guldberg quite rightly points out, citing Blatchford, Pellegrini and the Opies, that children have disputes; arguments are a part of life. How you deal with them is crucial and the fact that some adults do not take any notice of horrid stuff said about them and some take it to heart shows this to be true. In the early years space there are going to be disputes and things said; we need to give children strategies to cope and react and not leap in with the adult reaction. In Bilton (2004b: 29) there is an example of two children in disagreement but with an adult standing by in case their help is needed. This school teaches children to deal with such confrontations for themselves and not call on adults unless really needed. Sometimes what is said or done has to be dealt with by an adult, for example where the child cannot differentiate between play fighting and real fighting and always takes it too far (see Chapter 2 for a discussion about play fighting). But for the majority of

- Tom Mullarkey (November 2007), 'chief executive of the Royal Society for the Prevention of Accidents (RoSPA) warned against wrapping children in cotton wool' (Guldberg 2009: 60).

- David Yearly, Play Safety Manager of RoSPA, argues that judging risk comes through exposure to it (Jones 2007: 15).

- The Health and Safety Executive issue a myth of the month, for example for November 2008 there is this little ditty. 'Myth: Children need to be wrapped in cotton wool to keep them safe'. Answer from the HSE: 'Health and safety law is often used as an excuse to stop children taking part in exciting activities, but well-managed risk is good for them. It engages their imagination, helps them learn and even teaches them to manage risks for themselves in the future. They won't understand about risk if they're wrapped in cotton wool. Risk itself won't damage children, but ill-managed and over protective actions could!' (www.hse.gov.uk/myth/index.htm accessed 6.3.09 12.50pm)

- Lisa Fowlie, president of the UK Institution of Occupational Safety and Health (IOSH), on Sky News, 13 October 2007, suggests that safety is used as the lazy approach, no effort is needed to stop something happening but having to justify and make sure it's safe is much harder, so using the health and safety banner is the lazy approach.

- Mike Grenaway, Director of Play Wales, argues that you need to learn to deal with danger to become safer in the long run (Guldberg 2009: 62).

- The Heads, Teachers and Industry (HTI) organisation positively encourages risk. Schools who can demonstrate the attitude they are looking for will be awarded as a Go4it school. Its information pack says a Go4it school will demonstrate an over-riding self-belief, free thinking and 'can do' attitude. It will show 'a continuing commitment to positive risk taking which demonstrates an understanding that risk is part of the culture of creativity and success'.
  (HTI Heads, teachers and industry 2009)

- Ungar (2007) who deals with teenagers with difficulties says those children he works with are saying what they need most is to be able to take risks and be given responsibility. He considers by not giving this we are creating problems for teenagers and adults. 'A concerned parent provides scaffolding for growth, not just a life jacket for safety' (Ungar 2007: 4).

- Guldberg makes a 'positive correlation – that is, an association' (2009: 69) between the number of parents who would not let their child cross a road on their own and child pedestrian deaths. The former from 2002–6 has risen from 41% to 49% and the latter has risen from 10% to 18% in the same time frame, for children aged seven to ten years (Guldberg 2009: 69). She argues this may suggest that as children are allowed out less, when they are they don't know how to protect themselves and so then have an accident.

For more information on risk see Guldberg (2009).

Figure 1.4 Some sensible comments about risk

the time children can sort these disputes, if they are given the strategies. It is a risk to leave children to 'sort it' but we must trust them to rise to that challenge.

Children need to be outside to take risks and rise to the challenge to become more able and confident children and adults. Guldberg cites Dr Spock's opening line, which is: 'Trust yourself. You know more than you think you do' (Guldberg, 2009: 144). We need to trust children more rather than protect, wrap and prevent.

Learning through movement

Movement is probably the most crucial modes of learning for young children. It is the way children learn about their environment and themselves. 'Words are at first merely a way of pointing to things, and but empty sounds until the children have had a rich contact with the things themselves, and explored them with hand and eye' (Isaacs 1954: 74). Isaacs goes on to argue that children need to do and explore to understand meaning, by walking and stretching they come to understand 'far' and 'near' and so on.

> It is important to recognise the role of movement as common denominator of the total development of the child, and its integrating function. Movement is bound up with physical, intellectual, emotional development and a child's doing, thinking and feeling may be examined in movement terms.
>
> (Brearley 1969: 83)

Movement 'reflects the inner activity of the person' (Brearley 1969: 88). Although there is not a causal relationship between developmental coordination disorder (DCD) ('clumsy') and school achievement, there is evidence to suggest there is a firm relationship which demonstrates that children who show signs of DCD do less well in school than would have been predicted from their cognitive ability (Sugden and Wright 1996). Maude (2008) demonstrates that some children may not be physically ready or have reached a level of maturity in the structure and functioning of the wrist and hand to use such tools as pencils. It is not that they are being naughty when off task but that they are not ready. Through movement children can express their feelings, whether by skipping for joy, stamping to let out anger, or walking to get rid of tension. But more than this, success in movement can improve self-image (Gallahue 1989). This theme is picked up in Chapter 6.

From birth, children discover through moving themselves about and manipulating materials about them. The prime concerns for a baby are interaction with others and to be in a position to explore, hence the strong drive to reach, sit up, crawl and walk. This discovery continues until the three- and four-year-old wants to understand such concepts as 'near and far', 'heavy and light', 'lines and curves'. Their own movement and the manipulation of the world around them is their way of finding out about such concepts. For example, 'heavy and light' can be explored through pulling a truck with and without a child in. 'Lines and curves' can be discovered by making these with bricks, blocks or stones. 'Through movement and play, children learn more than motor skills, they learn to employ cognitive strategies, to understand their psychological self and how to interact with other children' (Zaichkowsky *et al.* 1980: 11). Each child has to build their own knowledge (Vygotsky 1978). It is, therefore, vital that children are able to access the easiest mode of learning and this can only be done by allowing them to manipulate the environment for themselves.

It needs to be appreciated, however, that there is movement and there is physical development; the former is a mode through which children can learn and the latter is one aspect of child development. By movement is meant walking, playing with another child, pulling a truck, building with bricks or being a reporter, and it is therefore more than just physical development. Movement evades all activity, can occur inside and out and is not just about physical development. Davies argues that 'Movement is so much a fundamental part of our lives that, understandably, those concerned with child care and education may not necessarily see the need to classify what must, after all, seem obvious' (1995: 1). Confusing movement and physical development as one and the same thing, coupled with statutory curricular guidance rating development (where physical development is often mentioned last), means movement can be lost in the world of education. We need to ensure we are aware of the distinction between physical development and movement.

This is why outdoors needs to be viewed as a learning and teaching environment, not a physical exercise yard. What the outdoor environment can offer, which indoors cannot, is the space for children to move freely, to move so that they can use their whole bodies in imaginative and fantasy play situations, to grapple with concepts which can more easily be understood and appreciated on a large scale. Hardeep in Figure 1.5 made a bridge/tunnel. He did not converse, had time to think his ideas through and was learning about width, height, comparative measurements, sizes and balance. He was learning through movement.

Hardeep pulled his truck up to a pile of crates and child-size ladders which had been left by the previous players. He started to pile the milk crates one on top of the other, with seemingly no focus. Then his body language changed and he became more intense. He made two stacks of milk crates side by side. He looked about him and spied the ladder, which he kept looking at, touching, but then looking to his truck as though trying to work something out. He placed the ladder on top of the two stacks and it fell off as they were not equal height. Hardeep took the stacks to bits and started piling up the crates again, this time further apart. Again he put the child-size ladder on the top, again it fell off as the stacks were not the same height. This went on for a number of minutes until Hardeep had two stacks of equal height and placed the ladder on top. He looked very pleased, took hold of his truck and went to go up to the stacks. Something was clearly wrong. Hardeep took the ladder from the top of the crates and pushed the stacks apart, he placed the ladder on top but now the stacks were too far apart and the ladder fell to the ground. Hardeep played around with moving the two stacks until the ladder fitted exactly on top. He took hold of his truck, pulled it through the stacks and under the ladder and out the other side. Hardeep had made a tunnel/bridge!

Figure 1.5 Learning through moving

Bruce (1987, 2005), looking at Bruner's theories, argues that the modes of learning for young children are the enactive (action), the iconic (graphic or visual) and the symbolic (abstract). She argues that the active mode is the most developed in young children and the most crucial. 'Most developed' means it is probably the most accessible vehicle for learning. Piaget's notion is that 'thought is internalized action' (Wood 1998: 21). Athey (2007) identifies schemas which are patterns of behaviour that are significant in helping children make sense of their world and learning. She argues that through movement children can secure information about themselves, the environment and the topological properties of objects, and understand shape, form and movement. Through movement children can find out about space, direction, laterality, dominance. All of these are important with regard to, for example, coping with writing, manipulating tools or crossing the road. Movement is about enabling children to get to grips with things so that they can eventually get to grips with ideas.

Matthews (1994, 2003), discussing drawing and painting, demonstrates that action and movement are important to thinking and feeling and thereby to visual representation and expression. Matthews shows that drawing is not narrow, simply involving pencil and paper. There is a whole process of discovery with all sorts of other materials – anything which children can lay their hands on – and that the drawing is a part of that discovery process about the world and how things happen and why. Children will be moving to help with their drawing and drawing to find out about the world. 'When they represent anything (using a mark, a shape, an action or an object) they make something stand for something else, and through expression (in speech, action or images) they show motion' (Matthews 2003: 9). Often children will talk and gesticulate as well as draw, because they are telling a story, so the movement is a necessary part of the process. Babies will play with spilt milk and through observing what happens learn to appreciate the impact they can have on their environment. This will eventually lead to making the link to symbols (symbols and pictures), so initially a mark is just a mark but then a mark can then represent something. When we think about outdoor play children have the space to create these ideas, whether it be on the ground with chalks or water or using fabrics and objects. The OMEP (2001) video shows a lovely example of a child chalking a train track on the ground but as he does so he tells a Thomas the Tank Engine story. Interestingly a programme called 'Art Attack' shows how one can make pictures using any manner of materials. The creation has to be viewed from above to be appreciated. Children given enough freedom will also do this. What we must remember is that when children manipulate (move) food, soil, puddles for example, they could be exploring that material and attempting to understand it and its properties; they could also be drawing with it, that is creating an image. So we must not narrow painting and drawing to the creation of an image, it is so much more than this. By watching children we can ascertain what they are doing and can support them in their efforts by ensuring others do not disturb them or their creations.

Figure 1.6 describes a child learning by doing. Apart from a brief functional conversation, Mario had not spoken, but this did not mean he had not been thinking. He had solved a number of problems and had foreseen another. Mario could not have solved the puzzle of fitting 13 crates into a truck if he had been asked to work it out on paper, but

Four-year-old Mario had a truck stacked with crates which were badly arranged and in danger of toppling over. In fact this was exactly what happened when another child crashed into the truck. Mario set to work and tried to stack them in a more orderly fashion but with the addition of the tenth crate they all fell down. Mario decided to take all the crates out of the truck and start from the beginning. He tried the crates so that the maximum surface area of the truck was covered. He eventually worked out that two flat, and one on its side, used the space most effectively. He then very carefully stacked the crates one on top of the other, ensuring they all fitted properly. The stacks got too high and Mario was confused as to what to do to be able to continue stacking. He then decided to use a chair to stand on. Having finally got the thirteen crates into the truck, Mario, without moving the truck, realised that the crates balanced on their sides would fall out unless he secured them in some way. He asked the teacher for a rope, and spent some time attaching the rope to the crates on their side and then feeding the rope through and attaching it to the securely standing crates. Mario moved off with the truck and the crates stayed in place. The whole process had taken thirty minutes (Bilton 1989).

Figure 1.6 An example of learning by doing

through this activity this is what he did. Movement can be 'described, promoted, supported, enriched and recorded' (Bilton 2004c: 92).

Children need to be exploring and manipulating their environment every day. If children only get periodic experience of something it is unlikely they will move on in their acquisition of skills; they will spend time simply retreading old skills, which is pointless and they are more likely to have accidents. Vygotsky's (1978) 'ripening structures' can hardly be catered for if some activities are only provided every other week. The benefit of outdoor activity is that children can explore and learn through movement.

Discussion

Out and in are different environments and we all (children and adults) behave differently in many and often very subtle ways in the two spaces. This means the two spaces offer different things to different people. We have to be acutely aware of this and become tuned into the differences to ensure we help all children. It is not just that children have different experiences outside but also that we, the adult, react differently to children outside (Stephenson 2002).

Overall, outside benefits children – emotionally, socially, physically, aesthetically and intellectually. Children benefit from being outside and being engaged in worthwhile activity outside. Outside is a healthy and health-inducing environment – children benefit from being in the fresh air, in sun and daylight. Through physical activity and learning through movement children learn to see exercise as a part of life, to exert the body and so keep it healthy. Taking risks and rising to challenges enables children to learn new skills and through success their self-esteem and confidence can increase to try yet new skills. Through movement children learn about themselves and the world about them. Being outside and being active can ensure children are ready to take part in more sedentary tasks later and can improve their mood.

Questions and ideas

1. Think about what you did as a child when playing outside. Share your findings with the staff group and then decide what you learnt from the games. Can some of those ideas be put into practice in your setting? If not, why not?

2. Are your children ever out of breath? If not set up games so they can get out of breath, for example simple chase games, or follow my leader. You are the leader and hop, jump, skip, run and everyone has to copy. Then a child can be the leader. Or set up an obstacle course made up of hoops, blocks, ropes and enable the children to go round the course at their own pace. Pretend to be horses at a race or at a stable. Make saddles and reins from material and rope and then play racing or gymkhanas. If the children have no knowledge of these events they can see images on the internet and in books.

3. Measure how much time your children spend outside. Why do you spend this amount of time outside? Having measured how much time your children spend outside, increase this by 5 minutes per week. In 4 weeks you will be staying out for 20 minutes more every day. Note down what children are doing at the beginning, then when you add 5 minutes and the next 5 minutes and so on. What discernable differences are there in the children's behaviour?

4. Collect rain-coats, gloves, hats, balaclavas, caps, Wellington boots so there are sufficient in case children do not have their own.

5. When you watch the children how do they present themselves physically? Could you describe the various types of jumping, for example, they can perform? If not, start finding out. Make sure you move every child on in their abilities and skills.

6. Take Stephenson's differences in behaviour inside and out (Figure 6.7, page 154) and use them to compare your environments of in and out. Do you have the same dimensions as Stephenson or different dimensions?

2

The environment for teaching and learning

Summary

Having agreed that it is important that children do use the outdoor environment, we need to come to an agreement about terminology and what it is we think the environment should look like and what should be happening. Therefore environment, organisation, management, teaching, learning, play and work are discussed.

The environment

Blenkin and Whitehead argue that 'the most neglected and misunderstood dimension of the planned curriculum is the creation of an environment or setting in which education is to take place' (1988: 35) (see also Whitebread 1989, McLean 1991, McAuley and Jackson 1992, Bruce 2005, Pollard 2008). Any educational experience is made up of children, a curriculum and an environment in which the curriculum and children are brought together. So there is a content, the 'what' of the equation (the curriculum), there is the 'who' (the children) and there is a context – the 'how' of the equation. All three components of this triangle have to have due regard paid to them. What makes a great teacher is how she or he brings those three components together, as Whitebread argues: 'The best teachers use a repertoire of various styles and strategies, it is not the strategies they use which make the difference, but the skill with which they use them' (2000: 1). So it is not what you do – it is how you do it that makes the difference. For example, the interactive whiteboard (IWB) should have transformed classes but the skill with which teachers use them is limited to mostly using them as a blackboard, and as Moss et al. conclude, the IWB in itself has not transformed existing pedagogies (2007: 6). Gura (1992) argues that how we organise time and space affects how children feel about themselves and others. Social awareness, social understanding and personal autonomy will be dictated by the way the class is organised and managed (Blenkin and Whitehead 1988). Aasen and Waters (2006) argue that the Norwegian example of including personal and social development and well-being at the heart of theory, policy and practice ensures quality in education. At the heart of policy in England, however, is test and profile results;

this militates against improving practice. Siraj-Blatchford states that 'the curriculum does not necessarily determine pedagogy' (1999: 21). So we need to think through how we are going to 'do' the curriculum to be effective in helping children.

It can be hard to see the outside as an environment for learning and teaching because it does not look like a 'normal' setting for learning and teaching. 'Frequent lack of attention to the external environment must come from some bizarre assumption that knowledge acquired indoors is superior to that gained outside' (Bruce 1987: 55). Outside does not have a floor, walls, ceiling, or windows but probably the easiest way to approach the planning of outdoors is to temporarily view outdoors in the same way as indoors. Pretend the outdoor area has walls and a ceiling, what would you have in it? You would have furniture and resources, children utilising those resources and the furniture, children and staff working together. Having accepted this, it then follows that the outdoors has to be part of the planning, it has to be on the long-term, medium-term and day-to-day planning grids. It has to be evaluated and children working in that environment have to be assessed. It has to be discussed at staff meetings. So, when working outside all the managerial and organisational issues we would address in the indoor class have to be considered.

Organisation and management

A successful teacher is going to consider how they are going to organise their environment and then how they will manage it everyday whether this be inside or out. Organisation is 'the way in which the class and classroom is structured to facilitate teaching and learning' (Pollard and Tann 1987: 102) and includes the way children and adults are organised, the use of time, space, display and the use of records for monitoring organisation. Moyles describes organisation in terms of 'the context and contents of the classroom setting, including the plans made for teaching and learning' (1992: 5). Management is the 'action part of the reflective teaching style' and this includes the day-to-day running of the class and the managing of every learning situation. It is about managing time, people and resources and is crucial in ensuring the success or otherwise in teaching and learning (Pollard and Tann 1987: 120). Moyles argues that management is about what teachers do in response to their organisation 'to ensure both the smooth running of the learning environment and fulfilment of intentions' (1992: 5). Organisation precedes management and both are totally linked (see Cleave and Brown 1989, Pollard 2008). The three-year study of children learning in 19 randomly arranged classrooms compared with 19 structured classrooms found that there were differences in learning outcomes and that spatial organisation did have an impact on learning. The structured classrooms were those where attention had been paid to the issues under the heading of environment and the space was deliberately arranged to promote learning (Nash 1981: 144). Children in the randomly arranged class showed less evidence of development than children in the planned classrooms. Children in the randomly arranged classrooms were often interrupted in their work and unable to move onto more complex tasks.

Blenkin and Whitehead (1988) argue that if the environment is not considered and planned for, the effect of this can actually undermine what the teacher is proposing for children's learning in the first place. So the place in which we expect learning to take place has to reflect the learning we are expecting. We send clear messages to children about what we think of activities by the way we organise things. If something is badly resourced with staff standing around chatting, that tells children reams about what we think of outdoor play. Management and organisation are at the heart of our work; they 'make or break' us. Wragg (1993) argues that the most imaginative teacher will fail if organisation and management have not been addressed.

Expectations

We need to make it clear to children what our expectations are, it makes children anxious if they are unsure what is allowed and expected and what is not. Looking to the ORACLE work, even though it is not concerned with nursery-aged children, provides some relevant findings (Galton *et al.* 1980). Here the pupils were found to want to please the teacher and do what she wanted and they tried to avoid high-risk situations, which might put them in a vulnerable situation. The conclusion from the study is that teachers need to demonstrate clearly what it is they want and value, otherwise children will not try out new and high-risk situations. Owens argues that 'It is not merely enough to provide stimulating school grounds if the children are not shown how to investigate and participate in them' (2004: 74). This small-scale research demonstrates that where children had first-hand experiences and staff had been truly involved with children to show them the potential of outdoors, children were more aware and involved with their surroundings. At De Bohun Primary School reception children are very clear what the expectations of the class are and they know that the staff are willing to pursue and develop their interests. Children come into the room confident and very willing to get going with their current interests. On the day I visited, I was impressed by the level of confidence and clarity with which children chose what to do. A huge range of games were devised and played out which involved mathematics, language and science. Real artifacts were made such as guitars, wands and football shirt numbers. Children were physically active on climbing ropes, moving up and down hills and when building with blocks. Figure 2.1 is a letter written from a parent about his experiences of this class. He was skeptical but is not now.

Children need to feel secure not vulnerable and we can make this happen by ensuring parents and children know what is expected and valued. They need to be told that it is okay to make mistakes and to get things wrong; that we will say 'great' when they do as this gives us a clue as to what help they need next. We need to let them know that we want them to get resources out for themselves, that we love creative ideas, that we do not mind mess (within reason!), that we want them to become independent. We need to reassure children that we love it when they come and talk to us and share ideas, that it's great if they have a problem as there are lots of people who can help. Equally we can get the children involved in deciding upon their shared expectations of the class and what

Having come from the Netherlands during the summer recess, we happily accepted the
school's offer to educate our two daughters. The school staff were hearty and involved.
The school had good Ofsted ratings.
Enthusiasm soon faded, not seeing any structure in the reception class. Children dropped
by their parents, shooting off in every direction. No teacher starting with a group welcome,
song or gathering of some kind.
This apparent lack of attention, supervision, teaching was not what we bargained for.
We were shocked, skeptical, worried and wrong! The child-induced way of discovering its
world stimulated by their guardian teacher. Heed the saying: 'we know what's good for
you, sit and pay attention' has worked miracles.
Our 5-year-old has mastered reading, writing, numbers, created a new social surrounding.
She did it completely stress free, just by playing, following her heart, her interests.
We being very Dutch critical parents, can only testify that the school's method works.
We hope this method will be extended throughout the years 1 to 6.

Figure 2.1 Letter from a convinced parent

they feel is okay and what is not. Finally, we need to be flexible and convey this to children not as a fault or to create insecurity but to be responsive to each day. For example rather than having a blanket rule that no one goes on the grass after 1 October, each day is taken as a new day to decide on the condition of the grass for going on.

Time

Under-fives need a flexible approach to the day and particularly time to play with few interruptions. If children are part of a class where interruptions are frequent they are less likely to settle to tasks. If they know that they have time to pursue activities they will be more motivated to concentrate, persevere and be successful. McAuley and Jackson argue that interrupting 'children's absorbed activity' can 'contribute to a culture which is almost as subversive of learning as allowing disruptive behaviour to become a tolerated norm' (1992: 46–7). In Paley's (1984) study of children's behaviour in her class, she found that when she increased the amount of free playtime, and spread it out over a longer period, the boys ventured to the table activities to do more work-orientated activities, rather than continue to play. Her conclusions from this observation were that the children had been given sufficient time to play and fantasise, the play had not been packed into a frantic time and so the children were happy to move on to more school-orientated activities. Children were able to go between play and activities (more work-focused teaching) in the knowledge that the free play was not to be taken away. The girls actually played imaginatively more than they had previously, but, given that they tended to do more of the work activities, they did not suffer in the school setting or in school tests. Holland (2003) found in her research into Superhero play that when there was a ban on war, weapon and Superhero play children would secretly still make weapons but they were seriously low level in terms of design and quality of thinking. The weapons were the outcome of not being allowed to do something and lack of time. When the ban was lifted and children were allowed to do something previously banned, positively encouraged to

be more inventive and had the time to be so, the constructions were much more complicated and enabled the children to work at a high level of thinking.

As well as not interrupting children, it is important that children spend time on
worthwhile activities and not on time-wasting tasks. Campbell and Neill (1992) talk about
'evaporated time' that is time wasted, time lost doing things of no importance, taking up
one-tenth of a week, that is half a day. Hilsum and Cane (1971), Galton *et al.* (1980), and
Hastings and Wood (2001) evidence how much time is wasted on 'housekeeping' aspects
of life in the class and it does not appear much has changed over time. Rogers and Evans
(2008) noted that children need time to negotiate and assign roles during play. Children
need time to develop ideas and should not be disturbed by adults and have one or
two children taken out as this breaks the play up (DfCSF 2008: 79–80). The *Early Years
Foundation Stage Framework* (2008) argues that children need time to play and work,
that practitioners need to be flexible in their planning, so children can follow an interest
and if necessary enable children to return to an activity at a later time.

In terms of outdoor play, then, this means children do not need to waste time lining
up to go outside, but need to be able to use both areas freely, thereby making sure they
make optimum use of both spaces and have uninterrupted time to pursue interests. Staff
need to plan it so children can access the outside area as soon as possible after they have
come into the class. Staff need to organise their time so that they are free to work with
those children they want to, and not spend time responding to problems which have
resulted from poor organisation. Jago (2002), looking at primary playtime, found that the
more time children had available to them the more active they were.

Child initiated

Child initiated activity has always been central to early years educators. Tina Bruce, looking at the pioneers of early childhood education, notes that they all agree that 'intrinsic
motivation, resulting in child-initiated, self-directed activity, is valued' (Bruce, 1987: 10
and Bruce 2005). Putting that in a modern context Bruce argues that we still see this as
central tenant of education and I would suggest this holds true whether the learner is
4 or 40. The findings of the Effective Provision of Pre-School Education (EPPE) Project
recommend that schools should 'work towards an equal balance of child and adult initiated activity' (Sylva *et al.* 2004: 6). Child-initiated activity has become central to the
government agenda for early years education, with a need for child-initiated and adult-
led activities being available but with a 20/80 per cent split when drawing evidence
about children, so that 20 per cent of the evidence comes from adult-focused activity
and 80 per cent from child-led (DfCSF 2008).

But what does child initiated actually mean and what does it look like in practice?
The dictionary definition of initiate includes 'to begin or originate' and initiative 'the first
step or action of a matter, commencing move' and 'the right or power to begin or initiate
something' (Hanks 1986: 785). Therefore, looking at it in terms of an attitude or disposition we are wishing to foster, it seems important. I want children to grow up into adults

who can take the initiative, do not follow like sheep, who are confident enough to run with an idea. This involves engaging the brain, thinking about things and then making an informed choice, which can be backed up by a rationale. A society which needs speed cameras is full of people who cannot control themselves, cannot think things through. So child-initiated activity is important for now and for the future as the child grows up into an adult. James Dyson, who has invented a number of things including the bag-less vacuum cleaner, would have spent a long time in following his own ideas, designing, redesigning and being criticised, but he didn't give up. On the James Dyson website there is this statement: 'Sadly, most education systems still encourage children towards academic subjects and away from "getting their hands dirty making things". (Strange from the country that started the Industrial Revolution.) It may take time, but Dyson hopes to change that' (Dyson 2009). James Dyson has to be self-obsessed to achieve what he has and not to have that interest squashed. Likewise children need the opportunity to follow through their ideas and interests, to experience both failure and success, to become confident in thinking for themselves, not interested in being controlled by others.

So during a day children need to be involved in both child-initiated and adult-directed activity. What this looks like in practice is that sometimes the adult may be running an experience, whether it be foot printing or gardening, but at other times children will be able to follow their own interests and ideas – interests and ideas which may be very context bound, wrapped up with the resources and playmates available in the setting and at other times interests which may be consuming to each individual, either a subject or a skill. It could be an interest that started at home or spills over into home life. This means there needs to be an environment full of materials which could be many things to many people. (See Chapter 4 for a discussion of versatile equipment and resources). As Bayley and Broadbent argue, cardboard boxes, blankets, telephones, walkie-talkies, masks and dressing- up clothes (2008: 47) are all open-ended materials which can stimulate play and spark off a play interest. The authors suggest that some materials by their very nature encourage engagement, talk and play.

To achieve this the environment needs to be one where children feel secure, are able to trust the adults and know that if they have a particular interest they will be able to pursue it. As Darling asserts: 'Once children see education as something that other people do to them … they lose ability to take any initiative or responsibility for their own learning … we could and should have classrooms where learning is largely self-motivated' (1994: 33). The ideas here are picked up again when discussing independence and self-regulation in Chapter 6. Children need interested adults, able to stand back and able to sometimes work alongside children. They do not need adults who stand around drinking tea and chatting.

But equally it shouldn't be an environment where adults are hovering to deal with anything and everything. Although discussing parents, Mercogliano could equally be talking about teachers when he says:

> 'helicopter parents' can be found hovering protectively over their offspring, ready to swoop in and rescue them at the first sign of trouble … They pave the way, fight

their battles for them, and generally deny them free rein to succeed or fail on their own.

(Mercogliano 2007: 5)

Children need to be left to get on in an environment which has the spirit of the zone of proximal development (Vygotsky 1978), that is stretching not boring, intriguing not sterile, where children know that if things get difficult they can struggle and it is okay but equally when things get too problematic they can return to the adult to seek help, advice and support. They need an environment where the adult is able to ascertain when the child needs to be challenged and taken on.

What child initiated does not mean is the repetition of skills already learnt. The use of bikes outside is a classic example of poor child-initiated activity, where the same children jump on the same bikes, ride round and round every day and learn very little. Children are choosing to do this and it is not an adult-directed activity. But that does not make it worthwhile. For child-initiated or adult-directed activity to be successful it needs to be worthwhile. Worthwhile can only be measured by the learning which takes place, not as generals ('oh they are learning to pedal') but as specifics ('They learnt to pedal yesterday, can pedal backwards today, tomorrow they may be able to pedal round a coned course'). So many children come to an early years setting and simply practise what they can already do.

Child initiated does not mean the survival of the fittest, where those who can push their way forward win; where the bikes rule the outside area or girls rule the home corner. This may be free choice for some but stops the rights of others. So adults cannot ignore child-initiated activity, they do need to ensure they watch and listen, intervene and support when appropriate, so those who wish to take part in an experience, or activity or game, can. If the outdoor area is the M25 on a bad day then those who want to play a game, which does not involve a bike, cannot do so. Child initiated can only go as far as it does not impact adversely on other children's experiences.

Child initiated does not mean adults ignore children. Some schools have choosing time, when children can choose activities to play with when all the important teacher stuff has been completed. What this means in practice is that children are given a small amount of time to choose from a poor stock of battered and incomplete toys and games, and then spend much of the time discovering what pieces are missing. It is a bit of a release for children but yet again it is not worthwhile. They do not learn much and if they do the teacher had not intended it, as they do not rate it as important as when they are formally teaching.

So choosing has to be an informed decision, based on knowing what is available within the setting and feeling confident to try anything. It is not based on staying in an area which one feels comfortable in. We all, adults and children, get caught in doing things we like or feel happy with and become anxious in new situations and with new things. You as the adult may know the painting area backwards, but it could be a child has never painted at an easel and so does not approach it, scared of this new thing. But that child has the right to experience everything on offer and if they are not confident enough to approach it themselves we need to help. It could be a case of simply pointing out that it exists; do not assume what you know about your classroom children know. It could be a case of working with them at the activity until they are confident to work at it on their own. It could be a case of incorporating the experience with something they do feel comfortable with.

So child initiated is about the child following his/her own current interest. It is about grappling with that interest to find out and explore. Child initiated does involve experiences which are worthwhile and move children on, not those where they continually repeat skills already learnt. It may involve struggle and problems, some of which will be solvable, some of which will not. Child initiated does not simply mean self-chosen but it does mean following an interest to learn.

Space

Pollard argues we need to consider the organisation of the space as this can impact on the kind of teaching, the attitudes of learners and the quality of learning (2008: 282). As discussed in Chapter 1 young children learn through movement, and space is essential for this. They are not yet at the stage of sitting quietly and learning, but at the moving-about-and-finding-out stage. Whether one and walking or five and running, children need space as they are very active, both physically and mentally, and also because their motor development is at a crucial stage. These children need the space to move freely and spontaneously, to learn to control their bodies. In a study of 4-year-olds, space, positioning and choice of activities revealed different aspects of the child (Cleave and Brown 1991: 131–2). Good use needs to be made of the outside area so children can work on a larger, more active scale than is possible indoors (DfCSF 2008). If the outdoor area is small the sheer 'feel' of being outside makes it seem larger.

Even such a simple thing as space or lack of space may affect boys and girls differently. Research by Brian Bates into overcrowding in a playgroup suggests that it has differing affects on boys and girls (Bates 1996). He found that as the room became more crowded the boys became more aggressive and formed into groups while the girls became more isolated and played alone. He points to other research which argues the same points, that the more crowded a class became the more solitary the children became, but if they did interact, it was more aggressively. He concludes that children are affected in the short and long term by the conditions under which we teach them and by the methods. Environment does have an effect. Siraj-Blatchford and Sylva (as cited in Rogers and Evans 2008: 102) note a direct and 'negative correlation between restrictions on indoor space and children appearing "anti-social, worried and upset" ' (2004: 719). Their own research project found that the space did impact on children's behaviour, including lack of space and children's physical size. Lack of space was seen as a constraint on role play and thereby needing containing – 71 per cent of the respondents felt this (Rogers and Evans 2008: 57). Where the role play was close to children doing 'formal' work they were restricted in what they did so they did not disturb the children 'working'.

Boys tended to control far more of the space than girls and go out of the designated role play areas to continue their play. Interestingly it is suggested children of different ages need differing amounts of space (van Liempd 2005: 17). Boys may need more space than girls (Rogers and Evans 2008: 103). Jago (2002) found that those schools with more playground space had children who were more physically active and therefore more involved in health-enhancing activity and more likely to reach the Health Education Authority recommendation of an hour per day of physical activity. If we are to pay due regard to children's well-being we have to consider such things as space both in and out.

Teaching and learning

An educational institution is about both teaching and learning. Education is about providing both a teaching and learning environment, a sentiment echoed in the Foundation Stage guidance (QCA 2000: 20–4), and The Early Years Foundation Stage statutory framework (DfCSF 2008 revised: 11) and to some extent in the government's *Learning Outside the Classroom Manifesto* (DfES 2006). This means that not only will children be explicitly taught by an adult they will be able to get on and learn by themselves and with other children. It means the teacher has to be able to de-centre and see teaching and learning through children not through their own performance, a sentiment echoed in Pollard (2008). It means assessment of children is paramount to this approach. For children to learn independently (as discussed above and in Chapter 4) means that teaching and learning have to have equal status, learning cannot be seen as secondary to teaching. But neither can it be sufficient to assume children will learn by chance. It means the environment has to be well resourced and carefully planned. Learning cannot be seen as a free for all, where assessment of worth is judged by whether children go to an activity or whether they say they like it.

It is, of course, quite difficult to divide the two terms 'teaching' and 'learning'. By teaching it is meant those times when the adult is giving specific input to a group of children or to an individual, when an adult is teaching a specific concept which by its nature needs an adult to be involved. The teaching component of play may involve bringing in a teaching point by adding resources which make the children face a new concept. It may simply involve 'fine tuning' (McLean 1991) the environment on a moment by moment basis so the play does continue and does not fizzle out because two children are at odds with each other, unable to solve the issue or vying for space. It may involve simply being in role and developing language or mathematical understanding, linking work done through a matching game, for example.

Children need clear adult input to reach their potential, for example, in movement skills (Gallahue 1989), and this is so in other areas. Moyles argues that teachers have to decide what to actually teach and what to allow children to find out for themselves alone. Some things are better taught, such as art techniques (1992: 123), and some are better discovered independently. She argues further that children can be given more independence if they are taught certain techniques, as they can then choose from a greater range of options or methods as to how to tackle a task. If children are taught techniques for attaching materials, such as using masking tape, glue, nails, then they can use these skills when they want to make, say, the instruments for their street band. Children when given more information about real life scenes can then use that information to get into role and make more of the play. Children can make the instruments for their street band if they have actually had experience of making things at the technology table thereby designing, estimating, counting, cutting and writing. The *Early Years Foundation Stage Framework* (DfCSF 2008) talks in terms of helping children to make connections in their learning and to think forward and to reflect.

Setting up an environment for learning means that children can work together or alone and can find out for themselves; it is about implicitly learning and not being explicitly taught. So, for example, learning to care for others starts with adults caring for children, learning to be independent starts with children being given responsibility. It means that the nature of the activity does not need constant adult input, but does not mean that adults should not be involved at all. Adults need to accept that children are capable of finding out for themselves and are able to manipulate the environment to make discoveries. The way to encourage learning such as investigation, creativity and consolidation are through play and talk. The environment therefore, has to be exciting and stimulating so that children are motivated to utilise the resources and learn. This in turn means that resources and activities need to be carefully chosen. It ultimately means that adults must use their skills of observation to fine tune (MacLean 1991) that environment; to know when to get involved in play, to decide what needs to be done in any situation and to note down difficulties and achievements.

Learning experiences or adventures

One of the ways to make the environment exciting is actually to make it meaningful, and this is where learning experiences come in. There is a place in education to be taught, to learn, to play and work but there is also a place for meaningful experiences, whether it be lying in the pram watching the light play on the leaves or, for a two-year-old, to examine every object on the ground as you go for a 'walk', or for the four-year-old to experience the smells, atmosphere and beauty of a forest walk. As Whitebread *et al.* argue, children 'do not just learn what they are taught; rather, they learn what they experience' (2008: 25). These activities are not really play, they are not work, they are life-learning experiences but they can easily feed into the play, work and taught components of education. If you want to play at garages, or being a flower-seller, it actually helps to see those occupations in action. If you want children to be observant they need to go on regular walks where things are pointed out to them – it is the pointing out which makes the difference. Whitebread and Coltman argue that children need intellectual challenge and this comes about by children 'actively constructing their own understandings' (2008: 10). Therefore, we have to ensure they have meaningful experiences which they can investigate. Interestingly, Moyles says she prefers the word 'experience' rather than activities 'because the latter smacks of just doing something without necessary benefit, rather than undertaking something which results in learning' (2008: 32).

A fantastic and inspirational teacher and founding head of The Coombes School in Arborfield, Sue Humphries has always offered learning experiences or adventures as she calls them. Sue described a couple of examples of learning experiences from the previous three weeks at the school, one to do with storying, the other to do with art. Sue was asked by one of her teachers to help the children understand the concept of 'settings' in writing and by the way could she do something outside on it! Sue stood outside and was inspired to tell the story of Little Dog Turpey. In the story there are hemp stalks and Sue decided to go on a learning adventure by actually using a tug of war rope made of hemp to help the children imagine the story and all its components. The children carried the rope into the playground swinging the rope from side to side over their heads as they said the alphabet and sang songs. She asked the children to really examine the rope and take an individual thread and see how brittle it was on its own. She described how rope once twisted and combined could become so strong as to hold anchors and pull boats. She asked the children to smell the rope as smell can elicit so many visions. Looped on the ground the tug of war rope became the basis of the drama from the story. After this learning adventure children were able to play with the tug of war rope during free time, with one proviso: the rope had to stay on the ground. Small ropes (using sash cord) were provided so children could use the ropes in a way the tug of war rope had been used or in new ways.

Sue described another learning experience, making models using clay. But the experience was extended into a project without the word 'project' ever leaving anyone's lips. Sue had the children bring in a brick and break it in class, thereby discovering the sand particles and the softness of it when broken up. She shared many artefacts made of clay. The children were involved in the digging out of clay from the school clay pit. They spent £80 on hiring a digger for a day which was used to dig the clay out, revealing to the children the various layers: topsoil, strata, subsoil and clay. The clay was brought out and placed in a builder's bag. Meanwhile a marquee/large tent with carpet laid inside was set up as an art studio to stay in situ for a number of weeks. The space had a number of tables arranged and the children were able to use the clay from their own school grounds.

The children had to make the clay useable before they could create with it. They took out all the bits, then rolled and moulded the clay until it became pliable adding water to get the right consistency. Every class in the school was able to use the clay and make models over a number of sessions. In those weeks children had experienced such a lot and used and refined a number of skills, for example:

- fine motor coordination through modelling the clay
- using their hands they learned to roll, grip, pinch, squeeze and so on
- gaining a range of knowledge and understanding about where clay comes from, how it is originally formed, its properties and how it changes when heated

- put real feelings into play
- work together when holding the rope
- work in pairs when using the ropes
- listen to each others' ideas
- create clay models together.

This would fit with Lilian Katz's ideas of project work as described in Chapter 6.

Finally, Sue talked about something as simple as the chair or shoe and how these items can be used to help children to become more observant. She described how she has hoisted chairs or shoes into the trees so they can be viewed from different angles. In this way the chair/shoe can be seen in a different light – at an angle, upside down, from the back. Children become detectives looking for the chairs or shoes, given time to really gaze at and describe what they see. In this way the child's eye is trained to note the differences. And it is through being able to note differences that children can be helped to read. Most letters are pretty similar, children have to note the fine differences between letters to be able to distinguish them and then read them.

Sue finished talking to me by saying: 'every experience becomes a story in its very being'.

Redefining work and play

Any educational establishment should involve work and play. The dictionary definition of play includes the following: to occupy oneself, free, light, freedom of movement, activity, fun, sport, to toy/trifle, perform, amuse (Hanks 1986: 1175) and work is defined as: physical or mental effort directed towards doing or making something, exertion, labour, toil, employment (1747). In some schools there seems to be this unhelpful view that children play at nursery but come to school to work; that children work in class and play at breaktime; that work is more important than play and play is the opposite to work. It is preferable not to see the two terms as counter to each other, but as separate; play is seen by children as a serious business. Froebel (cited by Isaacs 1932) described play as children's work. It is preferable not to view one as more important than the other. Nor does it help to view them as conflicting to each other but simply both parts of our lives whether children or adults (Moyles 1989). We need work and play in schools but we need to agree what the terms mean.

Rogers and Evans offer a debate about play and work and argue that the division of work and play so apparent in Western cultures is not as 'distinct' in non-Western societies (2008: 15). Play appears to have been hijacked by many Western cultures and government rhetoric talks in terms of getting an outcome from play, for example the Early Years Foundation Stage states that 'play underpins the delivery of all the EYFS' (DfCSF 2008: 07 Guidance). Play has been hijacked – it is a multi-million pound industry – ballet, swimming, football, after-school clubs, you name it you can pay for it and it will be organised. But in these clubs and lessons for the majority of the time children are not free and self-motivated as they should be when playing; often there is a lot of stress involved and pressure to achieve. Cunningham (2006), discussing the disappearance of childhood in the twenty-first century, notes the increasing regulation of play and cites the Opies who deployed such control: 'nothing extinguishes self-organized play more effectively than does action to promote it' (Opie 1969: 16). Guldberg argues 'the biggest barrier to children's free play today is the increasing drive to structure the activities' (2009: 83). Fagen (1981) suggests that animal and childhood play is similar in structure: in both it is self-initiated, purposeless and performed by infants and juveniles. He argues that if we impose our will on something which has the defining characteristics of being self-initiated and for intrinsic reward then it stops being play.

It also seems ironic that in the nineteenth century many children from a young age experienced work and exploitation, then in the beginning of the twentieth century philanthropic individuals felt children should not be working down the mines but having a childhood, and now childhood seems to have regressed to one of toil. Children may not work for 12 hours in the mills but they do not have much time for free play. They have so much work in terms of toiling to get through a system which expects them to jump over fences (tests) to get them into training for the next fence jumping (more tests) and the next fence (exams) and the next (degrees) to achieve the ultimate accolade of 'getting a job'. School for many has become a toil, not a rich learning experience.

But there is another type of work that has a social outcome. These 'work' experiences, often called 'chores' are about working alongside adults to achieve an outcome – clean clothes, a meal, a bookcase, a happy car engine! It includes such jobs as laying the table, cutting the grass, helping the old lady down the road. These are all experiences which can be hard, can be fun, but are fruitful. The actual product at the end is important. But what appears to have come about now is that play has been hijacked, requiring an outcome, a purpose (Cohen 1993: 2) and work in terms of a social contribution has been removed. These types of work experiences are by and large missing from society and schools. Children may do a bit of clearing up after a lesson, they may have monitors for some jobs but it is very limited in the types and breadth of the work experience. Some children expect to be paid for doing chores around the house and at the same time are having to learn in school how to be good citizens!

So not only does true play need to be brought back into schools and society but so too does useful work. We need to be aware that maybe playing with children is not viewed by all societies as a prerequisite to healthy childhood. Lancy (2007) argues that parent–child play is generally only found in the upper and middle classes in wealthy families (as cited in Guldberg 2009: 141–2). This would suggest that in some groups it is more important that children work alongside the adults, not necessarily play with them. But as Guldberg (2009) concludes, what is probably most important is to allow children to make up their own games with their own rules in their own fantasy worlds. And in this way as discussed in the section on child-initiated experiences, we need to trust children just to get on with it. So we need children to be good citizens by learning to help others and to be thinkers by letting them play without being organised.

The process and product of work and play

Wells (1987) describes children as 'meaning makers'. In one sense or another we are all meaning makers, but at an early age most of life is taken up with trying to make sense of the world. The adults around young children are there to help them to make sense and reach their full potential. This learning for young children will be easy or more difficult depending on the way it is presented. Children need the means to find out about the world around them, make sense of their discoveries and discover their culture. Lally (1991) and Edgington (2004) usefully describe play as a 'vehicle for learning', something children are naturally attracted to and which we can use to help and support children and watch and find out about them. She suggests that play can offer children opportunities to 'explore and discover, construct, repeat and consolidate, represent, create, imagine, socialise' (Edgington 2004: 127–8). Alongside play there is movement, talk and sensory experience, all of which act as a means by which to learn and are learning in themselves. Children move to learn but they also learn to move (Gallahue 1989, Davies 1995), they play to learn but also learn to play, they talk to learn and learn to talk, they experience to learn but also learn to experience (see Chapter 1 for a discussion about movement). Both 'learning to' and 'to learn' are inextricably linked.

Work can also be viewed in this way: children learn to work or help and through helping/working they learn skills. Jobs do need to be completed – clearing up, setting up the snack table, putting away the wooden blocks – they are an integral part of life. Sami reindeer herding people in Norway say that 'we learn by doing' and 'children learn by herding', what this means is that as the children work alongside the adults they learn everything they need to about their society and their role within it. Tidying up in schools needs to be viewed as important as the academic work. If we look at Cowgate Under 5s Centre's approach there is a direct link between doing and clearing up:

> if you choose to cook you choose to wash up. If you choose to do woodwork you choose to follow our safety rules, respect the tools and replace them safely. Everyone is able to access our curriculum materials but equally everyone must take responsibility for tidying them away.
>
> (Cowgate 2008)

So 'chores' or work experiences need to be planned for and seen as a significant part of the day.

Therefore, outdoor play is much more than just being outside and more than just play, it is about playing and working in a garden. Carruthers (2007: 177) offers a useful discussion about the approach in Norway citing a study of Norwegian kindergartens (Moser and Foyn-Bruun 2006) whose headteachers when asked about the outdoor curriculum stated that 'Nature is a curriculum'. So what this means and what Margaret McMillan (see Chapter 3) envisaged is that the garden is not only a play environment but a working environment, where children play at being gardeners but actually plant, tend and harvest plants, where they sweep up the leaves and prune the shrubs and fill the compost. You do not need to create curriculum content, it is there already. It is not about children learning little watching outside contractors doing the jobs and then going off to play for two minutes!

The importance of play

Each child's play is an expression of their individuality.

(Walsh 1991:10)

Useful early years texts on play include those written by Anthony Pellegrini, Sue Rogers, Janet Moyles, Tina Bruce and Elizabeth Wood and of course Lev Vygotsky. He so clearly explains how important it is for children to play: 'A child's greatest achievements are possible in play, achievements that tomorrow will become her basic level of real action and morality' (1978: 100). He demonstrates that generally children just get on with life, but in play they have to think about it. If you are going to be a baby, a dog, a waiter in play you have to consider what it means to be a sister, an animal or someone who serves. Guldberg (2009) tested children to look at their thinking and view of reality. A child was asked what was inside a tube of Smarties and said: 'Smarties'. When they found it was crayons and were then asked what they thought the next child would think was in there, they said 'Crayons'. Thoughts and reality could not be seen as different but 'once children are able to think about thoughts, their thinking is lifted to a different height' (Guldberg 2009: 78). Through play this happens. Play offers a meaningful context for children and it is only when a situation has meaning and purpose that children can function at a higher level (Donaldson 1978).

Vygotsky (1978) argues that in play children have to show great self-control; children cannot just act on impulse, they have to bow to the rules of the game whatever they may be because play is social and involves others. If you want to stay 'in' you have to 'play the game'. Pellegrini (2005) concurs with this and argues that children have a vested interest while playing with peers to stay 'in' but through the play learn such difficult and demanding strategies to co-operate, compromise and inhibit aggression. Through role-play, children are able to decentre (Bruce 1987 and 2005), to see something from another perspective and this is crucial for a society to function well. So without realising it children learn to do these things, or if they do not, they find they can be isolated. Guldberg (2009: 88) references *The Good Childhood Inquiry* which suggests that the number of teenagers without a best friend is rising. You cannot be taught how to make friends, you have to find out through trying it. We need to give children the space to practise. Holland, researching gun and Superhero play, concludes that 'there is more free flow play among boys and friendships have been made through Batman and Robin combinations' (2003: 70). Holland found that social skills and more imaginative role-play were enhanced through quality play. Whitehurst (2001) makes a clear link between play,

play outside and personal, social and emotional development. Haines (2000), making a comparison between nursery education in Denmark and England, discusses a Danish study about why outside environments seem so beneficial to children. This argues that it is due to the positive attitude of staff to outside, who consider playing outside is more valuable than time spent inside and that play outside gives children opportunities for social and emotional development that cannot be found elsewhere.

Singer and Singer (1990) indicate the centrality of dramatic play to young children's development, and Smilansky and Shefatya (1990) argue that children who can readily manipulate symbols in dramatic play are more likely to accept and use the arbitrary symbols of mathematics and written language. Generally for a child until they learn to read, a cup is a cup is a cup. But in play meaning and objects separate. So a box can be a television, can be a cage, can be a den. This is the beginning of understanding that there are objects and there are meanings; the two are separate. This is the start of under-standing written language. Much has been written about how important play is, but if it helps only to ensure children can write, read, cooperate and think, it is worth retaining. In conclusion Guldberg (2009) argues that both through play and formal education Vygotsky's (1978) zone of proximal development can be achieved. That is through both vehicles of play and formal education children can be taken from where they are and moved on.

Holland, researching into Superhero play, found that having a relaxed approach to 'war, weapon and Superhero play' meant that two major gains were improved: imagina-tive play alongside social development (2003: 77). She also argues that this type of play with careful adult intervention can help extend the imaginative play of those children who seem to display rather aggressive tendencies:

> My argument is that war, weapon and Superhero play can be used as a platform to extend and develop the imaginative capabilities of some of those hard-to-manage children identified as being at risk in Dunn and Hughes's (2001) work in order to avoid the negative social outcomes noted in those children at age of 6.
>
> (2003: 79)

Taylor (1980: 133), as cited in Gallahue and Ozmun, asserts that:

> one of the best and easiest pathways to a strong self-concept is through play. Play offers opportunities to assist the child in all areas of development. Its importance can be found in how he (the child) perceives himself, his body, his abilities and his relationships with other.
>
> (Gallahue and Ozmun 2005: 287)

So Holland, Taylor, Gallahue and Ozmun are making a clear link between movement and play, that children do need to feel confident in their movement abilities and this can be fostered through their play.

A play continuum

Pellegrini describes play as being on a continuum going from 'pure play' to 'nonplay' (1991: 215) rather than describing it as play or not play (see Figure 2.2). Pellegrini suggests we can measure play:

- in terms of dispositions (see Chapter 6 for a discussion about Katz's dispositions) for learning, meaning there have to be certain attitudes prevalent for it to be called play
- as a context, so what is happening right now has to be appropriate
- as behaviour displayed, what the children are actually doing – for example, building a tower, being a mum or playing snap.

But the more of the dispositions and context which are prevalent, the more it is considered pure play. It then means we do not have to dismiss a child completing a puzzle as it does not fit our view of what play is, nor to worry as children very cleverly swing in and out of play. But equally we cannot then suggest 30 seconds rocking back and forth on a rope swing constitutes play.

Play as disposition:

- intrinsic motivation – children play because they want to
- attention to means – not outcome driven, concerned with playful acts
- 'What can I do with it?' – need to explore first
- non-literal – it's about make-believe
- flexibility – rules are constructed within the play by those participating and can change
- active engagement – players are making up the game, it hasn't been determined beforehand.

Play as context:

- familiar – need to explore prior to play if you don't know the materials, people
- free choice – children choose
- stress free – free from hunger, illness, tiredness, unfriendly children or adults.

Play as observable behaviour

- functional – (sensorimotor) – using previously learned motor skills in new situations
- symbolic – (preoperational) – representing real life
- games-with-rules – (concrete operational) – following externally imposed rules.

Figure 2.2 Dimensions of play
Source: Pellegrini, A.D (1991) *Applied Child Study*. New Jersey: Lawrence Erlbaum Associates, 214. Based on the text of Rubin, K., Fein, G. and Vandenberg, B. (1983) 'Play', In Hetherington, E. M. (ed.) *Handbook of Child Psychology. Vol IV Socialization, Personality and Social Development,* New York: Wiley, 693–774. Reproduced with permission from Taylor & Francis Ltd

Analysing behaviour during play episodes

Pellegrini (1991) suggests how we can analyse children at play (see Figure 2.3) and how this tool can help us understand play and assess children while they are playing. He argues strongly that we need to look at both the social and cognitive aspects of a child's play to fully understand a child and their social and cognitive competences; which can help us form a true picture of that child. Vygotsky (1967) suggests that during play children tend to work at their optimal level when we can see what they can really do, as they are truly motivated and not fearful of failure. Viewing both social and cognitive aspects of a child also fit the findings of the Effective Provision of Pre-School Education (EPPE) research (Sylva *et al.* 2004), which note that where schools see education and social development of equal importance children do much better than where they do not. Only looking at the social or the cognitive aspects of a play episode can give a false picture of a child. Pellegrini argues that we cannot use the categories totally hierarchically, for example a child may play alongside others to then become part of the play situation, and that some solitary play such as solitary-constructive has been shown to be a better predictor of social-cognitive performance than measures of interactive play (1991: 220). However, generally he suggests that as children develop they are able to engage in more complex play episodes, being of a more dramatic nature. The ability to weave play events into a coherent theme is related to children's narrative competence (tell and comprehend stories). So this is very useful in helping children's literacy skills (Pellegrini 1991).

The play spiral

Following on from the discussion above regarding child-initiated activities, Moyles's play spiral (1989: 15–16) helps create a balanced understanding of child-initiated and adult-initiated activities in schools. In this framework Moyles argues that learning is

Child's name		Date			
Context					
Others present					
		Functional	Constructive	Dramatic	Games-rules
	Solitary				
	Parallel				
	Interactive				

Figure 2.3 Categorising play
Source: Pellegrini, A. D. (1991) *Applied Child Study.* New Jersey: Lawrence Erlbaum Associates. Table 12.2, page 220. Reproduced with permission from Taylor & Francis Ltd

repetitive and incremental, that is you have to come back to it. Learning builds on learning. In this way the children become more competent, so a teacher can build on what children may have gained from free play in a more adult-arranged play situation (see Figure 2.4). Therefore children may get different things from adult-led as opposed to child-led play. It is not that child-led is in competition with adult-led or visa versa. It is that one can observe child-led experiences, see children's interest and then maybe set something up to support and extend that learning. For example in Bilton (2004b: 33) there is a discussion about how one child's interest in fungi found in the garden led to a range of learning for two children. But it was the adult who was the catalyst for all the learning that occurred. Equally one can use an interest in one area to be a stepping stone for other learning. Pellegrini suggests 'play can be used as an instructional mode' (1991: 213) thereby helping the child understand something more easily through offering it in a play-orientated curriculum. For example, two children in a school were interested in digging and making witch's brews. The staff saw this as an opportunity to give the children more practice with their writing. The staff buried lots of 'treasure' (sea glass, shells, sweet wrappers, bottle tops) in the digging plot, and nearby placed big pots and a large range of spoons, ladles, chalk boards and chalks. Staff made up a story that something magical must have happened in the night as they had found some treasure in the digging plot. Children were quickly drawn to the area! Staff were easily incorporated into the play and one member decided to make an inventory of everything they found which caught the imaginations of children including the two boys they were initially

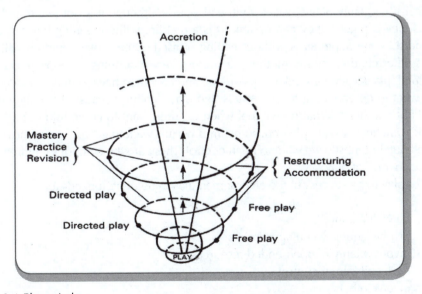

Figure 2.4 Play spiral
Source: 'The Play Spiral' from Moyles, J. (1989) *Just Playing? The Role and Status of Play in Early Childhood Education.* © The Open University. Reproduced with the kind permission of Open University Press. All rights reserved

wanting to pinpoint. Enthusiastically, children wrote out their inventories, their witch's brew and their recipes. In this way the two children highlighted were able to develop their writing.

See Chapter 7 for a detailed discussion of the role of the adult.

A supportive play environment

We do have to be wary so we do not kid ourselves and assume that choosing time equals quality play. The research by Bennett and Kell (1989) and Rogers and Evans (2008) makes it clear there is a mismatch between what teachers think they do in the name of play and what actually constitutes play. Only 6 per cent of the observations were classed as play, much was regarded as time filling with no challenge or purpose (Bennett and Kelly 1989). Similarly, Katz (1995), although discussing self-esteem, argues that much of the practice in schools is suspect. Activities 'intended to enhance it (*self esteem*) are more likely to foster preoccupation with oneself and achieved through helping children to cope with frustrations and negative comments rather than going over the top with praise and flattery'. She argues that self-confidence comes from making children competent, creating a learning environment where children are able to make proper decisions, where they can make real choices and have interesting challenges rather than quick success. Her discussions make for powerful reading and demonstrate that some of what is put out and done for children in the name of help is incredibly low level intellectually and sometimes an insult, which Katz describes as 'frivolous and cute' (1995: 140). Quality play engages children because although it is not real to us, it is as real as they can get – they can pretend it is a real fire without getting burnt, they can pretend they are Superheros without getting bruised. During play children will come across other children as say mothers saying not very nice things, 'shopkeepers' being unhelpful, planks getting stuck in an A-frame and they then have to make real decisions as to what to do and what to say. Adults find play difficult because it is children's real world but not theirs. What do we feel when children want to come into our adult real world? Sometimes we are pleased, sometimes we just want to get on, sometimes we feel pushed out, but mostly we want to be in control. These are the emotions children feel in their real world of play.

For play to be successful the environment has to be right. It needs to:

- be well planned
- involve adults, when appropriate
- involve plenty of open-ended resources
- have children in control
- involve others
- involve talking and listening
- have lots of time available.

The following scene may go some way to explaining the ideas above:

> Robert, Barry and Matthew parked three wooden trucks containing milk crates next to the school building. The children, by their actions, had obviously decided this was the milk depot. One of Robert's crates fell off. 'Oh, I must have been going too fast.' 'I've got more than you,' said Matthew. He then counted his crates and also Robert's. 'You've got more.' The teacher, when she entered the scene, was told: 'We're delivering milk. We leave the trucks this way' (Robert gestured) 'at night, and then turn them round in the morning.' Two other children joined the group. The teacher asked if she could buy some milk. 'Yes, and there's bread also,' said Robert. A discussion ensued about how much milk and bread was wanted, and the price and then 'goods and money' exchanged hands. The children went off. They returned to the teacher three minutes later. 'You need some more bread, milk and ... a present,' said Robert. 'I've got peas and veg,' said Matthew. The teacher and two other children bought bread and milk and the teacher took the present. Robert then tried to take Matthew's black crate which was the bread crate. An argument began and the teacher became involved. Suddenly, Matthew shouted, 'The bread's been stolen!' 'You need to go to the police station to report it,' replied the teacher. 'The police have stolen it,' Matthew declared. All the children involved laughed and the disagreement was forgotten. Scott joined the group. 'I've bought some shopping, here you are,' he said, and gave it to the teacher. 'It's ever so heavy,' replied the teacher. 'It cost one,' Scott said. The teacher gave him 'one'. Naomi joined the group. 'Can I buy some milk?' Robert replied, 'No! You can have it delivered this afternoon. Go home and wait.' Naomi went. By this time Matthew had moved away from the group and was lying on the ground mending his truck. As the teacher moved towards him he shouted, 'It's fixed,' and went off towards Robert. 'I've got fruit for sale,' said Matthew, and they went off together.
>
> (Bilton 1989: 40–1)

This play scene carried on for an hour and involved various children moving in and out of the play. Significant in this scene is the length of time it continued and that children were able to continue the play, despite difficulties they faced in it. These children knew they had time to play, they had space and resources and so the play could function on a complicated level. It was a very cold day, but the children were wrapped up warmly, they were moving and so kept warm, and there were no interruptions or distractions to their play. The significance of play to these children is shown by their desire to continue it and the skills they employ to do so. In the scene where Robert added a present to the second transaction with the teacher, it may be that he just wanted to add a present. But it may have been added to encourage the teacher to join in the play. The teacher had already bought milk and bread and may not have wanted to buy more, a present would be an added incentive. Matthew successfully defused the argument over the crate – which could have easily brought the game to a halt – by saying the crate had been stolen. Matthew also showed that he knew where he wanted the play to go, by rejecting the teacher's suggestion that they should go to the police station to report that the bread had been stolen; he countered by saying the police had stolen it. He was obviously wanting to be in control of the play and knew how he wanted the play to unfold. By telling Naomi to go home and wait for the bread to be delivered, Robert was extending the play and creating a scene where the children had to travel, rather than stay still.

Well planned

Play that children really become motivated by does not just happen, it has to be planned so it does happen. It may be no outsider including the children can see any evidence of that planning but it will be there. The teacher has to discuss with the team that play will occur and it has a high priority, the staff have to be supportive to play. Consideration has to given to the ethos of the class, what is and is not allowed. Is dough allowed in the home corner, are dolls allowed outside, can bikes go inside? And then staff need to be able to justify their decisions. Holland's (2003) research into Superhero play demonstrates the need for children to be reassured by staff about what it is okay to do. In one setting, Superhero play was allowed, but pointing at others with a gun was not. Staff need to consider the materials that are available, where children play and for how long. Children need some idea of the boundaries – too many and play will not get off the ground, too few and it can become survival of the fittest.

Sometimes practitioners change a play area overnight and children are expected to immediately fall into playing a new role. This is not helpful to children, as it is an imposition and may not fit their current interests. Staff can set up play scenes, alongside free-play scenes, but they need to be inspired by the current interests of children (as Moyles suggests in the play spiral, page 52) and slowly unfold. The pizza delivery scene mentioned in the planning sheet (Chapter 7) is an example of this approach. The staff and children devised this play together. Plans were drawn up as to what learning might occur, what resources and equipment were needed and what children could make themselves. Then children started to make pretend pizzas and garlic breads, design and eventually make and mass-produce logos and labels. Menus were written and rewritten and telephones made. With this came lots of talk about fast food and home deliveries. Then equipment was gathered and parents were involved in collecting things. A counter was made and stocked and children started to use it. The bikes were transformed to be the delivery vehicles. Staff acted out scenes that might occur in the shop and on the phone. Books were used to open discussions about the subject. And so, gently, the whole pizza delivery scene was opened. Over time the pizza delivery was added to and children devised their own play scenes within this broad scene. Children were able to think and were made to think for themselves, solving problems within the play. Children needed to cooperate, negotiate and interact in different ways. Staff incorporated maths work into the scenes, regarding prices, totals, quantities and so on. Staff and children were involved in long and complicated conversations. Lots of movement of various types was involved in the play – including using the bikes, packing the boxes, manoeuvring about the counter.

A lot of work went into behind the scenes planning, but it was worth it as children were able to think, discuss, be responsible, concentrate, persist, represent.

Adult involvement

Adults of course will sometimes be involved in play, but the approach needs to be one of interaction not interference. Adults are resources and that resource could be a pincer grip (because the child cannot manipulate a peg), a sounding board (so children can think through their ideas or problems), a playmate (being the invited poodle or a facilitator to ensure play continues). See Figure 2.5 for the multifaceted roles of the adult and Chapter 7 for a more in-depth discussion of the role of the adult.

Join in with children's experiences because:
- learning increases
- quality of play improves
- quality of conversation improves
- raises status of play, activity and participants
- raises esteem of those involved
- unsure children can be supported
- stereotypical play is reduced.

When managing the class day to day about
- furthering play situations
- feeding in ideas
- adding resources
- making sure play of one group doesn't encroach on another
- pre-empting problems
- encouraging children to try new ideas
- stopping children giving up
- making connections with subjects
- making sure children have choices
- encouraging children to put resources back once finished with.

When teaching remember:
- it is teaching not supervising
- the skills, knowledge and attitudes you are wanting to foster
- the developmental stages
- the patterns of expectation from activities and learning bays.

When setting up:
- don't do it all
- make sure children can get out things they want
- see it as being about feeding ideas, posing questions, teaching specific skills
- provide ideas bank – photographs of children at work to inspire children.

When tidying away:
- involve all the children
- consider the teaching possibilities
- build it into the planning and observations.

Figure 2.5 Organising and managing the environment for teaching and learning

Plenty of resources and versatile resources

Children need a range of resources, some of which are open ended and can be many things to many people, some of which are representational such as a doll. A toilet roll can be a telescope, a phone, a megaphone. Having objects which do not have a specific function ensure the play is not limited nor controlled by the object. Children need simple yet versatile resources and equipment which they can adapt to suit their needs and level of understanding. Pellegrini argues that 'general research suggests that different types of materials have very specific effects on social-cognitive aspects of children's behavior' (1991: 50). He argues further that 'more open ended materials (material and vague functions, such as blocks and clay) result in more sustained activity than more explicitly defined materials (e.g. puzzles)' (1991: 50). Where there are loose parts children have to be involved in more sustained play, so it therefore will impact on the level of learning. Of course children sometimes need representational toys, such as dolls, as these allow for more complex play (Pellegrini 1991). For a baby play scene to develop a toy doll is needed, which can be cuddled and fed and changed, with which the player will have a strong bond. A toilet roll tube would not suffice. It is interesting to note that in times gone by when children did not get hundreds of presents, usually the popular girl toy was a doll.

Children will not always need actual resources to represent something, for example, in the scene with the milkmen, the milk, bread, a present and money were all in the players' imaginations. But equally, children may want to make the resources. The trick is to not only get children to build with blocks and crates and material to create a structure they want, but also to use the materials from the technology table to make what they need. So, if children need binoculars they can make them, if they need maps they can make them, if they want instruments attached to themselves for a band-playing scene, they can make them.

Children need to know they can use materials from any learning area for their purposes, and that they can move in and out of areas for the play. It is hard to extend play and develop ideas if the sand contains seven dinosaurs with no option to use any other resources. Finally we must make sure some toys do not gain a high status and children vie to take control of that toy, which can often happen with bikes outside. (See Chapter 4 and 5 for more on this subject).

Children in control

If you talk to children they will say that the classroom is controlled by the adults, particularly the teacher, but outside is free from adult control. This is one of the reasons why children like to get outside, they are in charge and when you are in control you feel happier and less stressed, you feel there is potential and are more confident about yourself. The following scene looks at how children control their play. The staff had set up a train scene outside using hollow blocks, a steering wheel and an assortment of hats, whistles, batons and bags. Four children entered the scene and started to put on the hats, pick up bags and arrange themselves on the blocks. This scene lasted some minutes. Two other children joined and wanted to set up a cafe on the train. They disappeared to get milk crates and pieces of flat wood. These they arranged to act as cooker, sink, worktops and so on. They disappeared again to get cups, plates and saucepans, plus sticks and leaves for the food. The hollow blocks had string tied on for seat belts. This action caused a heated discussion about whether trains had seat belts. This was followed by a scene of people being on a train, buying food, eating it and moving about the train. One child who had been in the scene returned with a piece of material for a bed and a bag filled with various items for his journey. These children could not have reached this detail or level of play if they had not been allowed to adapt the original set-up and use equipment to suit their needs, for example, the crates for kitchen equipment. Children need to use their imaginations and to control, modify and change their environment. Only in this way can play between children develop, and it is when it develops that really imaginative play comes in. A ready-made environment with fixed climbing frames and painted vehicle lines cannot be controlled because it gives little scope for children to add to or change. When children are able to control their environment their behaviour changes (Ranzoni 1973). A changeable environment encourages knowledge-seeking behaviour and interest, and extends exploration (Overholser and Pellerin 1980).

Involving others

So much of life is about others and in terms of play it is a social preoccupation, so children not only need to learn the skills of caring and sharing but also to use those skills in play scenarios. Talking to adults about their own childhood play experiences shows that much of the learning is about how to get on with others, how to get your way without a fight, how to compromise and be satisfied, how to negotiate a path, how to consider another person's perspective. This is also true of play for children today. So through play and other activities children need to see adults negotiating and compromising so they learn to. They need situations which enable them to practise negotiating (for example during tidy-up time when older ones help the younger ones), of compromising (at the snack table when they have to have apple instead of orange) and through role play which involves working with others to be part of the group and stay within the group. The adult needs to support children by ensuring that some children do not suffocate others and that reticent children do not get pushed out.

Involving talking and listening

Of course if it involves others, play will involve talking and listening – both of which need plenty of practice and refining. Wood and Bennett (1997) noted one of the primary functions of play was to develop children's language (and social skills). So children need to be given as much information about real-life scenes as possible and need plenty of learning adventures as detailed above. If a cafe is a current interest children can be helped by looking at books and the internet about the subject, adults can role-play possible scenes, a visit to a cafe can happen, someone from a cafe could come in and talk about their job, the subject can be discussed as a group. There are endless possibilities.

Vygotsky (1978), Wells (1987) and Trevarthen (1994) argue that social interaction and communication are central to children's development; they need and want to communicate with other children and adults. Vygotsky demonstrates how socialised speech is internalised by children and structures their thinking and concept formation. Trevarthen demonstrates how important the fantasy world is to children at around the age of four, and how they are clearly able to imitate and act out a story. What is very important at this stage is for children to act out the drama as real people. This closely parallels Wood's (1988) theory that children are novices, adults being the experts, and so children need to play around with ideas, to be in the expert roles and to 'have a go'. This is about children using themselves as the players in socio-dramatic play.

Having time to play

One of the reasons children need time to play is that they need time to initially jostle for position and get into the play scene. Equally children cannot concentrate and show they can persevere if they are interrupted. Play works well if it is given time to develop. Some play can only be classified as mundane and rather pointless because children have been given no time to do much else with it. Children are being allowed to time fill and they are aware they do not have control over the situation, so it simply ends up in everyone's mind as time filling and time wasting (Bennett *et al.* 1997). Equally as disheartening play can become a reward (Adams *et al.* 2004, Rogers and Evans 2008) particularly where early years practice is mimicking Key Stage 1 practice. 'If you do your work then you can play'. What can also happen is those children struggling with their work never get to play as they end up struggling with their work, need help, still struggle and then watch those who find the work easy, do it and then go off and play! It almost verges on the inhumane to treat anyone like this. One of the findings from the Rogers and Evans research into role play in reception classes suggest that: 'extended periods of *uninterrupted* role-play would enable children to develop and demonstrate the sustained and complex narratives possible in this age range' (2008: 119).

A word about role play

Although one is anticipating all sorts of play happening in an early years environment, role play has to be seen as the most important type and one which should be happening all the time. Role play can be called fantasy play, pretend, home corner, imaginative or socio-dramatic, but the overriding term is role play, meaning 'shared pretend play between children in which they temporarily act out the part of someone else using pretend actions and utterances' (Harris, 2000: 30, cited in Rogers and Evans 2008: 3). Through the research into role play in reception classes Rogers and Evans (2008) demonstrate children's overriding desire to be involved in it. Frost and Campbell (1985) found that children aged four to six preferred an environment which encouraged dramatic play.

Play fighting

Play fighting (rough and tumble) and real fighting (aggression) are different and most children tend to be able to tell the difference, but often adults either cannot tell the difference or through their own experiences (and often this is along gender lines) cannot accept there is a difference (Pellegrini 1988, Connor 1989, Goldstein 1994, Schafer and Smith 1996). As adults we therefore cannot dismiss fighting because we do not like it. Schafer and Smith (1996) conclude that around 1 per cent of the pretend play researched descended into real aggression as opposed to around the 29 per cent suggested by the teachers. For those children who were socially less able or with more aggressive tendencies the figure was around 25 per cent, but again less than the teachers estimate. We need to learn to read situations and understand when children are play fighting and when they are real fighting. Women are more likely to call a play incident aggressive than men are and teachers tend to leave children alone if they are playing with gender specific toys. If girls start to fight, teachers are more likely to be concerned (Goldstein 1994). We also need to learn to trust children, as a child comments in the Holland research: 'This is not a gun, it's a toy – real guns kill' (2003: 85).

Holland (2003), looking at Superhero, war and gun play, demonstrates that actually banning gun play does not solve problems and generally causes greater ones. In settings where gun play is banned children still make them. It tends to be on the hoof, with a gun being constructed from two bits of Lego, away from adults, when 'bang bang' is shouted, an irate adult emerges saying 'we do not have guns here' and the children go off to find some other place to make them. In Holland's fascinating research she found that when Superhero play was allowed and when adults became involved more helpfully in children's play:

- the imaginative play developed
- the children's involvement in other activities increased
- those other activities improved in quality.

In a setting where Superhero play was allowed, the actual construction of 'guns' became far more complicated than when it had been banned, with the language used developing. Holland further argues that although she concurs with the findings of the Dunn and Hughes (2001) research which found that those children at age 4 with an interest in violent play themes demonstrated at age 6 less socially intelligent behaviour than those children who did not, she did not see this as a reason to ban Superhero play. She argues that we need to work with those children to help develop their social skills and their ability to negotiate through the fantasy play (Holland 2003: 38–9). Pellegrini (1988), through his own research and the study of others, notes that popular children generally know the difference between the two types of 'fighting'. However, those children he describes as 'rejected' (rejected in terms of relationships with others) were unable to differentiate between real and pretend fighting. Popular children were unlikely to escalate play fighting to aggression, but rejected children did. Popular children wanted to join the rough and tumble play fighting but rejected children did not.

Therefore, adults need to keep a beady eye out and support children who find play fighting difficult, to find ways to enhance their self-esteem and help them to 'read' situations. This could be through sharing images from books, discussing people's intentions by looking at their faces and body language. One could actually play fight with these children and show what is classed as play and what is classed as real fighting.

Blurton-Jones (1967) as cited in Holland (2003) demonstrates through his studies how rough and tumble play is not random but has specific moves; this is supported by Holland's (2003) observations:

> The human 'rough and tumble play', as I shall call it … consists of seven movement patterns which tend to occur at the same time as each other and not to occur with other movements. These are running, chasing and felling; wrestling; jumping up and down with both feet together … beating at each other with an open hand without actually hitting … beating at each other with an object but not hitting; laughing. In addition, falling seems to be a regular part of this behaviour, and if there is anything soft to land on children spend much more time throwing themselves and each other onto it.
>
> (Blurton-Jones 1967: 355, as cited in Holland 2003: 92)

This encourages us to appreciate that rough and tumble is something innate not alien and that there is a process to it (see Figure 2.6). Becoming aware of the various movements ensures we can support rough and tumble fighting not ban it, but equally know when it is about to move into being aggressive fighting.

Seven movement patterns:
1 running
2 chasing and felling
3 wrestling
4 jumping up and down with both feet together
5 beating at each other with an open hand without actually hitting
6 beating at each other with an object but not hitting
7 laughing.
Sometimes falling and throwing body onto the ground.
Taken from Blurton-Jones, N. (1967: 355)

Figure 2.6 Rough and tumble play

Pellegrini notes that rough and tumble helps with social skills in that sometimes a child is the aggressor, sometimes the victim, sometimes the chaser, sometimes the chased. In these games children have to decentre and find out what its like to be someone different and so 'get on' with the person. They also need to know how to be that person – whether victim or aggressor. Children learn to read the situation and then react appropriately; all of this is helpful to adulthood. By changing roles children ensure they do not get bored and the play is sustained.

Outside is a place ideal for rough and tumble play. We cannot allow our own prejudices nor lack of understanding to stop children play fighting. In a caring setting, children who are comfortable with play fighting and those who are not can both learn from being allowed to go into these Superhero roles.

Talking about play

Encouraging children to talk about their play may be a key teaching component of play and Bennett *et al.* (1997) suggest this needs to be recognised. The recent *Review of the Primary Curriculum* (DfCSF 2009) once again highlights the centrality of talking. Children need opportunities to simply talk about what they are doing as they play and what they have done when they have played. They need opportunities to 'tell the story of ...' when the adult writes the narrative. De Bohun Primary School reception class has found that the writing-down of a story tells reams about a child but also shows that one values their play and ideas. It helps children to make the connection between doing and storying and eventually to them writing. A discussion or review time needs careful handling and planning but may mean that children could 'become more consciously aware of what they are doing, learning and achieving in their play' (Bennett *et al.* 1997: 130). This could be incorporated into a general whole-group time and will clearly have links to both language and mathematical development. But it is also possible on a child-to-adult basis or small-group-to-adult basis and this would be the preferred approach, ensuring sustained shared thinking as aired in the EPPE project (Sylva *et al.* 2004).

These sharing times must not be forced. Initially children will find it difficult to talk and will give short answers, but given time they will become very able and proficient at sharing their play scenes. Play can seem somewhat divorced from anything else that is going on in the class. To consolidate ideas children need to express them in some way, and talking is one means by which they can express themselves. It will not be possible to have every child discussing their play every day but it should be possible to cover a class, over, say, a couple of weeks. Bringing play to a forum may raise its status and raise the status of those involved. Children could be asked to tell 'the story of ...' and be asked what they have learnt, whether they want the play to continue and where they want the play to lead the next day. They could also be asked to focus on a particular aspect of the play, maybe tell its story. This means children need to be clear, logical and reflective. The learning potential of such times is high: the teaching possibilities are there. But there is also the benefit of staff being able to assess what children have learnt and assess the potential of the play.

A supportive work environment

As described earlier we need to see school as a place to encourage work, but not work as in toil but as in community spirit. So helping, setting up and tidying away can be seen as important components of any child's school day. The lovely thing about these types of activities is the warm glow of success and achievement they bring. For work to be successful the environment has to be right. It needs to:

- be well planned and executed
- involve everyone
- involve instructional talk and action
- have lots of time available.

Well planned and executed

A supportive work environment is one which does not set the adult as the slave, forever clearing up for children. Children want to do real work, they want to feel important so there is no reason why they should not be involved with real activity which has an outcome. It has to be seriously well organised and adults need to set the ground rules of the activity or everyday jobs. As the example from the Cowgate Nursery (Cowgate 2008) showed, there is a clear understanding from the beginning that children have responsibilities. If children are involved in gardening they have to know and accept the plot cannot be used for just general digging. With this sort of job adults will need to be in attendance, or periodically in attendance or in contact with those doing the work. If children are putting PE-type equipment away then they need to have been taught the correct way to hold things and work together when holding equipment. If children are clearing up they need to know exactly what needs doing, in what order, where and so on. If we give children the skills and the understanding and the right level of adult support they can do lots of jobs and tasks.

Involving everyone

Everyone needs to feel involved in the work activities, so setting-up/clearing-up rotas are needed. For younger children it may just be a case of talking about what needs to be done. As children get older they can refer to picture and word charts. Older and younger children need to be combined so the older can support the young ones' attempts. Adults need to keep an eye so a few sharp ones do not get out of clearing up every day, this simply is not fair or right and should not be condoned by adults because they cannot be bothered to notice. If it is gardening, it is likely all children will want to be involved but they cannot all do gardening at the same time. Sweeping leaves could involve two children with child-size brushes and then two other children later putting the leaves in a wheel-barrow or into the compost. If too many children are involved at once, accidents can occur. Weeding needs children who are ready to take on such a responsible and time-consuming job. You can make identification cards, so children know what needs to be pulled up and why and what does not.

At the end of every session properly organised tidy-up time needs to be established. The rule of thumb is to start a couple of children off with the more long-winded jobs – cleaning paint pots, cleaning the clay table, putting away the gardening equipment, clearing complicated role play. The younger the child the more the adult needs to be involved. With older children they will be used to what is required and can actually be responsible for younger children.

Involving instructional talk and action

Children need clear instructions; thought has to go into the actual phrasing of these explanations. Children cannot be good explainers if they have not had good role models. Children need to be aware that what is asked is exactly what is required. Word or picture cards, showing the actions, support children in their endeavours. When the job is done children can feed back and say what they have done and maybe not done, to reinforce the language and understanding. For example if a child shares how they laid the table and the order of events, they have to be clear in their mind about the tasks and this helps with formulating thoughts, being logical, knowing what detail to leave in and what detail to leave out. If they have been gardening the adults need to have talked to them using the correct terminology so they can use it. Gardening is a very useful subject to help children use past, present and future tenses. For example if children have been thinning out they could talk about whether they enjoyed it, what weeds they found and these could be shown. They could discuss what is to happen next, how long it will be until the crop can be harvested and so on. Children have a real purpose for talking. Similarly after clearing up some children who may have had difficulties could discuss how they overcame that difficulty or may have suggestions as to how to make something more effective or efficient in the setting.

Having lots of time available

It is no good suggesting to children that they can do the job and then end up doing most of it yourself. I still see Year 6 children during a cooking session standing around watching the teaching assistant do everything. Early years children want to get involved and really do the job, so we need to let them. However, it is important to be clear about who does what, what they can do with as little support as possible. Consider what needs maximum support, what the optimum number of children is to make the activity or task manageable. Children will make mistakes, lots of them. But children and adults can only learn if it is accepted they may make mistakes and they may drop the flour, they may get washing-up water on the floor, they may put the bricks away in the wrong order. These are not big issues and can be rectified. Children only learn how to pour and cut if given enough opportunities to do so.

Discussion

As the Fun Boy Three/Bananarama song goes: 'T'aint what you do, it's the way that you do it, that's what gets results'. This holds true for any teaching and learning setting whether it be under a ceiling or beneath the clouds. To achieve learning outside the environment has to be carefully considered. Teaching should occur and learning cannot happen as an afterthought. Where resources are housed, what children can access, how long they can stay out, how children move from one activity to another, who has responsibility for that space, how the adults move into play are just some of the issues needing answers. Everything the adults do says everything about what style of teacher they are. Throwing a few bikes outside every day tells us that those staff responsible do not care about outside. The outdoors is both a working and a playing space, a place where children can play and develop their play and work to achieve community outcomes such as a weeded flower bed. The space outside is for all children, not just a few who want to control it.

Questions

1. Think of a time when you had no choice in a situation, you had to do whatever it was. How did that make you feel? Now think of a time when you did have a choice. How did that make you feel? Remember to ensure children have choices and control because you want them to feel in control, confident, valued and that they have potential.
2. Sue Humphries described every experience as 'becoming a story in its very being'. Are the experiences you provide children so interesting and absorbing that they are a story to be told?
3. Do staff work at all activities or concentrate on a few, thereby giving high status to some activities and low status to others?
4. Take Pelligrini's play dimensions (page 51) and observe seven incidents of children involved in play. Decide where the activity lies on the play continuum. Ask yourself what more could you do to move the activity further towards pure play.
5. Take Pellegrini's play categories (page 52) and have two members of staff observe the same play situations of two children. Then match your observations and see if you came to the same conclusions about the child's play. If you did does this confirm your other previous observations of the child or not? Is the child playing at a level expected for their age?
6. Read Holland's book *We do not play with guns here: War, weapon and Superhero play in the early years*. Discuss your settings approach to Superhero play and give reasons for your approach. Using Blurton-Jones's (1967) movement patterns to watch children play fighting, see if you can observe the seven patterns and (page 62) write notes.

Questions *(Continued)*

7. How much time is taken setting up with children contributing to the common good? How do you know? Take your timetable and note down the times when children are involved in work for the common good, what are the outcomes for children? Can you honestly say the children do the cooking, gardening and tidying up? What new skills and attitudes are you teaching or developing through the work activities you offer? Link these to the EYFS Framework.

8. How much time do you devote to enabling children to discuss their day and session? What quality of talk are you getting from the children? Is it just 1–5 word answers, using the same words everyday? Make sure you extend children's talk, so that the answers involve more than 25 words and incorporate new language regularly.

3

Historical and international context

Summary

I have always been intrigued by the fact that nursery schools and classes have an outdoor play area. It does not matter in what part of the country, whether a large or small class, nursery classes and schools will nearly always have this secure, outside, accessible area attached. The question is why? Where nursery classes are attached to primary schools, why is the infant playground not used, maybe at a different time? The answer could be that under-fives need the security of a fenced area, not being old enough to play in an unfenced area, as they could wander off and they may be too unsure to play with older children. Perhaps parents need the security of knowing the children are able to play in a separate but secure area. Although these answers do so partly, they do not fully explain why this area exists. Static and movable toys and equipment are provided in this outdoor area and there are different surfaces, trees and shrubs. Staff are expected to work and play with children here as the space is open for the whole session.

This outdoor area is not unique to British nursery education. The United States, Australia, New Zealand and many countries in Europe provide this outdoor area in their preschool centres and resource it in a similar way to the British nursery garden. So why is it that this strand of education differs from other spheres of education and particularly primary education? Why does this outdoor environment exist within the nursery? In this chapter how the nursery garden came about and why it continues to be a crucial part of nursery education are explored.

Influences

The answer to why the nursery garden exists appears to lie with origins. Looking back to the beginnings of nursery education in England, at the start of the nineteenth century, it is clear that the influences on it were different from those of any other sphere of education. Nursery education had very different roots from primary education and followed a different path. In part, nursery education grew from dissatisfaction with the elementary education system and came about as a direct reaction to this schooling.

Here children were not seen as individuals with particular needs, but were almost not seen, and they were expected to take what was offered, without comment. This was a harsh regime where children of three could be locked in a cupboard for daring to speak. The pioneers of nursery education viewed childhood and people's lives in different ways from those who ran compulsory elementary education. Their philosophy was formed from a number of differing influences which led to features unique to nursery education, which have come to be known as the 'common law' (Webb 1974) or 'the nursery tradition' (Pound 1987).

Nursery education, therefore, grew as a reaction to the poor and inappropriate quality of elementary education and was never a watered-down primary education. Likewise, outdoor play, which became a feature unique to nursery education, was a reaction to this inappropriate elementary education and was most definitely not a copy of primary playtime. In fact the garden was central to nursery education; it was its raison d'être. It is necessary to know about roots and influences to appreciate what outdoor play is and is not. Once understood, it is much easier to organise.

Interestingly, across the world there was an interest in young children's education, for example in the mid 1800s in Scotland with Owen, Foebel (of course) in Germany, Soerensen in Denmark and into the mid 1900s, Montessori in Italy.

Under-fives in elementary schools

Compulsory education came onto the statute book in 1870 and all children over the age of five had to go to school. Interestingly, the actual age of five was not chosen for sound psychological or social reasons but rather to enable MPs to wind up the business of the day in the House of Commons and so go home (Szreter 1964). In poorer families, children who had previously looked after their younger brothers and sisters found themselves compelled to go to school. Many of the younger siblings now found they had no one to look after them. Parents were either unwilling or unable to do so because they were working, childhood not being seen as something special. And so they were left at home or on the street. With nothing to do, these children started to drift into the schools to join their brothers and sisters. These young children, therefore, started to received an education which was geared to much older children, even though this was seen as inappropriate for the children it was supposed to be for. How much more inappropriate was it to the under-fives? Few schools attempted to gear the curriculum to suit these children's needs. Fifty to sixty children were expected to sit in tiered rows, for long periods, in cramped and often stuffy conditions. Children stayed all day at school; when they arrived they were already tired and hungry, and as school meals were not provided, stayed hungry. They were expected to stay still for long periods. They were expected to follow a very formal curriculum, to learn by rote, and were not to speak unless spoken to. Even the three-year-olds were expected to thread needles and do needlework. Matters were made worse because in some schools these children were then formally tested and, not surprisingly, many were found wanting.

By 1900, 43 per cent of children aged three to five were attending elementary schools (Board of Education 1912). Such was the concern about the schooling these young children were receiving that a report was commissioned to look into the conditions for the under-fives in schools. The Women Inspectors' Report on children under five years of age in public elementary schools makes for sad and alarming reading (Board of Education 1905). The report considered that the elementary schools were wholly inappropriate for under-fives and that the work being given to them was harsh and too formal, too much time was devoted to the 3Rs, and the discipline was too rigid. The conditions were unhealthy; the classrooms were not well ventilated and the children were restricted in their movements. The Report speaks of babies being 'dulled' and the discipline being 'military' and concluded that children between three and five gained nothing by attending school (Board of Education 1905). So, overall, these under-fives were receiving an education not at all appropriate, and so, some would argue, were the over-fives. The reaction to the Report resulted in the exclusion of under-fives from school, placing them back on the streets, with all its dangers, with no one to care for them and with no solution to their plight in sight.

An interest in childhood

The children belonging to the poorest families lived in appalling conditions, where working hours were long and money scarce. Each family lived together in one room, each room in a house being occupied by another family. Children had disease-ridden bodies, infant mortality was high, malnutrition very evident. The Boer War and the First World War clearly demonstrated the poor health of many citizens. There was a growing concern for the poorer sectors of society in both official and non-official circles and a desire for something to be done to help rectify the situation. There was a new interest in the health and welfare of everyone, but especially the young. There was a growing belief that many of the problems of ill-health and disease were in fact preventable.

There was also a growing concern for young children, with a changing attitude to the concept of childhood. Many began to see childhood as an important stage in life, with particular needs and requirements, and so wanted to give it more significance than it had hitherto had (Steedman 1990). Children could not be treated as 'mini-adults' and seen as cheap labour as they had been in the past. After 1918 half-time education was phased out and all children had to go to school all day and so the worst excesses of child labour came to an end. The establishment of the psychological notion of stages of development, work on language acquisition and the detailed physiological accounts of physical growth all helped to view childhood as something which must be nurtured. Children came to be seen as the symbols of a better future for all.

The work of Friedrich Froebel (1782–1852) influenced those working with young children, and kindergartens were set up in poor areas of cities in the 1860s and 1870s and they became official Board of Education policy from 1890 onwards. The ideas of the nursery pioneers were linked to the changing view of man and society and the pioneers drew their ideas from Rousseau, Froebel, Pestalozzi and Dewey. Margaret McMillan (1860–1931) was one of these nursery pioneers. She was influential in the nursery world and set up a nursery school in 1914, followed by a nursery training college. There were many others who set up nursery schools and also championed the cause of the poor, but her writings and talks made her stand out as particularly important in the nursery field. Through her work and political activities in Bradford and London she helped form Labour Party policy on childhood and the family. With other middle-class women she devoted herself to the poor and to children (Steedman 1990). She, with other concerned citizens, felt that improving the health of poor children was paramount. Among her many achievements, she managed to ensure that subsidised school dinners became available in 1906 and in 1907 a schools medical inspections service was introduced.

The nursery garden

The nursery school evolved over time but it began with the setting-up of outdoor camps in London. In 1911, Margaret McMillan, along with her sister Rachel, set up an outdoor camp for girls, aged 6 to 14, from the slum areas of Deptford. The children attended after school to have a bath, a meal and then to sleep outside. In the morning the children were given breakfast and then went to the Board school. The idea behind this experiment was to get the children out of the crowded, unhealthy conditions of their homes, in an attempt to improve their health, which it did dramatically. This work helped the sisters realise that outdoor living and the outdoor environment could have an impact on people's lives and help improve their health.

As a result of this work, the educational potential of working outside began to be seen. However, McMillan came to the conclusion that to have a lasting effect on these people's lives she needed to work with the youngest children, hence her desire to set up a nursery school for children under five. She had come to realise that health and education went hand in hand, which was in direct conflict with elementary education, which was only concerned with education and did not see a link with health. She felt, for example, that if children had nasal problems this could lead to not being able to speak properly, sight problems could lead to not being able to read properly, lack of exercise could lead to deformity, tiredness to lack of interest.

All of this is now taken for granted. So a healthy body was considered necessary for a healthy mind. McMillan also came to the conclusion that the environment in which education was to take place had to be conducive to learning. The large, cramped, colourless environments of the elementary schools, where children sat and learned by rote, were not considered at all stimulating, hence the desire to set up an interesting, enticing environment outside, where children could follow their interests.

The first nursery school was set up in Deptford in 1914, called the Rachel McMillan Open Air Nursery School. It started as an offshoot of the camps and began with six under-fives. The school was the garden; the buildings or shelters (as they were named by McMillan) were erected to support the work within the garden. This was in tune with

Froebel, who used the word 'kindergarten' meaning 'a garden for children' and not the word 'school'. One could argue that the word 'school' was irrelevant, as this was associated with being inside a building; 'nursery garden education' may have been a better description of what she was trying to achieve. The buildings were there to act as a shelter in poor weather, to store equipment and to house washing, cooking and toilet facilities. Musical instruments were displayed in the shelters and writing materials and games were available. The real learning environment was outside in the garden. This was not an ornamental, suburban or park garden as we think of today, but a children's garden. Visitors of the time were struck by the contrast the garden made with the squalid streets around. McMillan spent much time making this a beautiful oasis; it was designed with the learning of young children at the heart of it. And its relevance to our work today is that it was a planned space where adults played with and helped children. This children's garden was not 'thrown together'; it was not by chance that it was appropriate for young children, it was carefully thought about and organised, tended and managed with the learning of children at its heart.

The garden was divided into sections so that there were opportunities to discover, to play, to construct, to garden. Children were able to follow their interests without being interrupted. Staff did not spend anything like as much time as today in setting up activities because children were expected to select them for themselves. The garden was arranged on different levels, on grass and hard surfaces. There were paths, steps, logs, trees, shrubs, ponds, seats, tables, slides, ropes, swings, playhouses, planks, ladders, barrels, blocks. There was a kitchen garden, a wild garden and a rock garden. There was a plethora of natural materials – twigs, leaves, stones, bark, seeds and so on. The movable equipment included trucks, wheelbarrows and bicycles. Children used real tools. Sand, water and builders' bricks were available. Children had access to dressing-up materials. The garden naturally attracted birds and they were further encouraged with bird boxes, bird baths and bird tables. Animals, including chickens, tortoises, rabbits and fish, were kept. Children had access to scientific equipment and to small games apparatus.

> The garden is the essential matter. Not the lessons, or the pictures or the talk. The lessons and talk are about things seen and done in the garden, just as the best of all the paintings in the picture galleries are shadows of the originals now available to children of the open air.
>
> (McMillan 1930: 2)

All activities including movement, singing, painting, meal times and rest took place outside. The fresh air, the physical activity and the space ensured that the children did indeed become healthier (as she had hoped).

Alongside McMillan's writings, the works of Owen (1928), Cusden (1938), de Lissa (1939), Wheeler and Earl (1939) and particularly Isaacs (1932) all add to the general understanding of nursery education in the first half of the nineteenth century. In the garden, experiences were integrated and all aspects of development could be fostered. It was a natural, real-life environment and not a task-structured environment divorced from reality.

The pioneers stressed aspects of educational practice which included the importance of space, uninterrupted play, the social side of school, the enhancement of corporate activity, and self-initiated play (Owen 1928, Cusden 1938, de Lissa 1939). Learning through play in a natural and interesting environment was seen as the way to help young children develop (McMillan 1930, Isaacs 1954). It was somewhere children naturally wanted to go and was seen to offer first-hand sensory experiences. So, for example, the range of colours could more easily and clearly be studied in the garden rather than by looking at colours on a card. Outdoors is ever changing and its diversity raises questions. It was seen as an environment which could encourage 'corporate activity and corporate enjoyment' (Owen 1928: 86). Hence the reason the pioneers saw the need for children to play together, and encouraged this by providing scrap materials and movable toys for the children to work with and construct together. De Lissa talks about children engaging in 'experimental play' (1939: 49) with resources such as building materials which have many possibilities, enabling children to put ideas into action and so practising skills of planning, persistence, concentration and re-evaluation. This was very different from elementary education where all children were expected to do the same thing at the same time. Outdoors offered emotional support, either because it was somewhere feelings could be expressed or because it engendered a feeling of tranquility. In this environment children were able to benefit from the fresh air. They were able to develop a healthy body alongside a healthy mind, moving about vigorously and being energetic (Plaisted 1909, Holmes and Davies 1937, de Lissa 1939).

Teachers were seen as crucial. 'The whole value of the nursery school will depend, of course, on the teachers. They are the heart of the problem, they can give or withhold success' (McMillan 1919: 81). Essentially, it was how the teacher used the theory that made it successful or not, whether interacting with children, setting up an environment for play or involving children in deciding rules and expectations. But McMillan also came to see parents as important and central to the change in people's lives, feeling that the open-air nursery school would draw parents in and they could learn from watching the children at play. She set up the equivalent of a parents' room so they could be educated, being aware that not only the conditions in the slums, but also simple ignorance, created many of the health problems.

Decline of the outdoor play area

Over time, the centrality of the garden to nursery education declined and with it the amount of outdoor play decreased. As early as 1939, concern was being expressed about the misuse of the garden (de Lissa 1939). There seems to be three main reasons why the garden, which was viewed as the raison d'être of nursery education, was lost over time: first, nursery education came to be seen as a form of compensatory education; second, the provision of nursery education in classes attached to primary schools and not in separate nursery schools; and third, the general lack of nursery-trained specialists. The impact of these factors was compounded by nursery education never becoming a compulsory phase of education, and the consistent lack of funding which has dogged nursery education since its inception. By 1918, nursery education was on the statute book and this was a major achievement. However, lack of public funding prevented it from becoming universally available. Nursery education has grown over the years, but without overall planning. In some areas there is a good deal of nursery education and in others none at all.

Compensatory education

McMillan and others in the nursery field were very successful in improving the health of young children. They realised that children's health had to be improved before they could be successfully educated; cognitive growth could not be achieved without physical well-being. The emphasis was on outdoor living, with plenty of good food, exercise and rest. In the nursery schools children became healthier and more disease-resistant. As Bradburn argues in her biography of McMillan, many of McMillan's followers 'may have mistaken the route for the destination' (1976: 163). In a sense, the nursery movement's success was also its downfall. As nursery education was seen to dramatically improve the health of children, the conclusion drawn by some was that nursery education was not a new type of education but simply a compensatory education. Put poor, disease-ridden children in the nursery and they will get healthier. Unfortunately, in government documents, nursery schools came under 'special schools' and this meant they came to be seen as places to help children with special needs, as curative institutions to help some children, but not needed to help all children (Board of Education 1936). Whitbread argues that the nursery school was seen 'in terms of social and medical care, not as an educational institution' (1972: 68). So the garden was seen not as the learning environment but as a health-promoting environment. This compensatory theme continued, and in the 1960s and 1970s nursery education was seen as a solution to educational disadvantage, helping those children who were socially or linguistically disadvantaged. The rise in the 'programme' was evident; it was a case of giving nursery education to the disadvantaged and then they would be better, hence the increase in language programmes. Clark (1988) argues that language was a main justification for the expansion of nursery education at this time; it was seen as a place to prepare children for compulsory schooling, for special needs identification and to some extent it still is (see Hutt *et al.* (1989) for a discussion of the compensatory tag attached to nursery education). The significance with regard to outdoor play was that this compensatory education occurred inside the classroom and so the importance of the garden was sidestepped.

Looking to today, the findings of the Effective Provision of Pre-School Education (EPPE) Project, a longitudinal study into the effects of pre-school education on children, demonstrate that quality nursery education does help those children from disadvantaged backgrounds, by reducing the disadvantage and reducing social exclusion (Sammons *et al.* 2004). This government has as high on its agenda the raising of achievement of children from the most disadvantaged homes, therefore, they do view under-fives' education as compensatory. Alongside this is the government's desire to get people into work, even mothers, and once again under-fives education is not seen as simply good for all children but as being a childcare service so parents can go out to work (see the *Every Child Matters agenda* (DfES 2004) for a discussion of this).

Rise of nursery classes

Nursery education started life in schools, separate to the elementary school system. However, over the years, much of the increase in nursery places was in nursery classes attached to primary schools and not in nursery schools. With a drop in the birth rate, primary classrooms would become empty, and so, particularly in the 1930s and again in the 1970s and 1980s, primary classes were often adapted to house a nursery class, this being the cheaper option. On the face of it, this may not be an important change. However, in terms of the centrality of the garden it was highly significant. Immediately, nursery education was about adapting an indoor classroom, not about finding and building a suitable outdoor space. By paying attention to finding a room suitable for the nursery, the outdoor play area was 'relegated from first place in the order of priorities' (McNee 1984: 20). Time was taken in finding a room suitable for adaptation, with the minimum amount of cost. Most time, energy and thought would go into the adaptation of the indoor space. The garden was an afterthought, a space to be tacked on. The two areas were not considered together when trying to find the right space for the nursery class. Hence the reason why there are many nursery classes with what can only be described as unusual outdoor areas that are very small, a strange shape, on a slope, with only a hard surface, without shade, without sun, in part of the dustbin area, not even next to the classroom, and so on. The range of nursery outdoor play areas we see today is not a result of considered design, but chance. Because the nursery was part of the elementary or primary school it was affected by it both inside the classroom and very obviously in the use of the outdoor play area.

Teachers who found themselves with such 'interesting' or unusual outdoor play areas had to be very committed to outdoor play to make such areas work. Without this commitment such difficult environments did not get used in the way originally envisaged. Alongside this relegation came terminology relegation and as early as 1936 the garden was being described as the 'playground', where children had 'access to the open air' (Board of Education 1936: 20).

The lack of regard for the outside area when creating new early years' establishments continues. So often new build involves architects but not teachers who will have to work in the design. Where classes are to be adapted for the Foundation Stage little consideration is given to whether the space outside the classroom is the most effective or whether there might be a better space elsewhere within the school; the upshot being that I meet people who find it almost impossible to offer quality outdoor play because the space allocated is so poor. I have visited a number of children's centres where outside has yet again been an afterthought or considered immaterial to children's development;

with inside design occupying the minds of the architects or possibly even worse centre managers not wishing children to disturb their beautifully landscaped garden!

It is therefore surprising that the outdoor play space still exists at all today. Maybe this points to its fundamental centrality and importance to young children's learning.

Lack of trained nursery specialists

Nursery education was seen as different from elementary education and McMillan saw the teacher as the linchpin in the success of children's education. She set up a teacher education college, called the Rachel McMillan Training College, in Deptford, to ensure that nursery teachers had the specialist training required. This was not a version of elementary education but a completely separate training. With the death of nursery pioneers and the lack of universal nursery education, the nursery specialist became a rarity.

During both the First and Second World Wars nursery education was increased to free women to do war work. With the ending of both wars there was a dramatic rise in the birth rate and a shortage of primary teachers. After the Second World War, the government solved this teacher shortage by taking nursery teachers from the nurseries and putting them into the infant classes and replacing them with women who had received a short training in childcare (Blackstone 1971). The training emphasised the care aspect of the work and the fundamental aspects of nursery education, such as the garden, were not taught. During the 1960s there was a general shortage of teachers and the solution was to utilise nursery nurses instead of teachers in the running of the nurseries. On the whole, a nursery nurse training involves the care component of the work far more than the educational aspects. So, again, this has meant that those knowledgeable about nursery education have been few and far between, a situation which has been picked up by many government documents, including the Education, Science and Arts Committee Report (Great Britain 1988).

The lack of nursery specialists training students and the consequent lack of specialists in the field continues to beset nursery and now Early Years Foundation Stage education. Today, with an emphasis on subject teaching and increased time in schools, students can still leave college with only a general understanding of the EYFS and a hazy notion as to what outdoor play is about. Many staff may feel unsure as to the exact nature of nursery education and so provide a primary curriculum instead, with a clear division between work and play, and with the outdoors being relegated to a perceived lower order activity which staff do not get involved in.

In many infant settings, due to a lack of finances, teaching assistants instead of nursery nurses are being employed to work in the EYFS. Newly appointed teaching assistants can receive a four- to six-day training, covering such aspects as basic literacy and numeracy, special needs and behaviour management. This in no way gives in-depth knowledge about young children or how to assist in their learning, such as the two-year NNEB/CACHE qualification does. Within the private, voluntary and independent sector the adults may have little or no training at all.

Nursery education has always been beset by a lack of funds. The fact that nursery education is not a statutory phase of education means that many people not confident about its true nature may feel very vulnerable and replace nursery education with primary education. In this climate something as specialised as outdoor play can easily be pushed to the sidelines.

Learning from the past

From this brief look at the development of nursery education it can be seen that nursery education did not begin as a side-shoot of primary education and that the garden space is not akin to the primary playground. It is apparent that the outdoor play area is one of those 'traditions' unique to nursery education. The garden was central to nursery education and was the main learning area. From looking to the roots of nursery education it is apparent that this space was initially carefully designed and laid out and its use was carefully planned on a daily basis. It was not a place to run about in, after the work had been done inside, it was an area in which children were able to play for the entire session, weather permitting. It was an area where education and care went hand in hand, a wholly new concept at the beginning of the twentieth century. It was an area where a healthy body and mind could be developed. It was an environment in which teachers were expected to work and play with children.

The study of the development of nursery education has shown that the centrality of the outdoor learning environment did not decline because it was found to be a useless space, but because external influences brought changes to bear on it. Its centrality declined because nursery education came to be seen as a way to help children who were at a so-called disadvantage, to help with the next phase of education, or to help a child with particular mental or physical needs. In this way, outdoors became an area for physical education and to provide fresh air; indoors for compensating for that so-called disadvantage. It declined in importance because concentrating on providing nursery classes meant that attention was paid to providing indoor spaces and not developing an outdoor learning environment. Therefore, the range of outdoor play areas we see today is not a result of design but chance. One can see the direct influence of infant education, where attention is given entirely to the indoor learning area. Finally, the lack of people knowledgeable about nursery education meant that what went on in many establishments was more akin to infant education, with a division between work and play, with indoors being seen as the work station and outdoors as the much less important play area. In some quarters these attitudes still prevail.

Today

The Start Right Report (Ball 1994) recommended the ideal approach to the expansion of nursery education would be based on nursery schools and classes. However, with the introduction of the desirable learning outcomes and voucher scheme in 1996, the government was attempting to provide nursery education on the cheap by saying any institution providing care for under-fives, whether it be a playgroup, private/workplace nursery or LEA-run nursery could come under the blanket term 'nursery'. Overnight, privately run under-fives settings, who often do not employ trained workers, could gain status by being called 'nursery.' Outdoor provision was not given status under the *Desirable Learning Outcomes* and so was allowed to decline even further, seen in terms of physical development only and possible to provide in a local authority park. In 2000 *The Foundation Stage Guidance* was introduced for children aged three to five and the term 'Foundation Stage' replaced the term 'nursery education' and became the blanket term for any setting providing for the care and education of three- to five-year-olds. This included a nursery class attached to a primary school, a separate nursery school, a reception class, a rising fives class, a combination of reception, Year 1 and 2 children, a privately run institution, a playgroup.

With the introduction of the Foundation Stage in September 2000, outdoor play was given more prominence and inspections highlighted deficiencies in provision and practice. There continued to be a lack of trained nursery/Foundation Stage specialists and this was particularly apparent as reception children came under the Foundation Stage umbrella and not the National Curriculum guidance. Teachers had to make major changes in their thinking as the ways of educating children are unfortunately very different; with an emphasis on play and independence within the Foundation Stage guidance and an emphasis on prescriptive schooling under the National Curriculum. Many establishments since then have made changes to the actual outdoor play space in the light of the requirements of the Foundation Stage guidance. Some schools have created new outdoor areas and have indeed looked at not only the most appropriate room, but also the best outdoor space for the under-fives. Some LEAs have provided money for fencing. Some schools have been able to fundraise for the outdoor space. Some have been given a limited budget but still been able to make a difference (see Bilton (2005) for an example of improved outdoor provision in one local authority). However, as the research by Waite and Rea (2006) looking into teachers' views of the outdoor environment in a number of Welsh schools demonstrates, teachers still lack knowledge of or sympathy for the outdoor environment.

In September 2008 the Guidance was replaced by the *Early Years Foundation Stage Framework,* covering children aged nought to five (DfCSF 2008 revised). Even greater emphasis is given to outdoor play, that it has to be provided, that quality experiences have to be provided outside. However, Foundation Stage education is still dogged by a lack of trained specialists, inappropriate premises and a sense it is compensatory education able to offer around the clock care and education so parents can go to work without detrimental effect to the child. The EPPE Project notes from the research that, unsurprisingly, quality matters and that quality is mostly found in 'settings integrating care and education' and the majority of these are in the maintained sector, including children's centres (Sylva *et al.* 2004: 1). Staff qualifications matter also: 'Settings that have staff with higher qualifications have higher quality scores and their children make more progress' (Sylva *et al.* 2004: 1). As the Start Right Report suggested back in 1994 nursery/Foundation Stage education should occur in local authority-maintained nursery schools and classes. Research from Durham has found that 'a good reception year teacher makes the biggest and longest-lasting difference to primary school education' (TACTYC 2007: 4). But it is important to make sure the quality of the experience is appropriate and developmentally correct.

International dimension

Across the world, countries vary in provision for the under-fives. Looking to a report in 2002 it is interesting to note the similarities, for example of 20 countries looked at 'there was almost universal promotion of an active, play-based pedagogy within the participating countries, where self-management and independence were encouraged' (Betram and Pascal 2002: ii). The countries involved were Australia, Canada, United Kingdom (England), France, Germany, Hong Kong, Hungary, Republic of Ireland, Italy, Japan, Korea, Netherlands, New Zealand, Singapore, Spain, Sweden, Switzerland, USA (Kentucky, Massachusetts), United Kingdom (Northern Ireland), United Kingdom (Wales).

Building on practice from Denmark, Sweden and Norway is the Forest School experience and this is a growing phenomenon in this country. Children either go to the forest in their own school or they are taken to a local wood and alongside nursery staff and Forest School staff play in the woods, climb trees, explore streams, build dens, make fires and use real tools. A great deal of the work is about building confidence through achieving. In Denmark and Norway these schools are permanent, offering outdoor access to the forest at all times, whereas here the children are likely only to experience it periodically. Children are having experiences that many had in the past but not so many have now. Children have 'the opportunity to learn about the natural environment, how to handle risks and most importantly to use their own initiative to solve problems and co-operate with others' (Forest Schools 2009). What happens at Forest School and more particularly where it happens is good. Children should have experiences of the natural environment, all children should experience trees and shrubs everyday of their lives. But two aspects concern me. First, as Tovey (2007) argues, does this mean Forest Schools come to be seen as compensatory education? Is it viewed as only for those poor people who do not have lots of greenery around them? Second, I hear schools/classes saying 'we are a Forest School' seeming to suggest they have no need of the long tradition of nursery education in this country. It seems quite acceptable to have additions to quality nursery education, but very dangerous to side-step it completely. Likewise I experience settings who call themselves 'Montessori' or 'highscope' with worryingly poor components of practice. To critically analyse and take on aspects of these approaches whether it be Forest, Montessori or highscope seems sensible but not so that it suggests it has higher status.

Childhood

At the opening of *Toxic Childhood* Sue Palmer (2006) describes a twenty-first-century child, who actually looks like an adult, behaves like a wracked adult and knows probably a lot more at her age than her mother. The overwhelming reaction of the reader is one of sadness. But this was not always the view of childhood; childhood as a concept has not only emerged over time, it has changed over time. As Postman suggests, childhood over time has changed in line with the economic, religious, intellectual plus the moral setting in which it appears: 'In some cases it was enriched; in some, neglected; in some, degraded' (1982: 53). Childhood is closely associated with schooling, education and social literacy and even Shakespeare talks of schooling as being a bore – 'the whining schoolboy, with his satchel/And shining morning face, creeping like a snail/Unwillingly to school' (*As You Like It*). Given a lot of school is to do with literacy, Philippe Aries argues that it 'tended to restrain the high energy levels of youth' (as cited in Postman 1982: 46). He argues that book learning means that being quiet and immobile became highly prized with the natural approach of children seen as inappropriate. Where I am not wishing to knock the importance of learning to read and write I think it is important to emphasise that 'quiet and immobile' should not be seen as a norm for children and particularly not for children of say 36 or 48 months, hence my anxiety to get them out and moving. Wetton discusses the lack of movement opportunities within schools now and how children can become frustrated and appear naughty:

> More likely, and almost by way of compensation, the children try to find spaces where they 'are allowed to move' – as in life corners where it is acceptable to crawl like a dog or climb to wash windows or pretend to be a dancing Teletubby.
>
> (1998: 99)

We need to work with the natural approach of the child, view childishness as fruitful and not against it. Children are not mini adults, they do not need to wear adult clothing, nor know everything that adults do and as Postman suggests by becoming all-knowing they are 'expelled from the garden of childhood' (1982: 97). However, there is this bizarre dichotomy of children being seen as mini-adults but also of needing to be protected. Having been protected as children they are becoming, as adults, incapable. Clearly we do not want children working down mines, or in terrible conditions in factories as is apparent in other countries today. But equally we do not need them to be wrapped up in cotton wool. As Cunningham suggests: 'So fixated are we on giving our children a long and happy childhood that we downplay their abilities and their resilience. To think of children as potential victims in need of protection is a very modern outlook, and it probably does no-one a service' (2006: 245). Gill (2007) argues that the concern about making a risk-free society is that it considers the child as a 'deficit model' who needs to be protected. In Chapter 2 there is the suggestion that we need to ensure children not only play but also partake of activities that are worthwhile and for the good of the whole community. Children do not need to be exploited, no one does, but neither do children need to see adults as their slaves. In the past children had to fit with the needs of adults, now it seems, adults have to fit with the needs of children, with adults spinning round children, fussing as to whether they will be successful, safe, happy. This spills over into schooling with it serving the needs of parents for children to be 'successful and safe' and not to serve the needs of children. Cunningham (2006: 239) suggests that the state made factory work illegal only to replace it with another form of work, which is in fact unpaid: school. It is time to find a balance between ensuring there is a phase called childhood but not at the expense of adults and not at the expense of children.

Discussion

History has taught us that children's needs have not changed over the last 100 years. They still need a garden to play in and outside is a healthy place to be. Education and care go hand in hand and both have to be provided for at school. Viewing outdoor provision as identical to primary playtime would be a mistake, as the two environments are fundamentally different. Indeed, in Chapter 8, there are suggestions as to how to improve primary playtime based on the findings within this book. The outdoor early years' area cannot be seen as a suburban garden nor as an adventure park. It is a complete learning environment; once this is understood it is much easier to organise. Chapters 4 and 5 look to the specifics of organisation and management.

Questions

1. Do you see early years education as more important for some children than others? Or do you view it as offering something to every child and if so, what?
2. Do you view the outside as less important than the inside environment?
3. What qualifications do you have? Do you know enough about children and child development? What more could you do to get informed?
4. Are you offering care and education? What is your evidence?

Section 2 Making it work

The guiding principles for outdoor teaching and learning

Summary

When I wrote *Outdoor Play in the Early Years* I wanted to make outdoor provision as clear as possible, particularly for those who had no early years' training. I put together 10 principles as follows:

1 Indoors and outdoors need to be viewed as one combined and integrated environment.
2 Indoors and outdoors need to be available to the children simultaneously.
3 Outdoors is an equal player to indoors and should receive planning, management, evaluation, resourcing, staffing and adult interaction on a par with indoors.
4 Outdoors is both a teaching and learning environment.
5 Outdoor design and layout needs careful consideration.
6 Outdoor play is central to young children's learning.
7 The outdoor classroom offers children the opportunity to utilise effective modes of learning.
8 Children need versatile equipment and environments.
9 Children need to be able to control, change and modify their environment.
10 Staff have to be supportive towards outdoor play.

It is to these principles I now turn for discussion and elucidation.

1. Indoors and outdoors need to be viewed as one combined and integrated environment

Inside and out need to be seen as one space, inside being a half and outside being a half, together making a whole. If inside is seen at fifteen-sixteenths of one's time and energy and outside one-sixteenth then outside will be relegated to primary playtime and be of little use to the children. The two areas have to be seen as equals, in which children can learn, not that one is the work area – where the important 'schooly' stuff happens and the other a place where children do something of a lower status – that is playing and letting off steam. Outdoors cannot be seen as an add-on; it has to be seen as an integral part of early years' provision, so that when one cannot go outside it is seen as a pity, not a bonus.

> The adults planning for the class should be thinking about the indoor and outdoor areas not as separate spaces but as linked areas where a child involved in an activity may move between them, using the equipment and resources which best meet her or his needs where and when the play requires them.
>
> (Lasenby 1990: 5)

Although this was written nearly 20 years ago, this sentiment still stands.

So how does one view inside and out as a combined environment? The best thing to do is imagine the outside area has a roof and walls and think how you would deal with it. It would have resources accessible to children, adults sometimes working with and observing children, furniture, spaces created for play and work, different surfaces and textures, this is exactly what is needed outside (see guiding principle 3 for more detail).

2. Indoors and outdoors need to be available to the children simultaneously

Probably the single most important issue to address is when outdoor play is available. Lasenby (1990), McLean (1991), Lally and Hurst (1992), Dowling (1992), Gura (1992), Bilton (1993, 2002, 2004b), Bilton et al. (2005), Robson (1996), QCA (2000) and DfCSF (2008) all clearly argue for the combined indoor and outdoor environment. In fact, problems are created both indoors and outdoors if outdoor play is offered on a timetable basis (Bilton 1993, 2004b). By offering both simultaneously and as one, both will work well. By offering outdoor play alongside indoor play you are acknowledging that outdoor play is as important and as relevant to young children's learning and thereby fulfilling the first principle. By offering it simultaneously it naturally becomes an equal partner in the planning process and both areas can complement each other.

What this means in practice is that pretty soon after the children have arrived at the setting, the outdoor area needs to be available, not as an announcement but as a quiet affair of a door being opened and children choosing to go out or if there is a focused activity then those relevant to it being taken out and others following as and when. Announcing outdoor play to use present vernacular 'kills' it, because by doing this you are saying 'everyone out' which is not what you actually want. Sometimes no one goes out immediately, each day will be different. Even if the setting is on the first floor or above there is no reason why children cannot be allowed to freely move between the two areas, as long as they are able to use stairs on their own. There are schools and classes who are not on the ground floor and children quite happily and safely move about the building.

Children and parents will need a period of time at the beginning of the session when they can talk to the staff. This should be standard practice, but if the establishment has sufficient adults it could be that both in and out are available right from the beginning of the session. But if there are insufficient adults to ensure the parents and carers are given full attention then as soon as possible into the session both in and out need to be open.

Within a standard EYFS day, there will be times for whole-group work, for those children for whom it is appropriate. This might be a language or mathematics session, music, movement, PE. Children will then need to tidy up and there may be a story time to finish the session or group discussion. If the children are at school all day and therefore stay for lunch then the afternoon format will be similar to the morning. It is inappropriate for young children (who may be as young as 36 months) to have to be part of the whole school for assembly, lunch or playtime. They need to have lunch in their own secure space or in one particular space within the dining room together with adult support. Playtime is a difficult time as it is and should not be imposed on young children. They have plenty of years to get used to it. However, if it is unavoidable then providing toys to play with and having closer adult support would be helpful. It may be possible for these children to use the Foundation Stage outdoor area at lunchtime. In terms of assembly it is tantamount to cruelty to make young children spend possibly one-fifth of their time (half-day attendance) or one-tenth (whole-day attendance) being involved in a sedentary activity, which flies in the face of what is developmentally appropriate. Going to morning playtime is pointless if children are using their own outdoor area and cuts into precious time. Prior to the National Curriculum it was perfectly normal practice to give children a rest period after lunch. By the afternoon young children can be lagging and some are at a point of needing to go to sleep and some are at a point of just needing to stop. Thin mattresses and personal blankets can be provided for a rest period.

If you are in a situation where you cannot avoid but have a timetabled period outside then consider having it first thing, so children and staff do not see it as a reward for good behaviour or something to wait for, with the possible repercussion of children not concentrating on the activities inside. Ensure the period of time outside is as long as possible, 20 to 30 minutes is not a great deal of time to get engrossed and reach a quality level of learning. Ensure, just because it is timetabled, that the planning, the care, the attention is as detailed as for inside.

Difficulties with timetabled outdoor play

The story in Figure 4.1 is an example of how many outdoor playtimes are run, where bikes rule the space. This cannot be construed as quality learning. Looking to Figure 4.2 highlights the many problems created by having poorly planned timetabled outdoor provision, including the impact on inside experiences.

Once upon a time there was an early years setting where outdoor play was timetabled at 10 am for 20 minutes. All the children were sent out at the same time and no one was allowed back inside, while the staff tidied up the area. The staff on duty outside didn't like being out and huddled round each other chatting and drinking tea. They only responded to children when they had to, usually involving an issue with a bike.

A little while before outdoor play was announced, the atmosphere in the classroom changed to that of a 'stirring pot'. Some children, particularly a group of boys, although they couldn't tell the time, felt it, and 5–10 minutes before outside time was to start would move about inside unable to settle. The moment the doors were open there was a race to get outside. Younger children were knocked over in the race to get outside, children would forego getting a coat, and inside toys and activities would be abandoned. Once outside, the children were after one thing – the bikes. Not just any bikes, there was a definite pecking order, with some having top status and some having low status. Once on the high status bikes, children would do anything to stay on them. They would stay behind the shed, not moving until inside time was announced, they would become very deaf when asked to get off a bike, they would lie to get back on a bike pretending they hadn't been on a bike for at least two weeks. If offered a low status bike, they would decline preferring to do nothing until a high status bike became available. The space felt dangerous as though standing in the middle of the M25. Children (and staff) worried for their safety, more concerned to keep an eye on the bikes rather than settle to an activity.

Once inside time was announced there would be a rush to line the bikes up at the shed, some children on bikes would continue to be surprisingly deaf and some would have to be hauled physically off the bike, using the double-knee-clamp to stay attached to the bike. The children would then be sent in while the staff put the bikes back in the shed. There was always a child who would be able to play on the bike even though everyone else was sent in. Partway through trying to place the bikes in the shed the staff members would resort to throwing them into the shed, slamming the door finally shut, thinking gleefully: 'I don't need to do that until next Thursday.'

Figure 4.1 The bike story

A graphic effect of the timetabled outdoor play session can be seen indoors. The Gura (1992) research into block play found that children would abandon play activities inside so that they could get outside first. The play these children were involved in was high quality and offered them interest; they were therefore actively engaged.

- Too many children accessing too few toys and activities.
- Little new stimulation or new learning experiences.
- Staff unclear about the learning outside.
- Many disagreements between children.
- Some children demonstrate immoral behaviour.
- Some children become very bored.
- Children learn very little.
- Children only revisit learning.
- Some children hang around waiting for status toys.
- Accidents occur, particular knocks to heads.
- Staff deal with arguments and police area.
- Some children dominate the area.
- Some children are frightened of the space and won't use it.
- Staff and many children do not enjoy being outside.
- Indoor play is disturbed and sometimes destroyed.

Figure 4.2 Problems associated with timetabling outdoor activities

However, the pull of outside was too strong and the timetabled outdoor play actually caused much of the learning inside to abruptly stop. In this study, children would see others rushing to get outside – often it was those children who had had less to clear away – and in their frustration the children left behind would simply not complete their job and slip outside. Gura argues that the fragmentation of the day, where outdoor play was timetabled, created a 'hit and run' approach to play (1992: 184). Personal experience supports this finding: in one nursery, even though the activities available outdoors were very limited, children would abandon a snack to get outside and stay there for as long as possible.

Outside, if all the children are expected to go at a set time there is the prospect of too many children trying to access too little equipment and too few resources. This can mean some children are not doing anything other than wandering, which is fine if that is a choice, not imposed. There can be arguments about the few resources and a rush on some which can end in accidents. When children first enter the early years' setting they will take differing times to settle down to concentrated work. They may at first go to one activity but this may be through habit and for security, they may then move on to take up their preferred, first, sustained activity or it may take some time before they settle. Where the outdoor play is timetabled, children will move outside at the designated time, but will need a period of readjustment before they select their preferred activity. It could be that for some children this will take all the time they have outside and, just as they are about to settle, it is time to move inside again.

Bruce suggests that, by limiting experiences, for example using the climbing frame only once a week, or having only a short period outside 'skills are not encouraged and accidents are more likely' (1987: 59, reiterated in Bruce 2005). We all know what it is like to start something, to then be interrupted, and go back to it saying: 'now where was I?' We have to retread old ground just to pick up where we left off. Children will get used to the equipment or resource, but find that just as they are about to learn something new it is put away. Equally the excitement of wanting to use the equipment may be so strong that some children will rush at it and have an accident. The next week comes round, they start getting used to the equipment again and the same thing happens. Not only is this very dull, it is also very frustrating. They will spend most of the time revisiting, rather than learning anything new, and in fact their skill acquisition may regress. Cullen (1993), looking at children's use and perceptions of outdoor play in New Zealand, came to similar conclusions. She argues that children may not reach the levels of confidence or skills expected, simply because they are not in the outdoor area for long enough.

Timetabling outside play can create a situation where staff view it as though it were primary playtime, when staff have a break, and a drink, when indoors can be cleared away (see the Introduction and Chapter 3 for a discussion about the traditions of Foundation Stage education). Timetabling can mean staff feel disinclined to put much effort or thought into what is on offer and what learning could be achieved. Cullen (1993) found that the longer the outdoor play period the better the quality of play, especially creative play, and that the more complex forms of cooperative play were facilitated by the staff. She concludes that the reason for this is simple. The longer the children spent outside, the more the staff had to plan for. The more staff had to plan for, the more effort they put into the plans and so the more interesting the range of activities.

This would seem to make a great deal of sense where timetabling outdoors causes the problems displayed. When children are outdoors for a short period of time, faced with few toys to play with, staff may have to spend most of this time sorting out conflicts between children. These conflicts can be difficult to resolve as the resources are not available to help children move onto worthwhile play. In this climate, it is a case of the survival of the fittest, with some children unwilling to go outside as they are too frightened and others staying very close to the adult, almost for protection.

Although a study of primary playtime, the findings by Blatchford (1989) reiterate the findings here. In this study it was found that:

- many children were scared to go out at playtime
- behaviour was often poor
- children got bored with little to occupy them
- many hung around the supervising adult.

Primary playtime was designed in the 1800s to enable children to have fresh air and some exercise after the sedentary activities of the day: a far cry from an effective teaching and learning environment.

Where there is little to do, very little interaction with adults and no quality high level interactions, certain groups of children can become dominant, for example, boys, older children or the more aggressive. Behaviour can become static with children doing the same things, such as riding round and round on bikes every single day. This means that groups of children are being denied access to whole chunks of the curriculum.

Timetabling can also send very clear messages to children about how staff view outdoor play. By offering it for a short time and with little or no planning, children, staff and parents will see it as somewhere less important than indoors. This in itself can create problems in that children are more likely to demonstrate non-purposeful behaviour and not settle to anything, as it is not expected. Lally and Hurst suggest that having a set playtime can encourage the staff to see outdoor play simply in terms of physical development (1992: 86). Cleave and Brown's (1991) study into four-year-olds in infant classes clearly argues for children to be given time to pursue interests and have blocks of uninterrupted play (reconfirmed by Rogers and Evans 2008). Barrett (1986) recommends that time needs to be given to children so that they can think, reflect, consolidate and master what they are learning. Stevenson (1987) argues that, when children are given time to work at an activity, they can concentrate for a considerable period of time and the children in her study did so. But, to concentrate and persevere, children need to know that the time is available to do so. Edgington (2003) and Lally (1991) argue that 'a whole class approach is clearly not consistent with a developmental approach where individual needs are of paramount concern' (Lally 1991: 78). Children cannot be approached as individuals or learn as individuals if the routine of the nursery involves interruptions and blocks of time devoted to whole-group activities, such as all going out to play.

Dispelling the myths

Making changes to outdoor play so it is available at the same time as indoors can radically change the nature of the children and their learning. Figure 4.3 cites an example of changing from short timetable play to free flow. It is possible even with only two members of staff to run indoors alongside outdoors but the will has to be there.

A number of difficulties can be raised by teachers as to why outdoors and indoors cannot be provided simultaneously throughout the session. These include the weather, supervision, lack of space and setting up. Unlike the indoor class, the outdoor environment is affected by the weather; however, the most common climatic condition which affects the use of the outdoors is rain. The advantage of having both indoors and outdoors freely available for the entire session is that the weather can be worked round. When outdoor play is at a specific time of day every day, children cannot go out if it rains. However, if outdoors is available throughout the session children can go out when it is not raining, and utilise the best of the weather, whatever time of the day. Obviously, staff have to tune into the weather forecasts and be confident about the day's weather, equally also being prepared for a change in the weather. The day-to-day study of the weather can

In a class attached to a primary school outdoor play was timetabled, midway through the session, for fifteen minutes. All the children were expected to go outside, their behaviour was manic, they rushed around with little or no purpose. They were in essence doing what was expected, that is, 'letting off steam'.

Staff felt very dissatisfied with what was happening outside and wanted to improve practice. First the staff considered what learning experiences the children needed and what was an optimal number given the size of the space. They then incorporated the experiences into the overall planning. There was a lot of discussion, planning, design, redesign until the staff felt happy with what they were proposing. On the first day when both areas were simultaneously available, no announcement was made but one member of staff quietly opened the doors and went outside. All the children rushed outside as they always had! This continued for three days, alongside conversations with the children about how outdoor play was different now and what was possible and generally about how the staff wanted the area to be used. After three days of everyone rushing outside the moment the doors were open and lots of conversation with children there then appeared to be a sea change, with children going out when they wanted.

The staff found that when indoors and outdoors were available for the whole session, there was no mad dash outside, the play outside was much more sustained and effective and the previous manic behaviour simply ceased. Indeed, the staff were surprised at just how much the children's behaviour changed in such a short period. There was a clear connection between organisation and behaviour. The short, timetabled, compulsory outdoor play session caused the non-purposeful behaviour, while the planned, full session, combined indoor and outdoor learning and teaching environment created informed and concentrated play.

Bilton (1993)

Figure 4.3 Changing from timetabled outdoor play to free flow

prove to be a beneficial and real learning experience. Children can learn to study the clouds, the wind, light and so on and make predictions (see Chapter 5 for a discussion about environmental and scientific discovery). Some staff will argue that it can be too cold for children to go out, but there will be very few days when it is so cold that children cannot go outside. But for the rest of the time if children are wrapped up well, and have enough to play with they will not get cold. When staff play with children and are as active as them they also find they do not get cold. Classes need to be prepared for all types of weather and have boxes of spare gloves, hats, scarves, boots, shoes, and for summer long-sleeved tee-shirts and hats. Having these available means the move from indoors to outdoors can be easy. Figure 4.4 shows reasons why in and out need to be available together.

Some staff argue that the supervision of two areas is difficult and not safe when there are only two members of staff. But if both areas have been planned carefully and there are sufficient activities which children can use with or without adult involvement, then one adult indoors and one outdoors is possible. We also have to learn to trust children and not think that if we watch them all the time they will be safe; to be safe children need to learn to trust themselves (see Chapter 1 for a discussion on risk). I find this apparent concern for safety without substance, when the same people will allow children to race around on bikes and frantically attack a climbing frame with a large number of accidents occurring. Many classes do have additional adults, such as students, and, of course, parental helpers. Equally, staff need to ensure wherever they are, they are scanning (Kounin 1970, Pollard 2008) the area to make sure children are settled, to pre-empt any possible conflicts and be aware of any dangerous situations. With indoors and outdoors available at the same time, staff also need to have a flexible rota so they can respond to the children's desire to move from one activity to the next, indoors or outdoors. In this way, if a member of staff is working with one group of children and they wish to move their play outside and the adult to stay with them, this can happen. The member of staff positioned outside can then move inside without any children having to be disturbed. Research by Bilton (1993) found that one member of staff outdoors and one indoors worked well as long as the scanning, moving about and flexible rota were adhered to.

- Neither space is viewed as more important than the other.
- Children who prefer outside will feel valued.
- Children can utilise both workshop areas and work between the two areas.
- Children have time to learn and be taught.
- No activity is adversely affected by the opening of the other area.
- Children who work well outside can have sufficient time in it.
- Children who are reticent about working in either area will have time to 'discover' the other area.
- Activities are more likely to be well planned.
- There is time for observing children.
- Stereotypical play can be altered by careful adult intervention.
- The weather can be worked round.

Figure 4.4 Reasons why inside and out need to be available simultaneously

Staff need to agree how to manage the situation if an accident occurs, particularly when there are only two adults. The procedure for responding to an emergency situation could be rehearsed as the fire drill is. For example both adults could have a whistle which when blown signals that all children go inside, with one child informing the other adult what has happened. In this way all the children could be moved to one area, one member of staff could move into a supervisory role keeping an eye on all, while the other member of staff deals with the accident.

Some staff argue that the outdoor area is too small for it to be of much use and resort to using it on a fixed playtime basis. However, too many children, in too confined a space, can create problems such as aggressive and dangerous behaviour. But, if outdoors and indoors are provided together the small size of an outdoor area is not such a problem. If children have quality activities available both indoors and outdoors, it will only be on rare occasions that any activity will be oversubscribed, or that any area will be completely devoid of children. Even on summer days, children still like to spend time working inside and likewise on very cold days children want to spend time working outside. If children are following current interests and concerns this will dictate what they play with. A small outside space can in fact be made into a particularly cosy area by virtue of its size.

Some staff argue that setting up outside takes too long, and this is the reason they do not bother with the space. First we need to decide whether it is in fact necessary to set up the whole space. If we want children who make decisions, think through ideas and become independent then a ready-made environment is not conducive to encouraging these dispositions. Ready-made meals do not create cooks, ready-made environments do not create thinkers. So spending time on creating a resourced environment is necessary but not to creating a set environment everyday. Staff who have indoors and outdoors running as integral environments, and who plan the two as one, find that setting up is not arduous but very stimulating as they are always thinking of new ways to interest and entice the children.

Unattached outdoor area

There are some settings where the outdoor play area is not just outside the classroom. If the situation can be changed so the outdoor area is attached to the classroom this should be done. If not then adaptations need to be made. The difficulty perceived with this situation is that children cannot move freely between the two areas, and it is not appropriate to allow under-fives to wander from the class through an unfenced area to the garden. One answer is a secure pathway, with fencing on either side so that children can only move between the two areas without going astray. A path such as this may cut across a primary playground, but could be opened at certain spots so infant children can access their whole playground when at break. It could be that a member of staff has to be more of a floater to support children moving about or that children cannot move quite as regularly between the two areas as they would if it were attached. Having a split between indoors and outdoors does make life more difficult, but the difficulties caused by having a timetabled playtime are far greater.

3. Outdoors is an equal player to indoors and should receive planning, management, evaluation, resourcing, staffing and adult interaction on a par with indoors

See Chapter 7 for more detail about the adult role and Chapter 5 for more detail about how to organise the space.

It goes without saying that if both out and in need to be viewed as two halves of a whole then whatever you do inside you need to do outside. The planning of outside needs to be a part of the normal planning process, not a single row at the end of the planning sheet, which may or may not get filled in. It can be more effective to actually create a planning proforma which does not distinguish between out and in but simply deals with experiences, some of which may be in and some which may be out and some where it could be either or both. Staff cannot see their role as one of teaching inside and supervision outside; both areas are teaching spaces. Children cannot be let loose outside where there is a survival of the fittest mentality. You definitely want children to feel free and able to try, but this cannot happen when no one has planned for it. Staff need to ensure they are watching what is going on and particularly assessing the equipment/ resource/activity/experience, its positioning and child interactions through their observations of children. In this way one can ensure no one is being left out where they lack confidence with a particular material or resource; or no one is being unkind. A new resource may have been added, say a pile of branches and logs, and its use and positioning can be assessed. Sometimes an activity can be used inappropriately and can create dangerous behaviour simply because it has been positioned incorrectly. Likewise by creating a managed outside we can watch real behaviour and make observations of children's strengths and needs. The environment needs to be such that it is not one of children going crazy, but one where sustained concentrated play is happening so children can be studied, understood and catered for.

Children will be using resources and equipment from inside but they also need resources and equipment outside. Some settings are very unlucky in that they do not have a shed, but resources do need to be made available outside – boxes and trolleys, even rucksacks can be used to hold equipment. The containers and shelves need to be labelled with words and pictures and tidied regularly. Some resources can be left outside all the time, for example the stones, shells, corks, etc. Wood needs to be brought inside. In an area used to vandalism, resources may need to be brought inside and the classroom arranged to accommodate this. One school I visited, where they had plenty of space outside but had such difficulties with vandals, had a container from a container lorry as the storage space. No one was able to attempt a burglary or damage a steel box!

4. Outdoors is both a teaching and learning environment

See Chapters 1 and 2 for a discussion regarding child-initiated learning, play and work and Chapter 5 for the areas for learning.

There can be a view that inside is where children are taught and learn from adults and outside is where children just get on. This is just an excuse for staff to drink and chat outside! If it follows that out and in need to be viewed as one environment and that there is an equality of both then it has to follow that children can be taught and learn in both areas.

In Chapter 2 there is a discussion about teaching and learning. This indicates that children need to be taught and to be in a secure environment where they can learn, and that children have an entitlement to be taught in all areas of the curriculum, not that they are taught some things, for example to write and then just be left to attempt to teach themselves to throw a ball. This simply gives a hierarchy to children's needs with gross and fine motor control and coordination being low down on the list, with a sense they may learn nothing new, just revisit that which they already know. Anything we do with children will have both a taught and learning component. So it follows that we need to see our role as one of facilitator and resource wherever the children are.

To create a teaching and learning environment, there needs to be an understanding that every aspect of the curriculum will be taught in some way or another. Reading may be explicitly taught when an adult reads a book to a child and takes the child's attention to the words. The child in a learning environment may take a magazine or book in a role-play situation and mimic reading or reading to others as though in a school situation. Likewise, a child may be shown, by an adult, how to move about on the climbing equipment, to later practise moving about on their own. The former can be described as overt teaching and the latter learning by doing. Children need both. We cannot leave any learning to chance, this is not fair.

We cannot work from the premise that because a child does not go to an experience they do not need to be taken to it. This is never more so than with activity outside. We all find it easier to stick to what we know, some children feel very comfortable with drawing, some with construction but that does not mean we just leave them in their comfort zone. In terms of outdoor play, it means that an activity a child does not seem to approach inside may well do so when positioned elsewhere. In Bilton *et al.* (2005) there are a number of examples where children did things they had not done previously because the position of the experience was changed. In one setting not all the children were painting and this was seen as a concern. Two large painting boards were built outside as painting boards and quite miraculously those children who had not painted previously were inspired to do so. Sometimes it is necessary to involve learning within the comfort zone, for example taking writing to the block play, where a moving house scenario could involve the listing of equipment to be packed, the cost, addresses and so on. It may at times be actually necessary to ban some children from an experience to allow others in. Bikes or the home corner can become dominated by one gender, where the involvement of the opposite gender is actually resisted. This cannot go unnoticed. Either children need to be encouraged to work together and this may involve significant adult engagement, or children who are being too dominant need to be supported while discovering other experiences and activities within the setting.

Through observations and talking to children we can ascertain how they need to be moved on in their learning and what experiences this would entail. Viewing outside as a no-teaching zone means these teaching and therefore learning opportunities are missed.

5. Outdoor design and layout needs careful consideration

There is no such thing as a perfectly designed classroom and likewise there is no such thing as a perfectly designed outdoor area. Areas can be too small, too big, too thin, too sprawled out; they can consist of only grass or only tarmac, receive no sun or get no shade, have no shed, and so on. All of these factors will affect the learning and teaching which can go on in the outdoor area. And there are some classes which do not have an outdoor space at all. Whatever the drawbacks of the garden, the best has to be made of the learning environment: compensating for the constraints, exploiting the opportunities.

Some of the difficulties encountered in the outdoor area are created at the design and build stage; such problems can easily be avoided if the outdoor area is considered more carefully when the Early Years Foundation Stage class is in its initial design stages. Common difficulties include physical access to the class, the shape of the garden area, shelter from the weather and lack of storage space. Fortunately some of the difficulties can be overcome. So, for example, where access through the outdoor area is causing problems, the access point can be changed. However, changes such as these can be costly. But many difficulties can be diminished by making changes to present practice, or to aspects of organisation and management. In this way the design feature is not altered but adapted or worked around to make the outdoor play area more successful. So, where a design feature may seem insurmountable, with a little careful rearrangement of the structure of the day or careful use of staff, this problem can be overcome (see Bilton 1993). Some issues may of course require more ingenuity than others. As Dowling argues: 'Nursery design affects how adults and children work' (1992: 139); this being the case, staff have to control that environment.

When considering the design features it is of paramount importance to keep the mind focused on the needs of young children. Fisher argues that effort has to be put into considering what children need and not on the constraints of the environment. She argues that the most important question to ask is: 'What do young learners need most?' (1996: 65). This is the starting point for all decisions then made with regard to resources and space. So, when considering the arrangement of the outdoor area it is necessary to ask, given that children have a variety of needs, and class groups vary from year to year:

- What do young children in general need?
- What does this class group need?
- What do individuals within this class need?

Whatever the outdoor area is like, there are a number of issues which need to be considered, at the design stage or when making changes to present practice. These include:

- access to and from the outdoor area
- size
- layout

- fixed equipment
- the weather
- surfaces
- seating
- the look of the area
- storage.

See Chapter 8 for more details on how to develop practice and address these issues.

Access

Parents, children and staff need to be able to get into the room and also into the garden. It is preferable if carers and children access the nursery via the classroom not through the garden. This is a view shared by educationalists not only here but in Australia too (Walsh 1991). If access to the class is through the outdoor area, problems can arise. For example, resources and equipment which have been set up before the start of the session can be moved, changed or disturbed by children and their siblings coming to school. This is not wanton damage, simply changes made by children who see interesting play equipment and want to play. However, if staff have spent time setting up equipment and resources in a particular way for the benefit of the children in their care, not only can the original set-up be lost, but also the possible intended learning outcomes. It can be very disheartening to staff who have spent time setting up to see their work and effort wrecked. If this happens regularly, staff will more than likely give up with setting up outside.

The ideal situation has to be access to the establishment through a building, that is the classroom and not the garden, with the waiting area for carers and children being outside the classroom but not within the garden. In this way, children and carers can enter the class, be greeted and then start playing, finally moving to play outside. In this way, equipment carefully and thoughtfully set up by staff cannot be tampered with and the children can begin working with the activities, as the staff had planned.

If it is not possible to deny initial access to the class through the garden and children are likely to disturb equipment already set up, then discussions both with parents/carers and children may help lessen the problem. This is where close contact with parents is so important, this dialogue will have to be ongoing as the requests can be easily forgotten. But it is difficult for children to see play equipment and stand by and just look at it! Other solutions can be to erect a makeshift fence which acts as an alleyway through the garden so children and parents can get into the class but not play with equipment. Schools which have access to the class through the garden have solved the problem by setting up equipment and then covering it over. This is a case of out of sight, out of mind, but it also says that the activities are not to be disturbed. Some classes put small equipment to be used in conjunction with, say, the sand into a box until all the carers have left. It may be that equipment has to be partly set up, but then finally arranged once the parents and carers have left.

Obviously none of these solutions are ideal. It is much better to have the outdoor teaching area only accessible through the classroom, but when it is not, solutions have to be found, so that equipment is not disturbed and the staff's valuable time is not wasted and opportunities lost for children.

6. Outdoor play is central to young children's learning

If we acknowledge that the environment actually impacts on people differently, as argued in Chapter 1, then it naturally follows that the outdoor environment may suit some children more than others and it may suit some children for some activities more than others. Children are made up of a personality, a unique background, learning styles, dispositions, needs and additional needs, there is so much to them. So if one child feels more settled outside painting and is more successful in his/her learning then it should not matter to the adults that he/she learns there instead of inside.

But for some children, outside is their life blood, this is where they do come alive, so they need to be in the fresh air, the light, the space to function effectively. A 17-year-old, who was a complete and utter failure within the measurements of the educational system of this country, is now laying hedges and has responsibility, determination, courage, ability – all attributes he was told he lacked while at school. He succeeds outside where he could not seem to succeed inside.

There is a greater movement focus outside, so if children do prefer to learn while on the move then outside is the place for them. If children are inspired by mini beasts and shrubs then outside is for them. If they feel less inhibited outside then of course they need to be out. In terms of learning language, outside enables children to use and apply words in context. For example through role play, it is so much clearer to say 'we're going to be painters!' to a friend for whom English is not their first language and take them along, getting the brushes and the water and paint. In this way the friend is able to hear the language in context whilst not feeling under pressure to speak until they are ready to do so. If children feel more able outside and with a 'can do' approach we should not deny them the opportunity to excel.

Often boys are more drawn to the outside as they seem to be more movement orientated, but equally this dosen't give them the right to control the area.

See Chapter 6 for more discussion about children.

7. The outdoor classroom offers children the opportunity to utilise effective modes of learning

Children have to move and talk, it is not a case of maybe, it is in-built. By the time a child is around a year old they are up on their feet walking. It has taken them around 365 days to master this skill, from being born without the ability to support their own head. Around two years of age they can talk and listen. The desire to communicate and shift continue as driving forces within any human being and both are something children need to achieve and something they can learn through. So children learn to talk, and talk to learn, they learn to move and move to learn, they learn to play and play to learn, learn about their senses and they learn through their senses (see Chapter 2 for more discussion about play and movement). All of these are vehicles by which they can learn and all are more easily accessed outside.

8. Children need versatile equipment and environments

If we need children to develop their imaginations, think and reflect, we need to give them the resources to do this. If a child is always faced with resources that staff have chosen and they are not able to add to then they cannot develop their ideas and thoughts. Quality outdoor experiences mean children need to have, within reason, any resources they want to ensure their learning goes as far as it can. For example if a child is interested in the properties of water then it is no good throwing the dinosaurs in Monday, funnels on Tuesday, jugs on Wednesday, sinking and floating materials on Thursday and cups on Friday. I fail to see what children gain from this.

Figure 4.5 shares a story of two children, a hideout and a play episode. If the children had not been able to take resources where they wanted, and make materials they wished this experience could not have happened. But the learning is quite extraordinary. Staff were able to view detailed conversations between two children, particularly about solving problems. The two children had never worked together and both learnt about a new person and a different gender, so in terms of their own personal development they

Two children went over to the hideout, a wooden construction which could be accessed by a ladder to the first floor. It didn't seem apparent that they had any particular play in mind, as they went over chatting about simply playing in the hideout, they may have had, but I didn't ask. These two children didn't normally play together, but somehow had just 'bumped' into each other that day. The girl was used to playing in the hideout, but not the boy. Having climbed up to the first floor, the girl started to tidy which was her normal starting point. The boy spent time just looking about. In the hideout there was an old printer, two plastic chairs, a baby bath, various old shampoo bottles and paper. 'Hey how does the postman get to post the letters?' the boy asked suddenly. 'Err, they just put them down there', the girl said. 'How do we get it then?' 'Go down, I suppose', the girl replied. This then sparked off a whole play episode with the boy going off to find a rope and a bucket and him attaching the rope to a section of the hideout, throwing it over the side, attaching the bucket handle to the other end of the rope, so the bucket in fact became a post box. They then both went to the technology table and made letters and found some old envelopes. The two children spent a while with a member of staff playing post the letters, hauling the bucket up, opening the letters, writing more, posting them in the bucket, lowering them down. This took the majority of the session. The next day the boy went straight over to the hideout and started up this play again on his own. He went to the technology table inside and converted a shoe box into a post box, complete with a hole for the letters. He got a proper pulley and attached it to the climbing frame and showed the staff member and she played the game of posting letters.

Figure 4.5 A versatile environment – the post box episode

moved forward. Their confidence would have been boosted because they were success-ful in their endeavours. Both had to use and refine gross motor skills (climbing and moving about the cramped hideout) and refine and use fine motor skills (cutting, sticking, attach-ing, measuring, throwing and tying).

As can be seen from Chapter 5, there needs to be a range of materials that can be used in any situation. Carpet squares and blankets can be used anywhere for example:

- to make a hideout in which to sit
- to make an obstacle course, using the carpet squares as stepping stones and blankets under which to scramble
- to use as mats to sit on and keep dry when gardening on damp ground.

The more versatile the resource the better, for example a rope has so many uses. It can be used as a skipping rope, it can be used to tie a truck to a bike, to make a pulley for a post box. If it is shaped into a circle it can be jumped in and out of, as a straight line it can be balanced along and so on. A rope does not cost a great deal, but has so many uses.

Many of the resources are free or cheap and easily available such as carpet squares, old bits of plumbing equipment, off-cuts of wood, electric cable spools and fabric. It is just a case of asking. Those involved in the Brent Project (see Bilton *et al.* 2005) found that local shops and stores were much more generous than they had anticipated and actually more generous than the big stores. Parents can become involved in collecting materials too, even in areas where there is not a lot of spare cash, parents are willing to help out as much as possible.

Kritchensky *et al.* (1977) suggest there needs to be three levels of complexity to the resources used with children – simple, complex and super units. They argue all three types are needed but one should be erring on the side of mostly super units, otherwise children go from one simple to another simple level without being able to develop their interaction. Figure 4.6 details the three levels and suggests that one needs to look at all resources and decide what level they are at. If most of the equipment is simple, it is time to throw some out and replace with more complex resources.

Children also need versatile environments: this means the fixed climbing frame to which nothing can be attached is as stultifying as having dinosaurs in the water. So any fixed equipment needs to be adaptable, that is be able to have resources added to it. Climbing frames can have material thrown over, planks and ladders attached, props brought onto the platforms. Of course there may be issues to do with safety which will

> Simple – having one obvious form of use e.g. swing, bike
> Complex – having a double dimension e.g. finger painting at a table
> Super units – highest level of complexity, blocks, sand/soil patches where resources provided are for unstructured play and can incorporate many other materials and resources

Figure 4.6 Three levels of complexity
Source: Kritchensky *et al.* (1977)

need to be discussed as a staff group and shared with the children. Sometimes the rungs on a climbing frame are not a standard diameter for ladders and planks to attach, so you may need to find a home-made source of planks and ladders. Equally equipment can be adapted, for example using the climbing apparatus for water play (Tovey 2007). If you have a wooden house you must make sure you actually deck it out, not leave it with a few dilapidated toys. You can ask a group of children to fill it with resources for play, this could actually be an adult-directed activity or you could involve the whole class in this activity.

9. Children need to be able to control, change and modify their environment

As we can see from Figure 4.5 children were able to control, change, and modify their environment. As has already be shared in guiding principle 2, dispelling the myths, if we want thinkers we need to give children opportunities to think not create a ready-made environment. It is not necessary whether in or out to always set up the activities for children, they need to be in charge of the resources and environment as much as possible. What this means in practice is that children will come into the setting ready to create and construct: to create and construct a play situation, a piece of art, a building from blocks, a mobile phone from scrap material, a small world scene from Lego and Duplo. If you are given only one material to play with, you cannot allow your imagination to create and construct, it is limited by the material. If James Dyson, the man who created the bag-less vacuum cleaner, had been limited by what he could bring to his design, he would not have been able to build the revolutionary vacuum cleaner. He must have drawn and computer-generated his ideas. He would have talked them through with others. He would have then built proto-types using metal, wood, plastic and a host of other materials. If someone had said 'oh no we can't have you using wood on a Tuesday', how quickly he would have ground to a halt with his innovation. Children of three, four or five may not be Dyson, but they all have the potential to be that in the future and they all have a right to be as creative as possible now. Looking at some of the constructions children make shows their potential.

So children do not need a perfectly set out environment every time they come to school, they need an environment where they can create a bag-less vacuum cleaner, they can wrap ropes around the climbing frame because they are creating a dog rescue centre, they can lay every single blanket on the ground as they are creating a sea or they can put mud and petals in a bucket as they are making a soup. This approach by the children will only come if you take the lead and they come to understand how you want them to behave. This leads perfectly to the final guiding principle.

10. Staff have to be supportive towards outdoor play

As in most things in life, everyone needs to sing from the same hymn sheet; all the staff have to be supportive towards outdoor play. Margaret Edgington goes further and says if you are not interested in outdoor play you should not even consider working with young children. I agree with this sentiment. If you are more concerned with the state of your nails, the straightness of your hair or the height of your heels, then go and do something else. I sometimes say: 'imagine someone dressed in an old duffle coat, funny looking bobble hat rammed tight over their ears, a pair of holey gloves, boots with bits of paint over them and a scarf tightly wound round their neck. This is the vision you may look like when it's cold and you are playing outside with children'. If you do not fancy this look do not presume you are fit to work with children.

If we look to guiding principle 9 you can only get this type of approach if you take the lead and show children that they can use a range of resources and materials in different ways and mix materials and resources. For example, in one setting, they had Barbie and Ken dolls, and these could be used outside. Four children pretended they were Barbies and Kens. They based the character round different dolls and dressed themselves in a similar fashion. They sprinkled magic dust on the doll they were holding and this made them be that character. They went inside and out, into the house, onto the climbing frame and created scenes everywhere. If the staff had not allowed the dolls outside this quality of play would not have been possible. Likewise if we look at Figure 4.7 there is an example of children playing but using a variety of materials and the water tray which becomes an exploration of the movement of water. Again if it had to be dinosaurs only in the water this level of learning could not have occurred.

Staff working in the early years have to be prepared to face all weathers. They need to accept that there is simply weather not that there is nice weather which they will go out in and not nice weather they will not go out in. Staff have to be prepared for all weather for themselves and the children. We do not have the right to deny some of our children the opportunity to work outside simply because the weather does not quite suit us. Equally, outside is not the break area to catch up with the weekend gossip. This will have to occur out of children's time and will mean that the break has to be taken at lunch time. Although not ideal for some settings the only break during a session will have to be a quick dash to the toilet.

Three children decided they would go on a journey. This started off quite tamely, in a play route they had gone before – family scene going on a bus. Suddenly one child started to talk about the locks at Devizes, which it transpired they had visited a few weeks before. The children then spent considerable time creating not 29 but 3 locks, using broom handles fixed into the side of big boxes and material on the ground for the water and one complete box for their boat. This did involve the careful engagement of an adult. At one point the children who hadn't visited the locks didn't understand how they worked and so the staff member decided to show the flow of water downhill using a water tray and dividing it into two using a tightly fitting board. It didn't work particularly well as the fit wasn't completely watertight but it was good enough. So the imaginative play turned into a scientific experiment.

Figure 4.7 The journey

Infant outdoor provision

Children are supposed to start formal education after their fifth birthday, but over the years there have always been under-fives in statutory school. The plight of four- and sometimes three-year-olds in school has been of concern for many years (Cleave and Brown 1991, Sylva *et al.* 2004, Rogers and Evans 2008) highlighting the inappropriateness of both the content and approach of the education on offer in many school settings. With the introduction of the Foundation Stage in 2000 and the Early Years Foundation Stage Framework in 2008 there is a desire to ensure wherever children are they received the right approach and content for their developmental age. But there is much poor practice still in primary schools with young children being taught far too formally.

Under-fives in infant and primary settings should not having literacy and numeracy sessions but should be receiving quality early years education as suggested in this book and in, for example, Edgington (2004). Whether there are EYFS children alone or EYFS and Year 1/2 in the same class then the approach has to be Foundation Stage based with activities available in and out throughout the day. Children can easily have a menu/planner which indicates the experiences or tasks that have to be completed in that day or week. In this way there is a nice balance between what has to be done and what children want to do. It is preferable to have a fenced outdoor space whether the under-fives find themselves in a nursery or infant school, but if this is not possible then a chalk line or foldaway fence or expedient placing of furniture will be fine. It could be there is only one teacher in the class and they cannot always be out, but we need to learn to trust children to be at times outside or inside on their own. It may be that only parts of the curriculum can be offered outside; but whatever the space imaginative and constructional play on a large scale must be available. It may not be possible to offer a climbing component in the area, but there can still be some physical activity on offer, perhaps skipping or ball skills, or these aspects of the curriculum can be offered through structured PE sessions. It may be that the area has to be organised so that it is only for a limited number of children at a time, and on offer on a rotational basis, as part of one of the activities on offer for that day. This is not ideal and has to be monitored really carefully, so some children do not come to monopolise the area.

It is essential to work alongside children in the area, observe how the children are getting on and assess their learning. Given the findings of Chapters 1 and 2 children need to be able to work on all aspects of the curriculum in any space; this is not a case of formal work inside and play outside. The space will only work if all the guiding principles are adhered to as closely as possible.

Babies and toddlers and outdoor provision

If the setting caters for babies, toddlers and children there is no reason why they cannot coexist together outside. All ages need periods of time together and periods of time with their own age group ... Facilities should be designed to support the expanding autonomy and independence of each child' (ECA 2004: 11). The Brent Project

(Bilton *et al.* 2005), where a number of settings made improvements to practice, demonstrated that babies and children can work and play in the same environment for some of the time. If equipment and resources are highly versatile then it does not actually matter what the age of the child using them is. But the difference is the involvement of the adult. The younger the child the more the adult needs to be in continual presence. With regard to say an A-frame a five- and four-year-old would easily be able to climb on this equipment without adult help. A three-year-old may need an adult nearby to assist. The two-year-old and younger walker would definitely need help and would require being held under the arms while attempting to put one foot on the first bar, or being held completely as they motion climbing up. For the crawler they would use the A-frame to haul themselves up, or crawl through but the adult would need to be close by. The main concern would be the child falling forward and knocking their mouth on the bars. For the 'sitter' the A-frame might be used to sit them under with the adult close by. A cover could be thrown over the top to act as protection from the sun. For the baby the A-frame is likely not to be of use. However, Walsh suggests that the toddler garden should be separate from the older children and have a number of resources removed, such as woodwork and higher A-frames. She suggests that toddlers need: lots of toys to push and pull, light objects toddlers can carry, things to hide and store and lots of duplicates so there are no conflicts (1991: 99).

Playground needs for children with a disability

Children with additional needs should have access to outside but often their access is denied for reasons of safety. But the outdoor area can be the easiest place to cater for children with special educational needs as there is lots of space, mess and noise are not a problem and there are lots of loose parts which children can use at their own level of ability. But staff must make sure the area does not become cluttered so children cannot move around easily. Unstructured play materials like sand and water are readily available and through their use children can gain often immediate success and a sense of achievement (see Chapter 6 for a discussion about sense of worth). Outside there are a greater number of possible sensory experiences, which may be more tangible to children with additional needs. Outside one can practise over and over and over again. In play everyone can be included and it is simply easier to follow the gist of what is going on. By thinking about children with needs means that the garden can be designed for them, and so for example garden boxes can be created which are at the right height for children in wheelchairs. The role of the adult of course is going to be much more one-to-one, but when involved in play the participants can forget who is grown up and who is not. Walsh suggests using a plastic floor runner on which to run a wheelchair over grass, blocks of foam to prop a child in a sitting position in a sandpit or for story time and an easel cut out to suit a wheelchair (1991: 103). She also suggests a 'well designed moveable ramp with a flat, slip resistant surface and a handrail 500 mm high, can be attached to a climbing structure' (1991: 104).

Figure 4.8 A learning journey

But at last the ship was launched!

And the crew jumped on board!

But the boat wouldn't move, no matter how hard the children paddled, or how hard they pushed.

'It's too heavy!' yelled Alison. 'Just one at a time!' said Helen.

Everyone climbed out and Helen stepped in – and the boat floated!

Figure 4.8 (Continued)

A few other children had a turn before everyone jumped back in.

But the water kept coming and then ....
'Oh! Look!' shouted Helen.

Suddenly Jessica noticed a hole that was letting the water in. 'Don't worry, I can fix it!' she said.

Figure 4.8 (Continued)

The boat gradually filled with water
and fell apart.

'I'll squash it and put it in the bin!'

'We can make a new boat tomorrow.
Let's use bricks – they won't break!'

Figure 4.8 (Continued)

- Fenced, mostly tarmac, different levels – if possible.
- Earthed area, shrubs and trees.
- Simultaneously available with inside.
- No announcement of outdoor play.
- Accessible as soon as possible after the children have come into the setting.
- For as long as possible, at least an hour.
- Carefully planned.
- Workshop environment – children controlling, modifying and changing the environment.
- Good quality resources freely accessible.
- In and out activities linked.
- Child access to storage.
- Little fixed equipment.
- Focused and child – initiated activities.
- Adults working with children.
- Children viewing adults as a resource.
- Available all year round.
- Flexible staff rota.
- Lots of vigorous activity.
- A covered area if possible.

Figure 4.9 The basics

Discussion

In this chapter we have looked at the ten guiding principles for outdoor play. Figure 4.8 details the learning journey of a group of children and a cardboard box in a school where children can follow their interests and do not rush outside to get away from the pressure of inside, where staff work with, support and inspire children. The results are that children can make these scientific discoveries together and in harmony. Figure 4.9 suggests what outdoors needs to be like to get these results. For outdoor play to work well it has to be provided alongside indoor play. Both areas need to be seen, not as separate entities, but as combined, integral and complementary. It is apparent that many of the problems aired about outdoor play, including the problematic behaviour of children, the disturbance to indoor play, seeing outdoor play only in terms of physical play, are actually caused by having a fixed time for outdoor play. Having outdoors and indoors available at all times means that the problems associated with staffing, resourcing, the weather, children's behaviour are either removed or diminished. Timetabling outdoor play pays lip-service to it and can be of little use to children in their learning and development. One knows one is doing a good job when children do not charge outside the moment the doors are open, and even sometimes no one goes out for a while once they are open. If children are charging outside what are they running from? Where children move calmly between the two areas things are going well!

Questions

1. If you have to timetable using outside, and you go out halfway through the session try going out first thing. How does the behaviour of the children change?
2. Using the levels of complexity (Figure 4.6, page 100), analyse your resources. Make sure you have a large number of super units. Think about getting rid of the simple resources. Talk to children about resources and their many uses. Ask the parents to identify and bring in resources which have many uses.
3. How do you store the resources and equipment? Make the resources more accessible to the children by labelling up boxes, shelves and containers and ensuring children can get to the materials. Talk to and model for the children how you want them to use the materials.
4. Children do not always know what is available in the class and garden so play find the resource/experience game with the children. 'I spy a place that you can paint at. Where is it?' Children then have to describe where it is. Turn it around and describe a place: 'It's at the side of the garden, over by the sandpit and it smells beautiful'. Answer: the herb garden.
5. Look at the links between the curriculum, inside and out. How does the curriculum outside link with the curriculum indoors? Does it matter if it does or does not link? What is your evidence? If it does matter, what more could you do to make the links?

Learning experiences/bays

5

Summary

When a teacher takes over a new class the first thing they do is look at the environment to see how it will work for them. Given a new classroom they are unlikely to leave it as an empty space, but to start to divide the room up into separate units or areas for learning: the book corner, a painting area, an investigative area, a blockplay area and so on. The curriculum is divided across time and space. Hutt *et al.* (1989) describe these areas for learning as 'microenvironments', meaning environments which are created for a special activity or purpose. This term is further discussed by McAuley and Jackson (1992) and Robson (1996). Nash (1981) uses the term 'learning centres' to describe the areas which have been organised within the spatially planned classroom and Cole (1990) uses the term 'activity center'. Henniger (1993/4, citing Esbensen 1987) uses the term 'zones' when describing outdoor play in US preschools.

In *Outdoor Play in the Early Years*, Bilton (2002) uses the term 'learning bay', which encompasses all the above and simply describes an activity area, an area for learning, a micro environment, learning centre, each of which has a slightly different focus. Learning bays can appear inside or out. They may appear in actuality or they could just be a tool for planning and do not necessarily need to be seen as such in action, only that they have been considered and catered for at the initial planning stage. So how should one arrange the area outside? Looking below there are a number of examples of how different authors have chosen to divide the outside space.

Dividing outside

Margaret Edgington (2003) suggests the following:

- a climbing area
- space to run

- a wheeled vehicle area
- space to develop skills with small equipment
- a quiet area
- places to hide
- a wild area
- an area for large-scale construction and imaginative play
- space to play with natural material
- a gardening area.

Esbensen (1987) suggests there needs to be seven play zones outside. These are:

- transition
- manipulative/creative
- projective/fantasy
- focal/social
- social/dramatic
- physical
- natural element.

By providing these he argues that staff can ensure children have a variety of play types to participate in.

Hutt *et al.* (1989) discuss areas for:

- physical
- fantasy
- material play.

The Inner London Education Authority (ILEA) document discusses the need for:

- large and small equipment
- imaginative play materials
- wheeled toys
- environmental materials
- blocks and building materials
- natural materials (Lasenby 1990).

Within this document a planning sheet from a school divides the outdoor area into:

- scientific
- imaginative
- physical
- construction areas.

Manning and Sharp (1977) describe four categories of play for both indoors and outdoors. These are:

- domestic
- construction
- make-believe
- natural materials

plus one extra for outdoors – play stimulated by the outside environment.

Hill (1978) describes four categories of play and play space outdoors:

- physical
- social
- creative
- quiet.

Gallahue (1989) discusses five areas outside:

- one for large muscle activities
- one for experience with various media
- one for seclusion and quiet activities
- one for opportunities to observe nature
- one for opportunities to dramatise real-life experiences.

Walsh (1991 and ECA 2004) working in Australia suggests three spaces:

- quiet
- active
- open

within which various activities can be placed.

Or it could be divided by how children work and play, which is:

- imaginative play
- design and construction
- communication and language
- investigation and exploration.

Parker created the following areas of provision:

- the natural environment, wildlife and vegetation
- gardening
- physical challenge and sensory integration
- role-play

- transporting
- natural materials
- the construction site
- the creative arts
- meeting places (2008: 116).

There are similarities between all of the above, involving themes such as imaginative play, construction play, scientific work and physical play. I have divided my outdoor provision to cover those ideas. I suggest the need for a number of basic learning bays, which can be added to, depending on the needs of the children. These include:

- an imaginative play area
- a building and construction area
- a gymnasium area
- a small apparatus area
- a horticultural area
- an environmental and scientific area
- a quiet area.

In an effort to ensure clarity I suggest the word 'area' is taken away and we see the above as experiences. Therefore outdoors provision should be made for:

- imaginative play
- building, construction and material play
- gross motor development
- fine motor development
- gardening/horticulture
- environmental and scientific discovery
- creative development including art, drawing and music
- quiet reflection (see Figure 5.1).

So in this way to a large extent any part of the outdoor area can be used for any experience, for example if you happen to have a sand pit this could be the focus of a

- imaginative play
- building, construction and material play
- gross motor development
- fine motor development
- gardening/horticulture
- environmental and scientific discovery
- creative development including art, drawing and music
- quiet reflection.

Figure 5.1 Experiences outside

child-led or adult-initiated science experiment or, another day, the centre of an imaginative game. Experiences can and will be by children combined and may be combined as a day unfolds, building and construction moving into imaginative play for example. Of course, some areas by their very nature will have to be static, for example gardening. Once a gardening plot has been established it cannot be moved around the outdoor area, but will be stationary! But an activity such as construction, a ball game, or art can move about the outdoor area.

Space and place

Alongside this runs a theme from Tovey, which suggests that the space outside is more than just that, because once the space is created and devised it becomes a place. 'Place is space imbued with feelings and meaning. While space can be anonymous, place has significance and meaning in our lives' (Tovey 2007: 57). The importance of the natural world is being distilled by an organisation called Natural England (see Chapter 10), which is supplementing the work of the National Health Service. There are plans for them to look after the green spaces around hospitals and health centres, plans to build a 1.3-million-tree NHS forest and a 'scheme has been piloted by London GPs whereby patients are referred to parks and places for outdoor exercise' (Bird 2009: 23). The centrality of us all, including children, being close to the natural world is once again being realised (see Chapter 1 for more on this). Walsh talks in terms of considering the 'ambience' (ECA 2004: 10) of the outdoor space, which means it needs to be as natural as possible and should be aesthetically pleasing. This area outside, by becoming part of the children's lives every day, becomes important to them and thereby it needs to be seen as a significant and cared for. Tovey talks in terms of possibly having the following spaces to make that space into a place:

Designated and connected spaces;
Elevated spaces;
Wild spaces;
Spaces for exploring and investigating;
Spaces for mystery and enchantment;
Natural spaces;
Space for the imagination;
Spaces for movement and stillness;
Social spaces;
Fluid spaces.

(Tovey 2007: 59)

What this means in organisational terms is that one needs a three-fold approach to the use of the space of outside. First making the space into a **place** possibly using Tovey's (2007) divisions as above so there is a sense of belonging for children and adults, of ownership of the space, so it becomes special and is a place, not just a tarmac flatbed.

Then applying Walsh's (1991 and 2004) three areas: open, active and quiet. Open being a flexible space for the freedom of movement where moveable equipment can be set up. This might include flat areas, mounds and three-dimensional effects. The active area is for physically adventurous play, where climbing and digging might occur. The quiet area might include a sandpit, areas for more formal adult–child work, a children's garden and secret places. This area is for 'observation, exploration, discovery, reflection, solitude and small group interactions' (ECA 2004: 11). Finally, one needs to plan for provision using for example the suggestion of learning bays/experiences. So that within say the place where children can be in an elevated position as Tovey (2007) describes, they can also be playing imaginatively one day but exploring scientifically another day. In this way the whole curriculum can be on offer and the focus of the learning bays helps to ensure that a balance of activities is available and that the teaching potential of all activities has been considered.

In the course of the last 10 years since the publication of the first edition of *Outdoor Play in the Early Years*, I have become concerned with how many settings have divided the outside so it has become a series of too distinct bays, with little interaction between them and often so full of stuff no child is able to move! Therefore time has to be taken to consider this organisation – to make the space into a place and then time to decide what will be available for children and how it will be arranged. In terms of planning there has to be evidence of it, but also a flexibility to it so it can reflect children's needs and interests. Planning will be slightly different for each person. Within this organisation, mention will need to be made of the areas of learning and development, namely:

- personal, social and emotional development
- communication, language and literacy
- problem solving, reasoning and numeracy
- knowledge and understanding of the world
- physical development
- creative development (DfCSF 2008: 11).

By structuring the learning and teaching around experiences it will help ensure all learning and developmental needs are covered. However, if a different organisation feels more appropriate to a particular setting this is quite acceptable with the caveat that there has to be evidence of why we are doing things as we are. Having a rationale means one should have thought about why. When you have considered why you do things as you do, you will be a better teacher.

Flexibility

It is not sufficient to just provide these learning experiences: how they are used is important to children's learning. The learning bays have to be seen as flexible and a part of the whole learning environment, not as isolated units. Children need to know that they can move their play from anywhere they want; that they will be able to continue their play tomorrow, if they wish, once the session is finished; that materials can be moved from one bay to another. The only proviso is that children should not impede other children in their play, interrupt them, put other children or themselves in danger, or damage equipment. McAuley and Jackson (1992) argue that when organising space, the microenvironments need to be arranged so that activities are combined within them, but not so rigidly that children are unable to combine materials within and between the various learning centres. Children can be thwarted in their play simply because they are not allowed to move something from one area to the next. Hutt *et al.* (1989) describe how some staff would not allow the mixing of micro-environments, so, for example, a cake made of sand could not be allowed in the home corner. The authors suggest that this is a pity as children are being prevented from making connections in their understanding. Athey (1990) concludes that children do explore systematically and have 'schemas of action' and they need to follow their particular interests and concerns. Matthews (1994), discussing visual representation, describes how Ben followed an interest and both drew and built 'fire'. This child mixed drawing materials and toys, such as blocks, straws and a sleeping bag. It was an ongoing project/sculpture and the child's thinking would have been disrupted if the experience had been cleared away every day. Matthews argues that children need to be able to mix toys and materials and need time for these often individual projects to develop. Fundamental to this has to be enabling children to move play and materials between these learning bays.

Layout (see Chapter 8)

A study by Brown and Burger (1984) found that design issues which were important in affecting play in the outdoor area were:

- 'zoning' (positioning of equipment)
- 'encapsulation' (enclosing areas for separate activities)
- the provision of appropriate equipment (e.g. vehicles).

In one playground, there was no play at the sand box because it was positioned in a high traffic area. Anyone who has visited an outdoor play area where children on bikes are rushing around will know how frightening this feels and how it can completely hinder play by other children. In the playground which promoted the highest levels of desirable social, motor and language behaviours and the highest rates of equipment involvement, there were many enclosed areas; children had plenty of opportunities to use vehicles, they had space and the correct surfaces to use these vehicles. Also, the play structures there offered greater opportunities for physical activity and offered more variety of use by children. The playground with the lower ratings of children's behaviour seemed to have a lot going for it except that:

- there was too much emphasis on it being aesthetically pleasing
- it had a large play structure, and a playhouse

- the ground was terraced
- there was a vehicle path and a large area with painted lines designed for play with vehicles.

The conclusion of the authors was that there was too little the children could actually change in this playground and so the play was at a low level. The designers had done too much. This is a view echoed by research into the designing of a nursery class garden (Bilton 1994). This particular outdoor area had clear paths to follow, extensive planting and was lovely to look at. The paths and flower beds, however, limited where children could move and almost prohibited the use of wheeled toys as the path was too windy. In many ways the school had done too much to this nursery outdoor play area, the space was very controlled and little was left for the children to affect.

Which activity is placed next to which will depend on such things as mess, space, safety, number of children, noise and so on. Teets (1985) argues that the activity to take place should be considered before determining where to locate that particular centre. Some of these considerations will change from day to day and week to week, while some considerations, such as safety, will be permanent – ball games cannot be played on a boundary next to a road or unprotected window(s). However, there are ways round such difficulties; one simple remedy could be to provide soft, light balls for children to use. Positioning a quiet activity near the nursery building, such as a table activity or sand play, can encourage those children who feel rather apprehensive about play in the outdoors to venture out. They can be seen to be playing but at the same time watching what is going on in the rest of the play area. The movement of children's play will need to be monitored to see where the natural walkways are and to make sure these are not creating difficulties.

Moving from indoors to outdoors

For children's understanding to be successful they need to know they can move their play and materials from indoors to outdoors and vice versa (see Chapter 4 for a discussion about the combined in and out environment). Children's learning can be thwarted if told: 'You can't take that outside, it's an inside dolly' or 'That pushchair cannot go in the house, it's an outside pushchair'. It may not be possible to allow complete freedom of movement of materials between these two environments but there is scope for a good deal of flexibility. Bringing bikes and trucks inside may not be possible in some classes as it may be physically impossible to get them through the door, or the space inside may be just too restrictive. However, in the Hartley (1993) research one school did allow tricycles both indoors and outdoors, even though the space was limited. What is allowed needs to be agreed with the children and made clear to them, so that they know the reason for the rules. The rules have to be there for the benefit of children's learning: 'No dollies outside because they might get dirty' does not seem a sufficiently good reason for them not to be taken outdoors. In the Nash (1981) study the randomly arranged classrooms used 'housekeeping' criteria to decide how the space was organised, whereas the structured class used 'educational' criteria, which reflected learning objectives.

Although it is important to work within agreed rules, it is also important to be flexible and in some circumstances it may be appropriate to bend, or simply not follow, the rule. For example, for the sake of enabling a particular play scene to continue, a scooter might be allowed inside, when this is normally not permissible. In such circumstances talking to children about a decision is important. By being flexible, each situation can be taken on its merits; each can be looked at in terms of what the learning possibilities are if it is allowed, what they are if it is not, what long-term damage may be caused, and so on. Following the path of flexibility means that children can, for example, have an imaginative house-decorating-and-moving-scene where they can build with blocks outside, decorate the blocks with wallpaper using adhesive tape, add furniture from the inside home corner and bring cakes made from the sand in the sandpit. Similarly, children can go from being builders outside, moving inside to make and write signs, moving back outside to set up the signs. If children are not allowed to move their play from outdoors to indoors and back again, if they are not allowed to use materials from more than one area this quality of play and learning cannot occur. Even in winter such play can occur, but the children need to be dressed up warmly. In a setting where the only outside surface is grass, and specific shoes are worn outside, then children will need to be trained to take their shoes off while the play goes on inside and then put their shoes or wellington boots on when moving back outside. This is not ideal, but is a means whereby children are still allowed to follow their play and interests.

Resources

See Figure 5.2 for a list of resources

Just as with the indoor space, each bay/experience outside needs to have the relevant resources at hand. Ideally this would be in a shed of some sort. Otherwise trays, boxes or trolleys can hold resources. Children will need resources which are positioned outside for easy access, but equally children will be free to move resources and furniture between the outdoor and indoor areas.

Central to the planning of the physical environment is making sure there are enough resources at hand, just in case more children become involved in a play setting than was anticipated. There always seem to be enough pencils for children and they are not expected to share, but this does not occur with all materials. In the McLean (1991) study of Australian preschool teachers at work, she highlights one teacher who made sure she had plenty of resources initially and as the day progressed made sure that if conflict began over resources then either more were brought in or children were directed to other equally relevant and often associated activities. Another teacher provided lots of materials and open-ended activities and as a consequence children were cooperative and 'frequently worked together on projects' (McLean 1991: 68). As McLean argues, scarcity of resources can so easily lead to peer conflict. The non-productive behaviour of another

I have always been reticent about providing a list of resources and equipment as I worry that it will be seen as definitive. However, having been asked so many times for a list I do so with this caution. This is just a list of the basics that could be provided in an outdoor area. It does not contain any fixed equipment, nor bikes. What is provided under the heading 'imaginative play' is as long as one's imagination! The most expensive pieces of equipment will be the blocks, A-frames and trucks. Some equipment will be free, for example the material or carpet.

A frames/folding trestles – large and small
Wooden planks – small and large
Metal ladders
Child-sized wooden ladders
Play cubes
Milk and bread crates, or some sort of box for building, strong enough for a child to stand on
Hollow blocks and unit blocks
Clothes horses – old and new
Pull- and push-along trucks/trailers
Imaginative play equipment, including dressing-up clothes and accessories
Masking tape, elastic bands, string/rope (these are the equivalent of indoor making and sticking materials)
Large pieces of material
Pieces of carpet, carpet squares
Hoops and skipping ropes (without hard ends)
Tubing and guttering, from DIY or plumbing stores
A host of water and sand equipment
Chairs or seating of some sort
Balls and bats – various sizes
Drawing materials
Writing, reading and mathematical games and materials
Trolleys to hold equipment
'Weather boxes' (Ouvry 2003)
Tree trunk sections
Mini-beast resource box
Gardening tools and resource box
Reclaimed equipment, such as cardboard boxes, card tubing, cable spools, wooden slats from an unwanted bed
Folding climbing frame
(See Chapter 10 at the end of the book for more information regarding resources)

Figure 5.2 General resources and equipment list

setting where there were not so many resources could have been lessened had the children had a wider choice and more interesting selection of materials to use (1991: 33). Interestingly, she discusses the work of Lindberg and Swedlow who state: 'An understanding of sharing cannot be legislated suddenly; it must be developed in an environment where a child feels that many things that he needs will be available to him, although he cannot have everything he wishes' (1985: 220). This would seem to be a helpful suggestion for those who want to teach children that they need to learn to share, and avoid situations which result in the survival of the fittest!

Which resources are grouped together can have an effect on children's play and subsequent learning. Nash (1981) considered that children associated equipment and materials. If they were close by, children considered they could be used together. So in the spatially structured class, children used materials together in the creative area, including dough, threaded beadwork, rocks, wood, box structures, collage materials and paint. In the randomly arranged class, children painted on paper and did not combine materials. In this way children could only follow what was dictated, but in the structured class they could follow their own interest and so develop their imaginations. What is grouped within a bay, therefore, will affect what the children do. Carefully and clearly arranged resources will also affect play. Teets (1985) found that where art materials, dramatic materials and manipulative materials were displayed systematically and children could see how the materials were categorised, they made much better use of them. It follows, then, that if good quality play is sought there needs to be a sufficiency and variety of good quality resources which need to be well arranged.

Rather than fill the shed with tricycles, consider this space as a cupboard for children to access. Shelves, hooks and labels in the shed means resources can be stored and children can access them. Carpet squares, large pieces of material, tubing, clipboards, etc can be stored in a designated labelled position ready to be accessed by children and adults. Cycle sheds, purchased from the local garden centre, can be used to house blocks, sand and water equipment. Visit the garden centre with an open mind and see the potential of the various garden storage containers. Coupled with an attitude that we do not need to set up every play situation for children means that our time is used wisely.

Resources can be gathered from a number of sources or they can be hand-made. For example, cloaks can be made from a piece of light material attached to a length of elastic, fire crew breathing apparatus from a lemonade bottle and plastic tubing, with a mask made from a sleeping eye cover, and then strapped round the child's middle using a belt. Or materials can be gathered from charity shops and jumble sales, bags and suitcases. Children need to use real materials and tools, such as hammers, trowels, money, cups, bowls and utensils. Families may also be willing to gather materials, and most importantly, children can make resources beforehand or as they go along and in this way take part ownership and part responsibility for the resources.

Boundaries

Given the nature of the outdoors, the learning bays/experiences cannot be permanent fixtures, and will have to be almost entirely cleared away each day. Research by Teets (1985) into the relationship between environment and behaviour in day-care centres found that where boundaries to learning centres were set up, the number of interruptions was reduced. By virtue of having defined learning areas there was a reduction in the loss and misuse of equipment. Division does not mean, however, that the structure is permanent. It may be that the positioning/clustering of equipment will be sufficient division; or the space can be divided by the resource trolley, box or table, similar to indoors; a simple chalk-line on the ground can indicate to children that a particular area is for a particular activity.

Too much permanent division of the garden can hinder children's learning, so any fixed hedging or trellising has to be really needed. Alongside these arrangements children can be encouraged to use their own sense, be aware of others at work and know that they cannot go charging across an area with a truck where children are attempting to play bat-and-ball games. In fact, the games children play will create their own boundaries. If children are given a chance to develop and extend, for example, their small-ball skills there will be no need to control excited kicking and throwing of balls, as the skill training will control the play. Boundaries need to be flexible and reflect the current play activities of each particular class. Alongside this will be the agreed rules, agreed between staff and children so that everyone knows that care has to be taken.

Continuity of provision

One of the difficulties with outdoor play is that equipment in most establishments has to be put away at the end of the day, whereas the indoor equipment can be left out. However, to ensure that children are able to follow their current interests and follow through ideas not fully formed, it is important to set up outdoors with some degree of continuity. The arrangement of resources can act as a starting point for children's play, so we need to ensure those resources are clean, in good order and carefully stored in labelled space. In this way children know what is available to them and can get to it quickly. Alongside this we can add additional materials and resources that we collect or make with the children. Sometimes it will be appropriate to leave the resources in the trolley for the children to start with a clean slate and sometimes it will be necessary to set up something new or set up where the children left off the day before (Lindon 1997). McLean describes ongoing play scenes, including the 'Telecom boys' where children were playing daily using various props which included ladders, shovels, a very thick rope, a hard hat, discarded telephone equipment and porters' trolleys. Another group were digging up a 'mine' and the boys liked to play for some time each day at this digging. The author describes the play as 'productive and highly elaborated as they unearthed interesting rocks and other long-lost (and sometimes recently-buried) objects' (1991: 167). What a celebration of play this is! Children knew the play they started one day could be carried on the next day and it would not be put away or broken up. Edgington (2004) reports that teachers find where children are able to follow an interest over a period of time there is a great increase in motivation and concentration.

A learning experience such as the imaginative play needs to be available all of the time. However, it will be given a different identity as needs arise, for example, a pirate ship or rocket. Experiments that children get involved in, such as those using water, need to be out for more than one day so that children have plenty of opportunities to explore them. Children need plenty of opportunities to use and modify the activities. There are some settings which are tight for space outside so the solution, although not a perfect one, is to offer activities on a rotational basis over a week or more (Edgington 2004: 135).

Outdoors not indoors out-of-doors

To successfully provide outdoor experiences it is not sufficient to move the indoor resources outdoors; moving the sand tray and writing table outside does not constitute quality outdoor play. Outdoors offers opportunities not possible inside and Edgington suggests outside 'children should be enabled to work on a more active, larger, messier and louder scale' (2004: 135). It is much easier to make a mess outside, much simpler to throw a ball outdoors, it is less disturbing to make a noise outdoors and easier to manoeuvre large play equipment. Edgington lists a whole range of possibilities for outdoor play such as constructing models on a large scale, rather than the size of say Lego, painting with large brushes, being part of a marching band using saucepans and metal pipes as instruments, blowing bubbles and watching the impact of the wind (2004: 135–6). These things do not work inside.

Resources used inside can be used outside but often in different ways; paper blows away outside, if attached to boards or clipboards it is still possible to draw and write outside. Imaginative play can take on journeys – in vehicles, on animals, on foot. Scientific experiments take on a grand scale, using climbing frames to attach pipes to discover the many properties of water. Games of counting and rhyming instead of involving cards can involve running, jumping and climbing.

The curriculum outside

The following is a discussion and description of each of the learning bays/experiences for outside, which together ensure the whole curriculum can be offered out of doors. See *Playing Outside* (Bilton 2004b) for more detail on each area/experience.

Imaginative play

The first learning experience and probably most important one to accommodate outside is imaginative play. This will need resources which suit many possible permutations of play, whether it involves being a post office worker, dog catcher, plasterer, TV repair person, zoo keeper, construction worker, astronaut, builder or pirate. It should enable children to work cooperatively, to negotiate, share, discuss, contemplate and conclude; it needs to be available on a daily basis in the same way as the imaginative play area would be inside. The difference with this outdoor role play is that there is much more scope for movement and the play can be on a larger scale, involve the whole child and many children. It means that children can use wheeled toys for being milkmen, removal men, or a family. Children need equipment which can hold just one child, a number of children at a time, or materials. The important criteria when buying are that it has to be well made and sturdy (See Chapter 10). Such items can be used in conjunction with bikes by simply tying the two together.

Much of the equipment associated with this play will be relevant to the building and material experiences. Children can then use their combined imaginations to design what they wish or staff may set up an initial arrangement to spark ideas. The equipment used here is more versatile than, for example, the play cooker or sink as it allows children to use their imagination to make whatever they and the staff want them to be. This area also needs chairs and possibly a table as children and staff need somewhere to sit in play settings and it is not always appropriate to sit on a crate or tree-trunk section! If available much of this equipment will be in the well-organised shed. Sometimes the staff will set up an imaginative scene and position various resources and equipment, sometimes the children will start from a level playing field.

The equipment does not have to be expensive; for example the following would make a good camping scenario:

- a makeshift tent from a piece of material
- cooking utensils
- sleeping bags made from material or a blanket
- backpacks
- a primus stove made by the children from recycled materials
- sticks from the natural material collection to make a pretend fire.

You could provide utensils from the kitchen including the usual plates, saucepans, spoons, forks including plastic picnic 'crockery'. But more inviting is the larger industrial size saucepans and utensils, which can be sourced from the school canteen or local industry where there is a canteen. Dolls, clothing and bedding need to be provided; these are toys which cannot be substituted with equivalents. Pellegrini argues that children do need to play with real dolls as discussed in Chapter 1. Ropes can be used in a play setting and along with string, masking tape and elastic bands are the outdoors equivalent to making, adapting and sticking materials indoors, which include adhesive tape and glue. Rope/string, masking tape and elastic bands are so useful for outdoor play. One can throw a piece of material over an A-frame and keep it in place with string; it then becomes an immediate den or house. Masking tape can be used to attach signs to wooden, metal and plastic equipment. It will not stay in place forever but should stay long enough for the play scene. Ropes can be used to attach trucks to bikes, to hold boxes together in a truck. Clipboards with paper and pencils attached or white boards are writing materials which can be used in most weather. The list is almost endless, but has to not only reflect the experiences of the children but also offer new experiences.

If we look at Figure 5.3 there are a large number of suggestions for play scenes, which staff and children can set up. Any of these suggestions can be introduced so that the children have plenty of ideas to follow. Taking the fashion show idea, children could watch just a part of one on the television, someone involved in the industry could visit. Research for and with the children in books and on the internet and making a visit say to a local museum (which always have clothing on display) would all add to the knowledge and understanding of the subject. In London for example the Victoria and Albert Museum has a section devoted to fashion. Collecting a range of clothing, particularly through the parental group, means children have access to a good selection of outfits and accessories. In this way children can play for a sustained period of time, not just flit.

Resources
- trucks
- hay carts
- wooden pushchairs
- carts
- scooter carts
- wheelbarrows
- blocks
- wooden and plastic crates
- large cubes
- A-frames
- climbing frames
- planks
- barrels
- drums
- large cardboard boxes, industrial tubing, tyres and tree-trunk sections
- large pieces of material
- pieces of carpet
- ladders
- tents
- variously-sized pieces of wood
- large umbrellas
- clothes
- accessories including bags, hats, belts, sunglasses, hard hats, workmen boots, fancy shoes, police hats, suitcases, baskets, harnesses, backpacks, sleeping bags, home-made stretchers, fishing rods, wands, old screens and keyboards, jewellery, maps, eye patches
- tools such as fire-fighter breathing apparatus (home-made), tubing made into fire hoses, doctor's equipment and bag, tool belts, paint brushes, shovels, small spades, old cameras, telephones, personal stereos, binoculars, pulleys, mallets, containers, such as sweet jars or flower pots
- pegs, sweeping brushes
- crockery or utensils
- dolls, clothing, bedding
- number plates
- home-made cones and road signs can add to the range of imaginative play materials.

Figure 5.3 Imaginative play

> - Builder's rucksack
> - Explorer's rucksack
> - Treasure trove rucksack
> - Decorator's rucksack
> - Wedding rucksack
> See Bilton (2005) for more ideas of resource boxes

Figure 5.4 Rucksacks or boxes

Children need scope to set up their own role play scenes and there could be a number on the go at once, enabling children to follow their own interests. Some children do seem to have a real flare and almost insatiable need for imaginative play. Again, props are needed to extend the play, extra to those already available. Children could be involved in the making of such materials: fishing rods for the boat, patches for the pirate ship, large trees for the dinosaur land. Whether designed by children or children and staff, imaginative play areas need to be available for some time, otherwise children cannot extend any ideas from the day before, cannot continue work from the previous day and cannot build on skills learnt the day before, such as negotiation, collaboration and so on.

Some children really struggle with ideas for imaginative play, so need help, either in the form of adults or resources. For example a cheap backpack from a local supermarket filled with an old mobile phone, tiny notepad and pencils, a scarf, a torch and some money could really inspire a child. You can arrange several such backpacks on hooks or in a box with a variety of resources in each and which, changed regularly, will really inspire some children (see Figure 5.4).

Bikes

Given the limited resources in school, bikes are not the most important piece of equipment to buy as they can sometimes be more trouble than they are worth! In fact three-wheelers are not on my resource list, except for under-three-year-olds. I suggest that some teachers' fear of nursery education and outdoor play stems from what they have seen in poorly run settings – many children racing around a small area on bikes and scooters. It can be a frightening place for adults, let alone children, to have bikes being ridden about in a small area, making the area feel more like the M25 on a bad day. Children will not venture out as they see it as a dangerous place; others end up controlling the area, usually the boys. Bikes become a source of power and perceived self-esteem enhancement. Bikes have a pecking order of preference with some being better than others. No one has told the children there is a pecking order to the bikes, but there seems to be this belief whether in Scotland, Ireland, Wales or England. Staff end up supervising and being 'controllers of who has the bike next' (see Figure 4.1 for the bike story).

Figure 5.5 Two-wheelers

So what is the answer?

- First, consider getting rid of the three-wheelers, they are not the most important resource. If you are in an area where children do not have access to bikes then consider having them, but not lots, just a selection of bikes which also have attachments so two or more children can use them together.
- Decide on a bike place or bike time, so the riding about does not destroy other children's play.
- Have two-wheeler bikes but again maybe have a place to ride them, not the general play area (Bilton *et al*. 2005). See Figure 5.5.
- Incorporate the bikes into role play. For example on Teachers TV (2006) there is an example of a school using bikes in a Domino Pizza delivery. You can have dispatch riders, Interflora, supermarket delivery, postal delivery, linked to Ebay purchases.
- Consider having an exercise bike. Get an old bike, take the wheels off and attach it to a sturdy and heavy wooden frame. Children can pedal to their hearts' content without bothering anyone else.

Building, construction and material play

Children need opportunities to build and use materials, which enable them to explore current concerns with regard to basic mathematical and scientific concepts. They need

- wooden blocks, both hollow and ordinary
- plastic milk and bread crates
- planks
- cable spools
- cardboard boxes
- logs and tree branches of various sizes and lengths
- ladders
- ropes – various thickness
- plastic tubing
- guttering and hose pipe
- plumbing piping
- buckets and other containers – good range
- collections of stones, shells, twigs, seeds, leaves, bark, cork, bottle tops, pieces of wood, pebbles, gravel
- spades with strong shafts
- trowels

Figure 5.6 Building, construction and material play

to be able to use, design, build and adapt. In this area children need opportunities to work together for a common goal, as only in this way can children learn to cooperate and get on to achieve the end product. It may be working together to build a tower using wooden offcuts and mud, or building a bridge using crates and planks. It may be that some of the children's play will move into the fantasy area, move out again and so on. If you are concerned about the impact of tarmac on the wooden toys, gym mats, pieces of carpet or material can help to prevent damage. Community Playthings (see Chapter 10) make a whole range of blocks which can last decades. A simple booklet entitled 'I made a unicorn!' offers examples of children building with a range of blocks.

Water and sand play can be part of this learning bay and can indeed be a mini-environment within the overall learning bay. Water play can be on a grander scale outside and can incorporate guttering, a number of trays, long pieces of tubing and a plethora of buckets, thereby involving children in corporate activity. In this situation children have to work together, otherwise the play will not be fruitful. Rather than having the classic water tray, try attaching two pieces of guttering to a sturdy fence or wall, for water to travel down. Equipment can be added to this basic set-up.

And there is no reason why young children cannot use real tools, such as mallets, hammers and the like. A nursery school, highlighted in an article in *The Times Educational Supplement,* uses real tools and was commended by an OFSTED inspection (Klein 1997 and Bilton 2004b). Carpet and material or large pieces of cardboard can be a warmer and friendlier surface to work on during cold and damp weather. Such items will get wet and dirty and can be thrown away when they become too knocked about.

Natural materials can be used in conjunction with this area and with imaginative play. Many of these could be stored outside, as they are not damaged by the weather and are unlikely to be stolen! Collections of stones, shells, twigs, seeds, leaves, bark, cork, bottle tops, pieces of wood, pebbles and gravel can be housed in containers which will

Collections of:
- stones
- shells
- twigs
- seeds
- bark
- cork
- bottle tops
- pieces of wood
- pebbles
- sea glass
- cones
- conkers
- beads
- wool
- string
- feathers
- leaves/petals/grass (until it rots)

Figure 5.7 Materials to be left outside

not be blown over (see Figure 5.7). These materials can be used in a variety of ways. They can be materials for imaginative play, or they can be materials for making discoveries about density, weight and volume. Children of this age particularly like to transport things, in fact, anything! So using the little trucks or sturdy push-carts they can put shells, cones or wood into their truck and they are away. Children love to make potions and perfume from things like petals steeped in water. The natural materials might be makebelieve food, a building material, animals, they can symbolise anything. They may also be used to examine, draw and discuss as materials in their own right. These materials can be placed anywhere in the garden to be accessed at any time for any play.

Under the umbrella heading of building and construction there needs to be a digging patch, separate from the horticultural area. This would be for building and construction work, where children might simply want to see if they could build a structure using mud and bricks and wood, or it could be for imaginative play, where children might be tunnellers or be burying treasure. You do not need both a sand pit and a digging patch – having either is helpful. Resources here would include spades with strong shafts, trowels and the natural materials described above. When it is dry, children can sit on the ground and dig. Even on a damp day children can still use this area without getting wet clothes by laying down large thick pieces of card or material on the grass or soil for children to kneel and sit on.

Woodwork using real toys could come under the heading building and construction and the table can be placed outside under cover on a permanent basis. But as with many activities you need to see where it works the best. Interestingly, in one school the woodwork table outside created an unnecessary diversion and staff felt it was better placed just inside the door along with all other design materials.

Gross motor development

This is where children need to develop their gross motor coordination and can also be described as the gymnasium learning bay. This experience is essentially about physical activity and developing physical skills and abilities, such as balance, coordination, agility and strength (Chapter 1 gives more detail about motor development). Children need to practise and modify their movements in order to reach a mature pattern of movement, but also to reach a high level of self-confidence. Once again, many of the resources used for imaginative and building experiences can be used in the gymnasium learning bay. It may be that imaginative play will move into physical play and into building play. An A-frame or cube for climbing may then become a hiding place from a terrible monster! Children moving over stepping stones may be keeping safe from crocodiles. When separating out this area, it is very important to remember that movement occurs in all children's pursuits and not just in the gymnasium area. So much of outdoor play is about learning through movement and learning to move.

Equipment needs to be set up for climbing, balancing, holding on with hands or legs, for stepping, for manoeuvring around. Equipment can be arranged on different levels, at various angles, connected together to create slides, walkways, bridges, stepping-stones (see Figure 5.8). For example, there could be an arrangement of balance bars and A-frames, followed by hoops to jump or step into, boxes to step onto and off, ladders attached to the top of A-frames for children to hang from. Strengthening arm muscles is very important at this stage for the eventual development of finer muscles. Tree-trunk sections, carpet squares and tyres can act as stepping-stones. Cones or boxes can be arranged in intervals for running in and out of. Canes across crates can act as jumping poles or for manoeuvring under.

These kinds of obstacle courses are for children to work at alone or together, and are for children to practise and develop their own skills at their own pace. Children can

> - planks
> - slides
> - ladders
> - nesting bridges or A-frames
> - boxes
> - crates
> - barrels
> - tunnels
> - hoops
> - ropes
> - tyres
> - tree-trunk sections
> - carpet squares
> - cones
> - canes
> - monkey bars

Figure 5.8 Gross motor development

attempt whatever part of the gymnasium they wish, depending on their confidence and readiness. A plank attached to an A-frame, for example, can be set lower or higher depending on the child. The gymnasium can be laid out in a circle or in a line; there can be two gymnasiums set up, or the focus can be on vigorous activity: it can be a running course, with cones to weave in and out of, boxes to climb onto and jump off and lines to jump over. The set-up obviously has to reflect the needs of the particular group of children.

Porter (2005), when looking at primary playtime activities, suggests concentrating on muscle groups when making decisions as to what to provide outside for gross motor development. For example, swinging on the monkey bars means the shoulder, arm, hand muscle groups are going to be used (see Figure 5.9). Balancing along chains or a rope on the ground exercises the muscles that hold the arms out straight, around the hips, the feet and leg muscles. Climbing along a climbing wall or on some kind of climbing apparatus will exercise underarm muscles, thigh muscles and the back. Therefore, pay due regard to the muscle groups when deciding what equipment to provide.

The concentration involved in physical activity can be intense, but the children will set the pace, challenge and speed. Staff can also offer challenges which will enable each child to develop and try something new, in a different way or simply to go faster. Staff can give guidance, support and encouragement (see Chapter 7 for more information on the role of the adult). Staff can also use such an activity to enable children to use and feel such words as 'through', 'underneath', 'over', 'into' and many other prepositions. Again, this area can be changed and adapted by children as a session progresses.

Figure 5.9 Strengthening arm and finger muscles, De Bohun Primary School

It may be that there is a scarcity of equipment, or only a small garden. But there is always a way to provide for gross motor coordination. Ropes or planks of wood laid on the ground can be used for balancing. A ladder straddled across two large wooden boxes can be used for manoeuvring across (as long as staff are holding it in place). This is not ideal, but is one way round a lack of equipment. A lack of outdoor space may mean that gross motor coordination can only occur inside or in the infant playground or in the hall, however limited for space children have to be given the opportunities to develop physically (see Chapter 1 and Chapter 6 and refer to Gallahue and Ozmun 2005). Whatever can be provided, children need opportunities to develop their skills and confidence over time. Bruce (1987 and 2005) argues that if children only experience an activity periodically they cannot build up skills.

Through observations of children while moving staff can assess how children are developing physically. As McAuley and Jackson (1992) argue, when analysing the Hutt *et al.* (1989) research, combined physical and imaginative play can simply be overlooked; observers only see physical activity or imaginative play and do not see how the two are combined. The importance of outdoor play is that the play is at a physical level because children are using their whole bodies. This is not about playing with small doll's house figures, or standing to paint a picture; this is about being a milk deliverer, a telephone repairer or a street player. The whole body is used and physical skills are developed.

Allow children to set up this area. Ask children to set up a two concentric circle arrangement, or a square joined to a triangle arrangement. Get them to draw a plan and then follow it. You can draw an arrangement for them to lay out. Obviously the complexity of the task will be dependent on the child's level of understanding. A member of staff could take some reticent children out to set up the equipment and in this way get them familiar with the unfamiliar.

Fine motor development

Outside is the ideal place for children to practise and refine small motor skills, as there is space to use equipment, without anything getting damaged. Again, children need regular access to small apparatus, otherwise skills cannot be refined. If children are only offered opportunities to use balls periodically then skills cannot be built upon. A resource trolley with balls of various sizes, and hoops, quoits, beanbags, skipping ropes, bats and skittles is needed (see Figure 5.10). It needs to be positioned as far away from other

- balls – various sizes and weights and material
- ropes – with and without ends
- hoops
- bats – various long and short handled, make sure they are not too heavy
- bean bags
- baskets and buckets to catch balls in

Figure 5.10 Fine motor development

activities as feasible. It may only be possible to have a few balls used at one time because games can become too chaotic with lots of balls going wide of the mark.

Again, if the space available is limited then a small group could be taken to the primary playground or primary hall, or less bouncy balls or beanbags may have to be used. Although it is fun to throw wildly, children should be encouraged to throw carefully; throwing to someone, into something, through something, at something. A small game of throwing into a bowl or bucket can be set up, or a chalked target can be marked out on the ground or wall. Children can be encouraged to kick or bat a ball into a receptacle, at the wall or over a line. A simple grid with the numbers 1 to 10 can be chalked on the ground for children to aim at and staff can encourage children to throw at the number 5, number 7 and so on. Likewise, letters, names or words can be chalked on the ground to aim at, thereby developing reading skills alongside motor skills.

A washing line is an invaluable resource. For example a tennis ball can be put inside one leg of a pair of tights, the end tied up and the other end tied to the washing line. Children have an instant ball which is controllable. They can bat it on their own, have two playing with it. A hoop can be tied to the washing line to aim a ball through. Balls can be aimed over or under the washing line. A piece of material can be securely pegged to the line and bricks laid on the side left dragging on the floor and balls can be thrown at it and will to an extent bounce back.

Figure 5.11 demonstrates some of the arrangements which can be made with the A-frames or trestles. These can be used anywhere for any purpose.

Gardening/horticulture

Gardening is so easy to do with children and acts as a real topic/project. Through gardening children are learning scientific and environmental concepts, learning to care and tend, learning to do something for the common good, helping to develop their motor coordination. The ideal is to have a section of land in which children can plant, tend and harvest flowers and vegetables. If this is not possible or available then wooden boxes, tubs, plant pots, growbags, in fact any container, such as a washing-up bowl, a bucket or an old tyre could be used to put plants in. Wooden or brick tubs set at the child's level are particularly effective and enable children to plant, tend and observe easily, and particularly those who have motor difficulties or who are in wheelchairs.

The gardening area would benefit from some form of boundary, such as a low fence, a section of grass or a layer of bricks or pebbles laid as a path, so that children know this area cannot be used for play purposes. Initially this would probably have to be an area where children and staff work together. As the children grow in knowledge and confidence they could be allowed to weed and water without too much supervision. Children need access to real tools and equipment (see Figure 5.12).

This area can easily be organised into two cycles, one which progresses from September/October to April and one which starts in April/May and carries through to September (see Figure 5.13). Parker (2008) suggests start small when it comes to

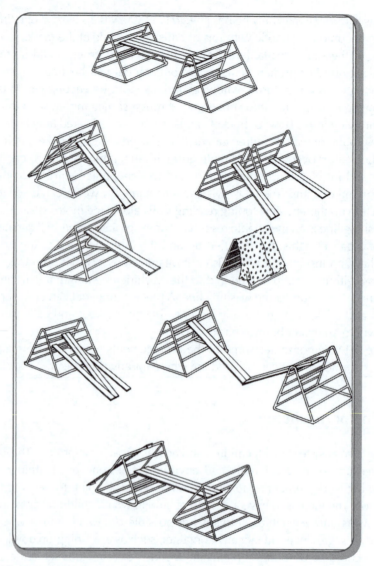

Figure 5.11 Various arrangements using the A-frames

gardening if one is a novice and discusses easy links with stories such as the Enormous Turnip which can evoke simple reenactment but also inspiration for growing vegetables oneself.

You do not have to be an experienced gardener. You may not be able to display in the local flower and produce show, but the fruit and vegetables will be of a sufficient size for children to see their growth and appreciate them; crucial is to see the cycle through. Another possibility is to grow herbs. See Figure 5.14 for an easily created child's garden.

Child and adult sized:
- spades
- trowels
- forks
- hoes
- watering cans
- water hoses
- canes
- wheelbarrows
- truggs
- plant pots
- gardening gloves
- secateurs

- seeds and plants
- outside tap
- water butt
- cameras
- writing materials

Figure 5.12 Gardening/horticulture

From September onwards,
for winter display: snowdrops
for spring display: daffodils, crocuses, tulips.
In May after last frost,
for summer display: hardy annuals such as alyssum, asperula, candytuft, clarkia, clary, lavatera, limnanthes, nasturtium, scabious, virginia stock, annuals: cosmos, marigolds and petunias; vegetables: beans, peas, marrows, potatoes, lettuce, cucumber, tomatoes; corms, bulbs and tubers: anemones, freesia, iris, *Liatris spicata*, dahlias.
In April/May, for cropping March/April following year: purple cape cauliflower

Figure 5.13 Growing cycle

Figure 5.14 Children's garden in spring

The BBC gardening site has all sorts of help, advice and knowledge for adults and children (see Chapter 10). There are suggestions as to how to grow a sunflower screen from April onwards, how to make a compost maker, to how to make a bumble bee box. Have a look at the jobs section and this will give you a month-by-month guide of jobs in the garden (BBC 2009); what a lovely way to start children using the internet and then using that knowledge outside! There is also a fantastic site called 'Dig in' (see Chapter 10) which gives step-by-step guidance on growing things like carrots, squash, lettuce and tomatoes. It has the most delightful video clips of 1–2 minutes long and the production is so child friendly. Children can quite easily follow the guidance because it is step by step.

It is also important to think about when the harvest is due, otherwise children who leave at the end of the term may miss the cycle of events. Children need to appreciate the life cycle and to record it, in words, drawings, photos, collage, paint and any other medium possible. The important aspect of this activity is the fact that something develops and changes over time, which can then be recorded. For this reason a camera is an essential item. Children can make their own books or joint books to record what they did and what happened. It means that children who prefer to work outside can be involved with writing, drawing, graph-making and so on, which they may not do so readily inside. Making a book would involve photographing stages – going to the garden centre, preparing the land, planting the bulbs, the first shoots emerging and so on. It could involve a time line which could be folded up in the book, but shows when things happened, and when nothing appeared to be happening. It can have children's drawings in it, and their thoughts and ideas written down. There can be graphs created on the computer with those children at a stage to do this sort of work. In this way the book can involve most of the children in some way or another.

The garden is an ideal environment to enable children to develop and use their senses and to hone one particular sense. A herb garden does not take much effort to make and yet children can be taught not only to experience the different smells, but also to describe them, compare them and ultimately use them in cooking. Flowers are ideal for sensory experiences, they can be looked at, smelt, felt and some can be tasted. Proper study of flowers, stems, leaves, seeds and bark can lead to excellent comparative work and a true appreciation of such things as colour and texture. Copying colour matches from nature can bring out interesting discussions, for example, red dots on white or yellow stripes on black. Areas which highlight different sensory experiences can be set up, which children can access themselves or a teacher can utilise for a teaching point: a sight area with mirrors and reflective materials, a hearing section with chimes, scented herbs and flowers for a smelling area, for touch various differently textured stones, barks and shells.

See Cooper and Johnson (1991) to check poisonous plants.

Environmental and scientific discovery

We are born with five senses through which we receive input from outside ourselves: sight, hearing, touch, taste and smell. Children need to use these senses to discover and explore, but they also need to learn how to use them. Children need help to focus in on each sense and so use it effectively. Through all experiences staff can hone children's senses but environmental experiences lend themselves particularly to this.

Children need to appreciate the world of plants and animals around them and we can help them in this by making environments attractive to certain species. Old rotten logs or a piece of carpet which is left in a damp, secluded spot will gather mini-beasts. This can be lifted periodically for the investigation and observation of such creatures. An old sink or bathtub can provide a habitat for water-keen mini-beasts, but beware that open water will attract mosquitoes. Bird tables, bird boxes and baths can be positioned so children can watch from inside. Ouvry suggests putting together something called 'weather boxes' (2003: 70). These are activities, resources, books, pictures, songs and poems all ready to be used if that particular weather feature occurs, whether it be wind, rain, snow or sun. This seems a great idea, as children need to have multi-sensory experience of these weather features – not be stuck inside looking at it! But for the experience to be really worthwhile it is very effective to have the ideas and resources at the ready. So for example, Ouvry suggests covering umbrellas with different materials ready to explore the sound rain makes on different materials. Bubble wrap, wool and foil covering three umbrellas will all sound different when the rain falls. She suggests putting a drop of oil on a puddle, followed by a discussion about colour and rainbows. Another idea is dressing two dolls, one in a rainproof material, one in woolly material, leaving in the rain and following up with discussions. Other ideas include bought and home-made kites, bubble blowers and bubbles, for the windy box; calibrated containers for the collection of snow, to allow the children to record the change in volume or to collect rain to see how much has fallen in a given time. These boxes could be added to, with ideas that children come up with and as more ideas are found.

A clear link with an indoor learning bay can be seen here: children will need reference books so they can identify and learn about the various creatures or weather features and these can be easily displayed in the book corner. Books can be made by staff which specifically identify the organisms the children are looking for and, likewise, children and staff can make reference books for everyone to use. The camera needs to be close at hand to record interesting sightings. Resources connected with this learning bay can be readily available on a trolley or in clearly labelled boxes (see Figure 5.15).

Parker (2008) discusses her experiences of making a bog garden with the children in her school and the high level of involvement given to them. Clearly the school encourages children to think and have ownership as they ask complicated questions about the bog garden, such as: 'Will we wake all the plants up? Can we splash in the bog garden? Will the birds come? Do spiders crawl really fast?' (2008: 113–14). I have to be honest, I do not know a huge amount about a bog garden, but this description of the work of the children inspires me to want to make those discoveries with children about bog gardens.

Katz and Chard (1989) suggest looking at the sayings of the weather, of which there are many. The discussions and observations and scrutiny over the year will enable children to become keen observers and highly knowledgeable. Again, books can be made about these sayings for all children to refer to. See Figure 5.16 for a list of some of

- inspection pots
- magnifying glasses
- gathering jars
- brushes to collect invertebrates
- pond-dipping equipment
- nets
- binoculars
- camera
- bird food – various
- squirrel-resistant bird feeders (RSBP)
- weather charts and identification of weather charts
- weather boxes
- writing and drawing materials, paper and pencils on clipboards
- reference books
- environments for:
  - animals (wildlife area)
  - mini-beasts (tree-trunk sections, old carpet, large flat stones, evergreen cuttings)
  - bats (boxes)
  - fish and amphibians
  - birds (boxes, feeding tables, baths, trees)

Figure 5.15 Resources for environmental and scientific discovery

the sayings. The Met Office has some activities for children such as making a weather station, a weather front, a cloud in a glass. They even have a form to download to record weather. The level is geared to young children and even if they do not understand what for example a tornado is, the actual experiment will be thrilling. This will heighten their

'Make hay while the sun shines'
'Red sky at night, shepherd's delight, red sky in the morning, shepherd's warning'
'March comes in like a lion and goes out like a lamb'
'April showers'
'No weather is ill, if the wind be still'
'Rain before seven, fine by eleven'
'A sun shiny shower won't last half an hour'
'Mackerel skies and mares' tails make ships carry lowered sails
    Mares' tales, storms and gales. Mackerel sky, not 24 hours dry'
'Every wind has its weather!'
'Cold is the night when the stars shine bright.'
'If smoke hovers low near the ground it is likely to rain.'
'When circle around the moon t'will rain'

'Whether the weather be fine
Or whether the weather be not
Whether the weather be cold
Or whether the weather be hot
We'll weather the weather
Whatever the weather
Whether we like it or not'.

Figure 5.16 Weather sayings

'Make a tornado in a jar

A tornado is air which is spinning very fast. It is made by a special type of thunderstorm called a supercell.
What you will need:
A clear jam jar or similar see-through container with a screw-on lid
Washing-up liquid or liquid soap
Food colouring
Fill up the container with water then add a few drops of the washing-up liquid and a few drops of the food colouring. Tightly screw on the lid.
Swirl the container around in a circle lots of times and then stop. Inside you should see what looks like a tornado. It will slowly disappear as it reaches the top of the container. Tornadoes in the real world are made in the same way'.

metoffice.gov.uk/education/kids/weather_station See Contacts and Resources

Figure 5.17 Weather watching
Source: Crown copyright 2009, the Met Office

curiosity and interest and to be motivated to ask questions and consider (see Figure 5.17 for an example of an activity from the site).

Creative development including art, drawing and music

Visual representation is central to young children, whether it be drawing, painting or making a design from blocks. Therefore, outside drawing materials need to be available every day. Matthews demonstrates how young children can put drawing and letters together to 'make free-flowing associations and multiple meanings' (1994: 93). He goes further in describing a particular picture, to ponder on whether it is the beginning of making puns and could indicate a child thinking about thinking, representing to reflect upon representation. This is higher order thinking and needs to flourish. Children need access to drawing materials, whether it be using chalks on the ground or pastels on old wallpaper or coming together and painting a picture on a large piece of paper. Group painting on a large piece of paper taped to a wall can be effective in encouraging reticent painters. Parker (2008) discusses the work of Andy Goldsworthy as possible for young children to emulate, using natural materials for sculpture. She suggests Jackson Pollock is appropriate for young children to explore involving splattering paint.

Artwork which involves mess can be planned for outside as mess outside is not usually a problem. Outdoors provides the perfect spot for foot printing, no worries if a child strays off the paper onto the ground! Clay, a natural material which is not used as much as it should be, can be set up more easily outdoors, as any difficulties with mess can be cleared with a bucket of soapy water. A music corner can mean that children can really make sounds without disturbing anyone. A music table, with instruments and resources

- Paper, various sizes and shapes and weight – wallpaper is good to use outside
- Pencils, various thickness, well sharpened
- Charcoal
- Pastels
- Clay
- Paint in pots
- Oil paints
- Clipboards with pencils attached
- Chalks – particularly thick ones
- Collecting baskets
- Old board for oil painting
- Sand

Figure 5.18 Creative development including art, drawing and music

used in a group music session, will enable children to practise and try out ideas from the music session (see Figure 5.18).

Quiet reflection

Indoors there are quiet spots for reflection, or for doing activities which require little movement; such spots are also needed outdoors. A table and chairs in a shaded or cosy spot would be preferable, but seats from indoors, a couple of crates, a blanket, a piece of carpet plus cushions would all suffice. However arranged, children must be aware that this is a quiet spot. A proper wooden seat enclosed either with a pergola or surrounded by shrubs would be useful, as this can act as shade in the summer and a windbreak in the winter. Even in the smallest outdoor area, a quiet spot can be established. A box with books, tape recorder, soft toys, paper and pencils, language and mathematics games can be set up here.

It is not always possible to set up outdoors as picturesquely as indoors, but it is still important to provide this spot. At other times, a board game, a threading activity, books on a particular topic can be offered. In this way those children who are reticent about venturing outdoors have a secure spot to go to, while those who work confidently outdoors but need time to have a quiet and settled period are also provided for. Any child who wishes just to watch what is happening outside is also catered for. It means that those children who are not confident about the more formal aspects of school work can have a go in an environment in which they feel secure (see Figure 5.19).

Other experiences out of doors

The learning experiences mentioned previously are but the beginning, and ensure that there is a balance of activities available. But what is offered outside does not have to end

- Books – some old favourites and some new ones, fiction and non-fiction
- Walkmans with taped stories, rhymes and songs – particularly those told and sung by you
- Comics and child magazines
- Dictaphones
- Soft toys
- Games which cannot blow away
- Writing and drawing materials

Figure 5.19 Quiet reflection

there and other experiences and learning areas can be set up. Group reading, music, dance, movement, snacks, meals, rest can all be offered outside, and in this way the outdoor area becomes just the natural half of the whole environment (see Figure 5.20). You can make a decision as to whether today it is okay to have the snack table outside or a dance session or for telling a group story. As with provision for inside, what we can and do provide outside is dependent to a large extent on the imagination of the staff. Figure 5.21 lists a host of possible ICT resources to use outside. Children can become real live newsreaders, journalists, camera operators as they go round the garden commenting on what they see. Or they can perform in the outside just as singers and bands do. These are very simple ways to get children to talk and listen and for good reason.

- group reading
- music
- singing
- dance
- movement
- snacks
- meals
- rest

Figure 5.20 Other experiences out of doors

- dictaphones
- headset
- walkie talkies
- radio mike
- karaoke
- intel digital blue movie camera
- hand-held metal detectors
- mp3 players
- battery operated cassette recorders

See Bilton *et al.* (2005) for more details on ICT and outdoors

Figure 5.21 ICT resources

Figure 5.22 A possible layout

Figure 5.22 gives some idea of what an outdoor area might look like. There are seven bays arranged:

- Imaginative: which is a supermarket delivery depot, with trucks, large cardboard boxes, cones, plank and tables with a large number of different containers from shops. Children have chalk-drawn a road.
- Construction: partially arranged by the staff, but children to build as they wish. Also a digging plot with tools – large hole made.
- Gymnasium: A-frames, planks, crates, barrel, mats, log sections, carpet squares.
- Small apparatus: trolley with variously sized bats, balls, hoops, ropes. Chalks to mark out targets.

- Horticulture: tools, outside tap. Plants in various stages of development, seeds to be put in.
- Quiet area: chairs, cushions, carpet squares. Tree for shade. Books, drawing pads, tapes, games.
- Mini-beast area: log, carpet squares, tree trunk. Cardboard squares for stepping stones.
- Shed: children can easily access more resources as shed is well arranged and labelled. By the classroom wall there is a collection of stones, pebbles and wood for use in any play.

Discussion

Outdoors has to be somewhere children enjoy being so there is a need to create a sense of 'place' as Tovey describes, this can be created either by planting of trees and shrubs and creating nooks and crannies, or if this is not possible, by our attitude. Children can still see it as a special place even if it is not Kew Gardens because we demonstrate our love of the space. You need to love it, for the children to love it. Generally there need to be three styles of area: open, quiet and active (Walsh 1991). Within this the learning desired has to be considered. We have to decide what is important to our children and provide activities within that special place. Divisions within the space maybe in your mind and on the planning sheets, or they may be more evident. Even if learning experiences are starting points they help children to get started in their play, they give a focus which they may or may not follow. The bays help to make sure a broad and balanced curriculum is offered and that no important component is left out. The experiences need to be seen by everyone as flexible and play needs to be allowed to move freely across the combined environments of indoors and outdoors; similarly it has to be allowed to progress from one bay to another. Figure 5.22 is one possible layout, showing some of the learning experiences children have had in a day; some of which have been decided upon by staff and children and some which have been invented by children.

Questions

1. How can outdoor provision be improved in your situation? What are the long-term solutions, that is, where do you want to be in 5 years' time? What are the short term solutions, that is, where do you want to be in 6–9 months?
2. Is your outdoor area both a place for children to call their own and somewhere they can learn? Look at the space and place divisions above, create your own place and relevant experiences.
3. What are the needs of your particular children? How can you provide for them in your educational space both indoors and out of doors?

Questions *(Continued)*

4. Get an old pair of tights, cut one leg off, put a tennis ball inside, tie the end and then tie the other end to a washing line – a permanent hanging ball for children to hit, which is not going to get lost.

5. Rather than have all the learning bays does your outdoor area provide for imaginative, physical, constructive and scientific experiences? If not make sure it does. Within the whole area are there quiet, active and open spaces? If not how can you provide for these?

6. Look at the continuity of experience over a period of time. Dos it matter if an experience/activity only lasts a day/morning? What is your evidence? How can you make an experience/activity interesting and effective for learning for a week, 2 weeks, a month? Use a particular experience/activity to demonstrate your thinking, for example imaginative play.

7. Look at one curriculum area, knowledge and understanding and break it down into its components: history, geography, science, and ICT. What are you trying to teach children under the headings? What experiences/activities could you offer outside to help you teach these ideas?

8. Take the layout in Figure 5.22: how could you improve this space? What more does it need, thinking particularly about the need to create a 'place'.

Children using the outdoor environment

6

Summary

This chapter attempts to demonstrate that the outdoor environment is a different place to indoors and how children behave in this space is often very different to how they behave inside. But there are even more subtle differences: this can be a space where some children ensure others do not get equality of opportunity. This is a space where boys often get a better deal than girls. Even who they play with and how they play can be altered by minor changes to practice. We have to be acutely aware of these issues so we can then address them. Outdoor play may suit some children more than others, but it may also give all children the opportunity to develop the necessary dispositions to help them to become learners, including a sense of self-worth and self-regulation.

When I talk to teachers and trainee teachers all comment about how their children are different – some like outside, some do not, some change when outside, some do not, some prefer certain activities outside and some do not. Some can be quiet and reserved inside and but quite extrovert, social and assertive outside. Children will not all gain the same thing being inside or being outside; what they learn will not be uniform. Margaret McMillan considered that all children would benefit from nursery education but that they would all get different things from it. The children from the affluent parts of Chelsea were nicknamed the Kensington Cripples by the middle-class parents, who set up the Open Air Nursery in the 1930s, because they had everything done for them by servants and could do little for themselves (Whitbread 1972: 72). McMillan felt these children could benefit from simply doing things for themselves when at nursery.

A sense of worth

Being outside helps children develop a healthy view of themselves. Children need to have a sense of 'who am I?' Gallahue and Ozmun describe 'self' (who I am) as being made up of self-confidence (belief in self), self-concept (awareness of self), self-esteem (evaluation of self) and self-image (perception of self) (2005: 280). So why am I talking about this in a book about outdoor learning? Because how you can move affects self, as there is a general valuing of being good at sports, games and play. 'Perceived competence and actual competence promote self-confidence, which has the potential for enhancing dimensional aspects of one's self-esteem and self-concept' (Gallahue and Ozmun 2005: 285). So we can be instrumental in helping children not only be physically able but believe in their abilities. The authors cite research that argues those children who take part in sport consider themselves as more competent than those children who do not take part in sports (cited in Gallahue and Ozmun 2005: 284). So this suggests a link between physical competence and one's positive sense of self. Interestingly this link is not as apparent in younger children although their participation in sport does have a clear link to their physical skills. Research cited in Gallahue and Ozmun (2005: 284–5) dealing with younger children found that participation in sport did not affect children's perceived physical competence – what they thought about themselves or others but that for those who actually did participate in sports they were more able physically, in terms of motor development. So we cannot leave it to chance at choosing time or play time for children to get involved in physical activity, we need to ensure all children are participating and helping them in the process, for actual physical competence now and for later perceived competence.

Children as adults need to feel a sense of success, that they can do things and that if they try something new they will be successful. We need children who say: 'I can' and 'I did it' not 'I can't' and 'I'm useless'. In terms of movement we can support children in having a strong 'I can' approach. Looking to the research by Stephenson (2002) she found that outside was a 'look at me' environment as opposed to inside which was more of a 'look at what I have made' environment. So children and staff were actually choosing to use the two areas in different ways. It is therefore possible to tap into this natural interest to be physically active, to encourage and develop skills and therefore self-worth (Chapter 1 looks in more detail at this research). It takes years to learn to read but it takes but a few days to learn to achieve many physical skills, for example skipping. At an infant/nursery school in Reading, one class decided to have the children skipping every morning, for around ten minutes. The children were aged 4, 5, 6 and 7 years. What was staggering was the speed at which they did learn to skip. It took even the youngest only three to four days to master skipping. The stages children tended to go through were as follows:

- throwing closed rope over the head
- throwing the open rope over the head
- throwing the open rope and jumping at the same time, but at the wrong time to get over the rope
- throwing the rope and jumping at the right moment to get over the rope. At this point children were so surprised at their success, they stopped!
- skipping continuously.

Children then moved onto skipping for as long as possible, skipping to different rhythms, skipping backwards, skipping with a friend, throwing the rope sideways before opening it, skipping in a rope being turned by two people. But significant was the speed with which the children mastered the skill, whatever their age. With this comes the very important self-confidence, leading to a healthy view of self. Children can get this sense of confidence from achieving many physical skills – whether it be climbing on apparatus, swinging on monkey bars, throwing a ball, riding a two-wheeler (see Chapter 8 for a discussion of primary-aged children's playground challenges). What is important is that children do achieve relatively quickly and so success is seen to be achievable. As Walsh (1991: 11) argues:

> Initially the young child will find it easier to have an impact on their physical rather than their social environment. This is because the physical environment is more predictable and clear cut whereas a social environment is more complex, shifting, and at times overwhelming to a young child.

See Chapter 7 for further discussion about motor development in children, what the adult needs to be looking out for and how they can help children succeed.

Self-regulation

The Cambridgeshire Independent Learning (CINDLE) in the Foundation Stage Project has studied and continues to explore the development of independent learning in young children. It argues that independence is a key skill that young children are capable of achieving and a skill that needs to be fostered as children move through the educational experience. Interestingly, Williams-Siegfredsen (2005) reveals that the Danish curriculum sees self-regulation as a learning process that teachers need to foster in children. Whitebread et al. (2005) found that children, given the opportunity, can self-regulate and can take responsibility for their learning. Whitebread's work stems from the findings of the psychologist Flavel, who created the model of metamemory and metacognition. This is about having an awareness and control over one's own mental processes so that one can say how one worked something out. Whitebread's findings suggest that there is a significant difference between those children who are taught explicitly and those who are not. The 'instructed' group 'had limited ideas, failed tasks and gave up quickly' whereas the children who were allowed to play and had control were 'more inventive, successful and persistent' (Whitebread 2008: 3). It is suggested that this ability, or lack thereof, is responsible for the differences in children's development as learners. The authors suggest four principles to help a teacher engender an environment of self regulation:

- emotional warmth and security
- feelings of control
- cognitive challenge
- articulation of learning (Whitebread et al. 2008: 27–30).

The implications of this work are that we need to give children plenty of opportunities to be involved in meaningful activities, which they have control over.

Children are more
- inventive
- successful
- persistent in an environment which encourages self-regulation. Absorption in play doesn't teach self-regulation but allows for it to flourish.

The environment needs:
- emotional warmth and security,
- feelings of control
- cognitive challenge
- articulation of learning.

Children need:
- play without interruption
- to be able to talk about what they are doing, so they can articulate their ideas
- opportunities to plan activities together and alone
- no adult-made role play areas
- access to a range of resources.

Figure 6.1 Self-regulation
Source: Whitebread *et al.* (2008)

Once again the outdoor environment lends itself to this type of experience, particularly as children feel that grown-ups do not control or own this space, therefore the sense of 'I can' has to be stronger. The research suggests refraining from creating adult-made role-play areas, instead making sure children have access to a range of materials to use as they wish. Ensuring they can continue to play without interruption ensures children have time to develop their ideas. Asking children to plan activities alone and together and encouraging through modelling self-commentary enables them to think through ideas and problems (Whitebread *et al.* 2008). Further it is argued that children are at their most self-regulatory when absorbed in play. So although play does not teach the skill, the process of playing allows for self-regulation to flourish (see Figure 6.1 for a précis of this information). All these ideas fit with the themes in Chapter 2, particularly with regard to child-initiated learning and learning experiences.

If self-regulation is not fostered children become overdependent on the adults, unable to function without constant support. This then causes the teacher to crisis manage, constantly reacting to problems and not being able to be proactive in teaching and assessing. Long term this lack of control means children do not function as well as they could and cannot reach their potential.

Dispositions

Leading on from Whitehead's research is the work of Katz and Chard (1989) who argue strongly for specifics in a learning environment. They conclude that children need certain dispositions to succeed both in a learning situation and in later life. The authors argue that although children can initially achieve success when given academic tasks and yield positive results, long term the success does not hold out. Knowledge, skills, feelings and desirable dispositions need to be fostered simultaneously; 'It is clearly not very useful to have skills if the disposition to use them is undermined in the process of acquiring them' (Katz and Chard 1989: 31). They would argue that having the disposition without the skill is equally pointless. What is needed is for the acquisition of skills, coupled with useful dispositions that then evoke the use of those skills. Worthy dispositions include 'curiosity, creativity, resourcefulness, independence, initiative, responsibility' (Katz and Chard, 1989: 30). But they also argue that interest or the ability to lose oneself in an activity, plus effort, mastery, persistence and challenge-seeking alongside helpfulness, charitableness and an appreciation of others' efforts are also worthy dispositions (see Figure 6.2 for a list of dispositions). Williams-Siegfredson, looking at Danish early years' education, talks in terms of competences that need to be fostered in children, such as the disposition to 'attend, concentrate, co-operate, reason, imagine possibilities, inquire – try to understand' (2005: 3).

Alongside dispositions is, as Whitebread argues, for children to be intrinsically motivated which means we have to be very cautious about reward, praise and recognition. Katz and Chard (1989), having looked at the research, demonstrate that when children are rewarded by others they then consider their efforts are due to others. If they are doing something because they are interested and then they are rewarded this can put them off being interested. Equally, if children have to work for rewards they can desist from working towards something risky or too challenging. Offering rewards after teacher-directed activities are completed can also have the opposite effect and the bonus activity can be seen as less interesting; the exact opposite of what is wanted. So we have to be very cautious in our use of praise, particularly when children are engaged in experiences they are truly interested in. Much more useful is offering very clear comments about the work and questions to get children thinking (see Figure 6.3 for a list of possible questions and Figure 6.4 for a list of possible questions children can be encouraged to ask).

> - curiosity
> - creativity
> - resourcefulness
> - independence
> - initiative
> - responsibility
> - interest
> - the ability to lose oneself in an activity
> - effort
> - mastery
> - persistence
> - challenge seeking
> - helpfulness
> - charitableness
> - an appreciation of others' efforts

Figure 6.2 Worthy dispositions needing to be fostered
Source: Katz and Chard (1991: 30)

Why do you like doing that?
Do you think you will make it differently next time?
What would you do differently next time or would you do it the same?
If you/we do … what do you think will happen?
I have no idea what we should do next, do you?
What will you be doing to it tomorrow/later?
If you were me what would you suggest?
It is worth thinking about making/designing/creating a …?
How about trying …
What do you think?

Figure 6.3 Questions to elicit positive dispositions in children

Katz and Chard's research is confirmed by the EPPE (Effective Provision of Pre-School Education) project (Sylva *et al.* 2004) which has established that children are helped to move forward in their learning when the adults are truly engaged with the children over time and through real conversations. 'Interest and capacity for absorption can be strengthened when children are encouraged to engage in projects that call for sustained effort and involvement over a period of several days or weeks' (Katz and Chard 1989: 35). The authors argue for what they call the project approach in teaching, when children can be involved in projects over time and which are not tied to one specific subject but where many subjects are involved. This could be a project one child or a group has become interested in and the adults facilitate the learning. This is in part what the cross curricular/creative curriculum is about and which is being suggested in the *Review of the Primary Curriculum* (DfCSF 2009), the logic being if children can become absorbed and lose themselves in a project over time then the dispositions we want them to have will be easily fostered. It focuses on ongoing learning and learning with others. Figure 6.5 shows a day in the life of a number of children as they used the outdoor environment almost exclusively to follow their current interest of building (houses in particular for one, whose family were building a house). This project lasted the day and included deep consideration of problems and the solution to those problems, conflict resolution as children wanted and others did not feel they could accommodate their needs, discussions of ideas and styles between children whose only common language was English (at one point three children came together who all spoke a different language at home). Children did write and draw as well as build and staff captured that narrative by writing

Can you help me with this?
Would you explain it again?
May I do another one?
Do you think if I did … then this would happen?
Could you help me think what I should do next with …?

Figure 6.4 Questions children could ask to further learning

Figure 6.5 Using dispositions and skills needed to be a rounded person

it down as the child told it and valued the discussions round the drawings children did about their work.

Reviewing Katz and Chard's work they argue there are definite ways of working with children but that one cannot have one single teaching method. With only one approach it is likely a number of the children will fail, as the method does not suit them. So again it is important that children are able to work outside in this different environment. In this way those children who feel more at ease or more interested outside can learn. And outside is an easy place to develop many of the dispositions. For example one has to persevere, and put in the effort if one is trying to make something at the woodwork table (see Figure 6.6), or enable a vegetable to grow, this happens over time and with a lot of tender loving care. Chapter 7 describes the adult role in more detail and the implications of the findings on adult behaviour.

Children working indoors and outdoors

Tizard *et al.* (1976a, 1976b), looking into four-year-olds' play in preschool centres, found striking differences in preference for outdoor play between working-class and middle-class

Figure 6.6 Woodwork – persevering to make a guitar

children, with the working class choosing to spend 75 per cent of their time outside. The authors noted that the play of the working-class children outdoors was more mature and they talked more than when indoors, where these children tended to be on their own more, games were shorter and less complex and social play was less advanced. If the working-class children had only been observed indoors then their play would have appeared less mature than they were capable of. Cooperative group play was more likely to be found outdoors and contact between adult and child and non-social play with creative materials more likely indoors. In conclusion, the authors found that the working-class children were removing themselves from the educational intentions of the staff.

Henniger (1985), looking into preschool children's behaviour in the indoor and outdoor settings, concluded that the indoor environment may inhibit some children socially. He found that the dramatic play of boys and older children was strongly influenced by the outdoor environment where both groups engaged in more play of this type. Henniger also found that cooperative play, the highest level of social play, was observed in nearly equal amounts indoors and outdoors. He felt that the lack of significant difference between the amount of cooperative play indoors and outdoors was important, as some children can be inhibited by being indoors, because of the limitations of space, floor covering and allowable noise levels. These factors may prevent the more active types of play which encourage boys to engage in the higher levels of social play. The only significant difference was that the younger children preferred cooperative play indoors.

A study by Whitehurst (2001) into her own practice found that pretend play was the most dominant form of play outside and that personal, social and emotional development was very much in evidence outside. Social skills and self-esteem were in greatest evidence followed by enthusiasm for learning, attention and persistence. The author makes a clear link between play and personal, social and emotional development, arguing that play contributes to this aspect of learning. However, she further argues that for this to happen children need to be able to access the area independently, have time to play and have resources freely available.

The Northern Illinois University research into visual–motor integration found that children's behaviour indoors was different from that of children working outdoors. Children working outdoors became 'strikingly assertive and imaginative' (Yerkes 1982: 4). Hutt *et al.* (1989) found that boys spent more time than girls outdoors on physical play and girls spent more time on material play. The activity span for boys was slightly longer than for girls when outdoors and boys tended to exhibit the longest activity spans in physical play outdoors; for girls the highest activity span was on material play indoors.

Parker (2008) highlights her points about the outdoor learning environment with a number of photographs of children playing outside. The overwhelming sense is of children in child-initiated activity, doing real work, of being very capable, motivated and engrossed. They are fantastic examples of quality outdoor activity. Parker gives two examples of children at work outside: the first self-selects because the activity is outside and the second displays a need for movement, which would likely not have been possible inside. The author demonstrates how the environment lends itself to certain activities, for example, stories with an outside theme – such as 'The Gruffalo' and '3 Billy Goats Gruff' – play with natural materials which enhance small-world play, and active role play. These experiences can happen inside, but outside explodes the potential of them.

Stephenson (2002), looking into the relationship between indoors and out in one setting in New Zealand, describes major differences as listed in Figure 1.2 (see page 16). Looking to the detail of the differences they may not be the same as seen here, but what is significant is that children and adults saw there were differences and behaved differently in each space. Figure 6.7 notes some of the differences as perceived by the adults involved in the setting. What is striking is the fact that there are so many differences and all involved feel there are differences. Some are quite obvious such as it is possible to make more mess outside, but others are less so. For example the staff felt that children were more accommodating of them joining their play and staying a playmate outside, whereas inside if they did get involved in the play the children tended to subjugate themselves to the member of staff. These subtle differences could be completely context bound and only relevant to one setting. But what this tells us is we have to be sensitive to our own very subtle differences within our setting. In a small-scale classroom-based research, a teacher found that the two children he observed were particularly keen on creative activities, working alone and preferred to be inside when doing this type of activity. They were happy to play and work outside but did not like the open nature of it nor the heat of outside (Gater 2009). He found this out through his close observations.

Gender

Equality of opportunities suggests that all children have a right to equal access to all activities and people in the class. This does not always appear to be the case. As Murphy argues when analysing gender differences in assessments: 'These achievement differences can therefore be understood in terms of children's opportunity to learn rather than

OUTSIDE	INSIDE
Transporting schema	Different schemas
Children physically active	More sedentary
Longer term projects	Short-term experiences
Fewer rules	More rules and regulations
Changeable environment, noticed by the children and staff	More constant environment
Nosier	Quieter
Messier	Not messy
Younger children on more fixed equipment	Less variety in what children did
Older children on more moveable equipment	
Play – open-ended, fewer fixed outcomes	Specific outcomes
Direct teaching of skills, particularly physical skills	More facilitation as opposed to direct teaching of skills
Bigger groups of children	Smaller groups
Staff able to dip in and out of play without destroying it	If staff dipped into the play children tended to want them to assume responsibility
An environment that was: <ul><li>accepting and less controlled</li><li>incorporating change and unpredictability</li><li>lacking the security of enclosure and surrounding walls</li><li>dynamic and open-ended</li><li>unpredictable and even threatening.</li></ul>	An environment that was: <ul><li>predictable</li><li>constant</li><li>secure</li><li>routine led</li><li>more intimate and had more physical and emotional contact with staff.</li></ul>

Figure 6.7 Differences in behaviour in and out
Source: Stephenson (2002)

their ability to learn' (2002: 324). So children are not doing as well, not because they are not able but because the environment for learning is not conducive. She further argues we need to pay attention to 'children's ways of knowing' (2002: 326). Skelton and Francis argue that gender as 'relational' (2003: 13) means identity is not fixed, that boys and girls are actively involved in learning to be a boy or a girl, (we are all involved in creating the person we become and the changes that occur during our whole life). So the context children find themselves in can and does impact on gender identity, there are no generalisations concerning boys and girls and that the becoming of a boy or girl is a long process. Connolly (2003) argues that all children are active in creating their gender identity. Significant from the above research is that how we behave can impact on children and has to concern gender as much as any other aspect of the creation of the person. If we always react negatively to girls who are being stroppy or boisterous but accept this same behaviour in boys then we are going to have an impact on both, for one we are saying something is not allowed and for the other it is allowed. Either stroppy and boisterous behaviour is okay or it is not and is not dependent on whether you are a girl or boy. So we need to actively intervene as the adult; adult behaviour is picked up in the next chapter.

'On entry to pre-school girls generally show better social development than boys, especially in co-operation/conformity and independence and concentration. Girls show better cognitive outcomes than boys' (Sylva *et al.* 2004: 03). Walkerdine argues that the reason girls show early success at school is that they take up the right 'positions in peda-gogic discourses' (1996: 300), while boys do not take part in this discourse: they stay silent, and do not take part in the domestic games which are being taught by those who are used to a domestic play setting. Walkerdine suggests that boys clearly do not feel at home in domestic imaginative situations, as girls have the controlling hand. She found that boys wanted either to remove themselves from domestic play or change the play because they were subservient. Walkerdine further argues that boys rarely played domi-nant father roles when the girls were present, but did when they were playing only with boys. The Leverhulme Numeracy Research Programme shows how the National Numer-acy Strategy has impacted on boys and girls. The strategy promotes 'performance, com-petitive learner style' (Skelton and Francis 2003: 55) but this is at odds with most girls' general conformist behaviour. 'The National Numeracy Strategy is generally about under-standing processes rather than the right answer, which is highly commendable except for one thing, it is causing issues for girls. '... evidence from the Leverhulme Programme suggests that *generally speaking* this practice is more easily taken up by boys than girls and that boys are more prepared than girls to "do things their own way" ' (Skelton and Francis 2003: 53). Furthermore the research findings argue that girls are more concerned in trying to remember what the teacher has said and following instructions and boys can cope with the idea that there are a number of ways the same problem can be addressed. It can also be added that the competitive pace the NNS encourages, discourages chil-dren who do not want to speak out and who do not find it easy to work it out in their head. These children know the answer but not in a whole-group setting and are quite capable given a pen and paper and making a few jottings. So the NNS approach can be counterproductive to many children, whatever their gender.

Benjamin, looking at the evidence of gender and SEN, argues that there is a strong link for boys between success at football and success in school. For those with additional needs there is a strong desire to reach success on the football pitch as they do not have success elsewhere in the school system. SEN boys can therefore be keen to make 'infor-mal 'macho' performances' (2003: 104). In terms of girls Benjamin suggests that there may not be as many girls as boys identified as SEN, as the girls do not set themselves up as having SEN. As the Walkadine research above indicates girls set themselves up in the right pedagogic discourse position and seek out support from others without recourse to official help through assessment and SEN identification, whereas the boys display their needs for all to view. Noble *et al.* argue that more boys than girls prefer the kinaesthetic approach (learn and remember by doing, moving and by touching), but that 'English schools tend to put heavy stress on the other two styles' (2001: 99) of learning that is visual (learn and remember images, shapes and colour) and auditory (learn and remem-ber voices, sounds and music). In this way boys are not able to access the curriculum through a style they find easy. But this research needs to be viewed alongside that of Benjamin (2003) and Walkerdine (1996) which indicates girls make sure they help themselves in learning more so than the boys do. So even in terms of additional needs children can create a different discourse for themselves dependent on gender.

Millard (1997) argues that reading is seen as an activity more appropriate to girls than boys, that the narrative fiction most valued by teachers is that which is favoured by girls and that boys and girls create different educational experiences for themselves. Boys create more discipline problems for teachers; they take more of the teachers' time; actively oppose teachers giving girls equal time and emphasise the negative aspects of female sexuality. They do this from an early age. Paley (1984) came to the conclusion, in her fascinating study of boys and girls in her classroom, that the curriculum she offered suited the girls better than the boys. She found that the girls would go to the table activities associated with 'work' much more readily, while the boys would avoid these activities. She talks about the fact that girls are at an advantage because they are able to achieve more quickly and easily than boys. Boys get easily discouraged from the work associated with the table activities, because they are concerned about failing. For girls, the work at the table is play, and they will use the equipment whether the teacher is there or not. The boys do not find it so easy and so they, having tried the table activities, go back to the block play and more vigorous imaginative play that is associated with being a Superhero. Paley found that not receiving an immediate sense of achievement makes boys give up more quickly than girls. O'Sullivan (1997) discusses research which argues that boys are treated more often as part of a group and not individually, whereas girls are treated as individuals and this does not help boys in their overwhelming need for individual recognition.

Recent sophisticated scanning techniques are now supporting the above findings. The lack of male role models and coursework have been blamed for the reason many boys do not do as well at school, but with this scanning major discoveries are being made, particularly in the area of processing information, which boys and men and girls and women do differently. But processing information also impacts on perception of the world and how one learns. Brain scans show that indeed men use only the left side of the brain when reading and women both sides. See Figure 6.8 to note some of the differences. There are implications for these differences in terms of classroom practice. Through the Leverhulme Primary Improvement Project at Exeter University, Wragg and his associates found that boys start school four or five points behind girls in the NFER Reading Tests. And this level hardly changes by the end of the year. So for example to help this, Moir (cited in Salmon 2009) suggests asking boys to pick letters/words out of a container rather than write them by hand, as they find difficulty with the skill of writing. Boys need to be at the front of the class, so they can hear. Girls are encouraged to climb trees, because they need to be encouraged to take more risks, so they may be more comfortable with taking risks when they are older (Salmon 2009).

But we must also not loose sight of the fact that girls and boys can and do like many of the same activities. Holland's (2003) research into Superhero and gun play noted that girls do want to play Superheros and they do know a lot about the characters and themes, although they were rarely seen to initiate the play. Although the girls showed no interest in weapon construction they were interested in the chase and victory of the Superhero games. It is not true to say that girls are disinterested in Superhero games, a sentiment

Attention
- Boys are more interested in how things work, the mechanical world, sport and action-packed fiction.
- Girls love to learn about how people work, the emotional world and emotionally packed fiction.

Brain maturation

Girls:
- The verbal areas of the brain matures four to six years ahead of boys.
- The fine motor area matures four to six years ahead of boys.
- Emotional control matures three to six years ahead of boys.

Boys:
- That part of the brain controlling abstract reasoning matures two to four years ahead of girls.
- Gross motor control matures two to four years ahead of girls.

In both sexes it takes a long time for the limbic, emotional generating areas of the brain to become connected to the planning and advice area of the brain. These connections develop around age 16–17 in girls and 20–22 in boys.

Figure 6.8 Girls and boys
Source: Salmon (2009)

echoed by Pellegrini and Smith (1998). Holland also noted that boys were more willing to cross the border, as Holland phrases children moving into spheres they are not expected to. In establishments where Superhero play was fully allowed, boys who wanted to dressed up in girls clothes. She suggests that the new regime gave children the knowledge that they were accepted and not judged (2003: 58) and so were confident to move into different spheres of exploration.

Wragg (1997), Neumark (1997), Millard (1997) and Burstall (1997) argue that schools should be more accommodating to the needs of boys so they are successful, but I would argue not at the expense of girls. Schools need to consider children's individual needs whether they be a boy or a girl. If boys and girls are sometimes different and learn in different ways and sometimes actually like the same things and if we do not want a culture of 'super-girly girls and disaffected boys' (Parkin 1997: VI) then we will need to intervene and help. Figure 6.9 is an example of a girl being allowed to follow her interest of setting up a circus and using the bricks to make a tightrope which two boys are then able to use. No one is better than anyone else. Ann Moir, neuropsychologist, argues we need a 'gender-neutral education', so we look at children as individuals not as a gender and 'classes are organised on a child's brain-based needs' (cited in Salmon 2009: 18), where there are girls who have more boy tendencies and vice versa.

Gender and outside

The sense of inequality of opportunity seems particularly acute when viewing outside. MacNaughton (1999) argues that playgrounds are dangerous spaces and can be places where domination and subordination occur (see Chapter 8 for more on this).

Figure 6.9 Children playing happily

Connolly (2003) suggests that self-directed play tends to favour boys who are more exploratory and experimenting than girls and when girls behave more like this they can be discouraged and punished. In the blockplay research, Gura (1992) argues that, indeed, territory and dominance are linked and that boys dominated an area of the class environment, namely the blockplay area; a finding which also comes through in the Halliday *et al.* (1985) research from New Zealand. Hart (1978), in a study of sex differences in the use of outdoor space, found that boys tended to modify the landscape more frequently and more effectively than girls; when girls modified it, it was more often than not in their imaginations, so bushes became walls, lateral branches became shelves. When girls did get involved with building, it was with boys and it was the boys who organised it. Boys tended to build the outer parts of the building (walls, windows, roofs) and girls dealt with interior design. But particularly significant was the finding that when boys came across girls building, they would take over and the girls would become subservient. So there appears to be an unhealthy dominance, with girls taking on a lesser role. Hutt *et al.* (1989) found that boys were more competent and decisive in their choice of activities than girls. Tizard *et al.* (1976a) found that boys tended to dominate outdoor play and girls tended to play more with fixed equipment (climbing frames and swings), while boys tended to play more with the movable equipment (wheeled toys and larger constructional materials, such as crates, tyres and ladders). Cullen (1993) found that girls and boys used the outdoor area in different ways and that the differences followed stereotypes of girls' and boys' play found in other studies. The boys played with the more active equipment and the girls tended to stay with the quieter home-type play.

Holland (2003), looking at war, weapon and Superhero play, demonstrates that girls are more sedentary than boys but that the adults do not tend to concern themselves with the girls who are being compliant and settled and cause no problems. But as Holland argues this is not actually right nor fair. Holland goes on further to say that we may be doing more damage to girls if we stop Superhero play in boys, as we are 'preventing girls from understanding that resistance is an option and boys from understanding that girls can be active and resistant' (2003: 27). She also suggested that by allowing and developing Superhero play we are helping children to gender mix. We need to pay far more attention to encouraging girls to be confident in being physically active and to view it as okay to be boisterous and have a voice. She further argues that we need to create an environment in which we do not see the need to repress children and that all children feel they have a voice, to say no and not feel they have to be complicit. This goes across gender. Jago found in his study of activity in primary playtimes that the boys were more active than girls and 'boys spend more time promoting their cardio-respiratory fitness during play than girls' (2002: 175). Girls' obesity is growing faster than boys and in playgrounds Stratton (1999: 79) highlighted that boys got more cardio-respiratory fitness than girls. Equally if as suggested in the Connolly (2003) research boys tend to dominate outside then girls have even less opportunity to be physically active. Jago (2002) found that the boys gained more through his intervention than the girls and boys became more physically active than the girls. His interventions included placing activity cards in the playground with activity ideas, a skipping demonstration, parental information packs, CPD, a physical education lesson and a science lesson based around the importance of exercise for health. He concluded that the girls were not as interested as the boys in the activities on offer. Looking to Chapter 8 there are suggestions as to what adults need to do to address this anomaly.

Even more worrying than basic differences is the research which indicates that girls are actually getting a worse deal than boys outside. Ross and Ryan (1990) found that girls were often expected to be subservient to boys and understand the boys' needs over their own, actually sacrificing their wants and desires when there were conflicts over space (see also research above). Blatchford (1998) argues that girls learn to consider themselves powerless. Learning to accommodate others is a worthy characteristic, but one that all should learn: boys and girls. Connolly (2003) through his close study of three contrasting playgrounds found incidents:

- of male aggression and violence and sexual harassment of girls and boys
- of girls being excluded from football games
- of boys being excluded from skipping.

By virtue of controlling the outside area and achieving success in such things as football the boys can be viewed as more successful than the girls and so believe themselves to be more powerful (Benjamin 2003). Interestingly, there were variations in the form of masculinity and femininity that came to predominate in the different schools (Benjamin 2003: 124–5).

Connolly (2003) makes a number of suggestions to improve playground practice including providing more equipment, developing places to play different activities, getting the staff involved to watch and analyse and intervene if necessary. For example banning football actually did change the social dynamics of the playground. Increasing the adult involvement did get more children keen to join in. He also suggests that we get the children involved in discussing what is happening to thereby improve the practice.

We need to be providing an equality of opportunity for all children, not one gender-domination, otherwise schools are failing in their duty. Schools will be reneging on their duty to follow the *Every Child Matters* agenda, with the emphasis on equality, health and safeness, if some children are dominating the space and limits are made as to who joins in with what.

Who children play with when outside

Research over the years has demonstrated that outside in the playground children tend to play with the same sex friends and males and females tend to play different games when outside (Opie and Opie 1969, Roberts 1980, Blatchford 1989, Evans 1989, Boulton 1992, Thorne 1997, Connolly 2003). A small-scale study conducted in a rural Oxfordshire primary school in 2008 concurs with these findings (Milligan 2008). In this study a group of 9- to 11-year-old children were observed generally in the playground and then on a static large ship climbing construction. Children were found to have nearly six times more same sex interactions than opposite sex interactions. Clearly children as adults enjoy the company of their own sex; the concerning aspect is that the games and resources available may be helping to create this segregation. The games most played by the boys were ball games, running/racing games, and wrestling/fighting and these were the activities the girls had the least to do with. The girls on the other hand sat and talked, and used the swing and slide the most. Boys were eleven times more likely to engage in fighting and wrestling than girls and girls were nearly five times more likely to sit and talk than boys. Looking at the generals of the games it is clear that the boys preferred the competitive games and the girls the games which required cooperation. The lack of activity on the part of the girls is a very worrying feature and their tendency to stay with the static equipment fits with the research above in the previous section; nothing appears to have changed over time. The lack of boy engagement with clapping games and role play which involves the playing with and use of language and words is worrying also. Chasing/it games, the use of the swings and slides had much more equal usage by boys and girls and where girls and boys tended to play together.

The research into gender preference has mostly been focused on playtime, not outdoor play in the early years, and children do become more aware of gender as they get older. However, much of that division can be seen in the early years' outdoor area, with boys tending to play on the moving bicycles and girls role playing or simply gathering at the fixed equipment. It is important to make observations of behaviour outside to then make changes to what is available. For example in the Connolly (2003) research the observations meant that football was banned and behaviour changed and improved.

Children – outdoor play and playtime

Quite intriguing is how children can change their behaviour dependent on what type of outdoor play they perceive they are in. For example children in an early years' setting where they have both outdoor play as part of their curriculum entitlement and then play-time as the standard break time can behave differently in both situations. They can be quite responsive, responsible, active and engaged when playing in the outdoor area during a free flow period in the nursery/Foundation Stage classroom. Then at lunchtime they are either expected to play in their own garden or the school's playground and suddenly behaviour changes. Children become unresponsive, irresponsible, active but distracted. They can even have the same equipment as when playing during the free flow period, with the only difference being the existence of dinner ladies/lunchtime controllers and suddenly poor behaviour surfaces. It would seem the children behave almost as they are expected to behave and even consider they can 'get away' with actions which would not be acceptable during a free flow period. They choose to behave in particular ways dependent on what type of outdoor play they perceive it to be – outdoor play or break time play.

A partially sighted child using the outdoor area

DJ was a partially sighted child with sickle cell anaemia who came to nursery just after he was four. His mother was concerned as to how he would fit into this environment with its bustle and activity. A teaching assistant was assigned to DJ and there was a teacher and nursery nurse for 26 children. The nursery operated so that indoors and outdoors were available simultaneously.

DJ could make out shapes and shades of things and tended to move about using this knowledge. Initially, DJ was very tentative and stayed close to an adult and needed, rather than a helping hand, helpful information about what was around him and a warn-ing if he was going towards something he had not seen. DJ's favourite area was outdoors and he played outdoors every day for a good deal of the session. He found indoors frustrating as he bumped into tables and chairs, but outdoors he did not have the same difficulties. This was interesting as the indoor space was very large and uncluttered. The difficulty he had outdoors was that the equipment tended not to be in exactly the same place every day and so the staff helped by telling him where the equipment was before he started to play.

Once DJ had settled into the nursery, he did not need to be told where the equip-ment was but simply stopped, looked, and pinpointed the positions himself. In particular he enjoyed playing on the climbing frame when it was set up as an imaginative play situ-ation. He not only played on the equipment, he also manoeuvred boxes, planks, barrels, and the like, to design, build and make himself. If he got into difficulties, for example getting a plank caught and not being able to see what was stopping it, he preferred not to be helped and often got quite upset if an adult intervened. DJ enjoyed climbing, he would use the gymnasium set-ups, and would be happy as long as he could go at his own pace. He could even run but never fast. He enjoyed working in the wild area, where insects were studied close up. He could follow a ball but if something else crossed its path, he would often not see it and this is when bumps would occur. In terms of PE lessons in the infant hall, DJ was initially supported by one member of staff who stayed close and gave helpful information. By and by, DJ did not need this help and got on with what was asked. He learnt to cope with children moving quickly about the hall, say, for example, when they were asked to run and change direction. He was helped in this because the other children were 'DJ-aware'; they knew that they had to be aware of him and not to run at him. But equally, DJ wanted to do whatever was on offer, and never said he could not do anything.

DJ had two illnesses which one could say made him unsuited to outdoor play but he needed and wanted to work outdoors. Outdoor play gave him a good deal of confidence, and laid the foundations for later learning. His mother was understandably very anxious and sometimes over-protective. Outdoor play gave him opportunities to do things that his mother would not have felt confident about him doing, but the staff in the nursery were able in a very supportive environment to give him the experiences that he needed. Outdoors also gave DJ a freedom of movement he could not find indoors. The importance of talking about DJ is that outdoor play is for everyone and any child should be able to access it.

Discussion

In 1972 Hutt argued that boys and girls were different and needed to be treated as such: this would seem to be a message which needs revisiting. Neither gender should be up for preferential treatment, both have needs, they are just often different. We need to see children as individuals and seek them all out, including quiet girls who cause no problem and can go unnoticed. Education is more than just knowledge to be gained, more significant are the skills and attitudes needed to ensure one can approach any learning situation and be successful. Outside organised well is a space where children can become engrossed in play and work and develop the ability to run themselves, to become independent. This is a space where children can be much more active and achieve physical prowess which helps them not only in terms of motor development and coordination but also in terms of self-worth and confidence.

Questions

1. How do you want your children to look when they leave you? What skills, knowledge and attitudes do you want them to possess when they leave you?
2. When they are using the equipment, say for example, the blocks or sand, what would you expect the younger or older children to be doing?
3. Look at outdoor play from the children's perspective; put yourself in their shoes. How do the children feel outside? What is your evidence? What do they think outdoor play is all about? What is your evidence?

Questions *(Continued)*

4. Do you set up the environment so children can create their own imaginative role play situation? If not, consider collecting lots of resources, as suggested in Chapter 5, and make sure children can create their own role play. Note the difference in children's behaviour.

5. Take the dispositions listed in Figure 6.2. Put the dispositions into a list. Discuss with the staff group what behaviours demonstrate each disposition, so you end up with a list of behaviours for each disposition. Using this information make observations of children and note where you think they are demonstrating the dispositions. Where there are gaps decide what you are going to do to improve practice.

6. Note what your boys and girls do outside. Note who plays with whom outside. Note when girls and boys play together. Note who the staff play with. Use the involvement proforma as in Chapter 7 (pages 196–198) to make observations. Having done this what patterns of behaviour have you noticed? How can you improve things?

7. Sheridan (2008) is a useful book and I would advise the buying of it. She indicates the general milestones in a child's life to five and in less detail to seven; this book serves as a very useful reference when working with young children, to support one's diagnosis and suggestions.

The role of the adult

Summary

The success of outdoor play rests with the staff. It is only when the whole staff support and enjoy outdoor play that it will work. A teacher said to me that she was not keen on imaginative play and so she did not have it! Sadly this can be the fate of outdoor play. When viewed as a peripheral activity which may or may not be provided, then outdoor play will only have a peripheral effect on children's learning. Where it is seen as a crucial part of education then it will be well provided for. As McMillan (1930) argues, the success of children's learning rests with the teacher. Lally maintains that the role of the nursery teacher is a complex one; she sees it as a 'dynamic occupation' and one which requires continual investigation of themselves, the children and their families (1991: xi).

The quality of the interaction between child and adult is central to higher-order functioning (Vygotsky 1978, Wells 1987). Higher order functioning is involved in play where children really have to think through ideas, analyse and work with others to solve problems. This is about the development of intellectual self-control and leads to the development of thinking which is characteristic of logic, perseverance and concentrated thought. Play is not an easy game and requires a great deal from adults. For it to be successful adults need to interact, collaborate and, when necessary, facilitate and interpret. The interactionist approach highlighted by Bruce (1987 and 2005) places a responsibility on adults to make sure children have a partnership role. Staff, therefore, have roles to fulfil before, during and after children have been in the setting. Beforehand, staff need to think about the needs of the children in the setting and then plan accordingly. They need to think carefully about how materials, resources and equipment are to be set up. While children are using the environment staff will be working with them. At the same time the staff will be assessing the effectiveness of the experiences and observing the children absorbed. Afterwards, staff need to reflect on each day in preparation for the next day's experiences. The staff role is therefore the same as when working in the inside class, and involves bringing the children, the environment and the curriculum together.

A study such as that by Stephenson (2002) highlights the importance of actually thinking about one's practice. It cannot be a case of just dumping a few bikes outside; one needs to consider one's pedagogy. Stephenson discusses how the staff in her study had 'philosophic difference in approaches' (2002: 32) when dealing with out and in. They saw the two spaces as being different and that meant they needed to be approached differently. So for example they felt outside was more to do with a changing environment whereas inside was more constant. This meant that more changes could be made outside than in. Staff felt they had control over outside as opposed to what is suggested in the general research findings. Stephenson cites Gilkes (1987), Bilton (1993), Davies (1997) and Stine (1997) as indicating that because of the nature of equipment staff feel they have little control over it. In these studies fixed climbing apparatus was seen as something which could not be changed. But in Stephenson's study staff felt they had complete control over developing the space even if it did have fixed apparatus. What this seems to suggest is that staff need to have considered very carefully what the outside space is all about and how it can be developed to help children. In the Stephenson study the staff saw outside as being able to offer them 'opportunities to respond to children's interests and needs in the way they set up that environment' (2002: 33). So they did what they did for the children's benefit, not for their benefit. Viewing outdoor play as when staff have a break is about the needs of staff not children.

Planning for and evaluating learning

Staff have to plan carefully, evaluate what has occurred in a day, observe what children are doing and saying, and evaluate the effectiveness of the resources. To ensure that the maximum is achieved from all learning experiences, all will require adult involvement at some point and part of the planning is about where adults need to work. The planning needs to cover the provision of all the experiences and whatever else the staff may feel needs to be provided outdoors. It is not sufficient, therefore, to have a planning sheet for indoors with one small square devoted to the whole of outdoor play: the planning has to be as detailed as for indoors (see Figure 7.1). Once the two areas are viewed as one, then planning for both becomes much easier. Activities indoors can then support activities outside, and vice versa. But most importantly an activity can be placed in the position which will give the most to children, thereby making best use of all the available space. Whitehurst argues that practitioners need to plan activities and identify how adults can 'model, interact or play with children' when outside (2001: 66) and that these features make for successful learning.

It is important to guard against listing the fixed structures in the outdoor area, such as the 'sandpit, climbing frame, house, boat', etc; then listing activities for each structure. This means the curriculum planning is centred around a structure and not necessarily around learning. It is much more effective to list areas of learning or development and then decide how a fixed structure will be used within it. So, for example, an imaginative play scene may be a pirate's ship, and it may be thought that the climbing frame will extend this play by being made into an island. So the materials and resources are set up on the climbing frame. But another day the climbing frame may support some mini-beast project.

This weekly outdoor planning sheet demonstrates the link with the indoor curriculum and indoor play, offers starting points for play in each area, shows where staff will be supporting named children, what activities have been set up from the children's interest, how activities can be spread over a week, and what aspects of the activity staff may like to concentrate on. Obviously many other play situations will occur and staff will respond as the session progresses. There are 3 members of staff at this nursery and they decide on the day where each will start working and what their specific responsibilities will be.

Outdoor play	Monday	Tuesday	Wednesday	Thursday	Friday
w/b 1st June Notes	Connor and Megan's parents to bring in bits for imaginative play. Bring in mini-beasts from home!	Observe Jagdeep and Hardeep – physical skills	Potatoes		
Imaginative	Linked to indoors – moving house, available all week, changes made dependent on children's play . . .	Trucks, ropes, boxes, furniture, material, sticky labels, check-list of furniture for children to tick off . . .	Lunch boxes, thermos, extendable tape measures . . .	Staff input needed, particularly with children reading checklists and writing labels	
Construction	Filling in space – linked to moving house	No set-up. Saima and Em to make own construction with staff member	Filling in space. Using blocks, bricks – fitting into large wooden cubes, boxes, den	No set-up – Laura and Gina to make own building, staff support	Respond to children's ideas from the week
Gymnasium	Linked to story about bridges – moving around figure of 8 set-up without touching the ground	2 figures of 8 set-ups, one higher and one lower	Nests and ladders – strengthening arm muscles and tunnels, stretching horizontally	Combination of Monday and encourage Wednesday arrangements	Arrangement to encourage use of prepositions – under, over, in, out, etc
Small apparatus	Chalked letters, throwing ball onto named letter	Chalked letters using children's own initial letter	Writing letters on walls – to aim at	Bats and soft balls – batting practice for different levels – throwing ball to child and getting some to bat against wall	Open choice

Figure 7.1 Reflective planning/assessments

Science	Following on from Jagdeep's and Junser's interest in mini-beasts' habitats – setting up dry, wet, covered and uncovered habitats to look at on Friday	Make books ready for recording information on Friday – special activity inside			Look at and record habitats
Gardening	Weeding, what constitutes a weed, gardening books	Weeding	M, R, J and E putting in potatoes	Billy, Ruth, Megan and Connor putting in potatoes	Planning sheet to decide what work needs doing next week
Other Activities				Tape recorders and story and poetry tapes	Pastels and thick paper, big mats, canopy if sunny

Figure 7.1 (Continued)

Nursery class planning sheet – mid term, for 2 week period. This plan works very loosely from a theme This plan concentrates on progression through the learning bay, for example the gymnasium has very specific movement intentions – be it balance, speed, endurance or attitudes such as perseverance. In this way by the end of a year children can be said to have experienced clear progression of learning. The plan reflects the seasons – for example the planting calendar and drawing of bluebells. This is but a fragment of what actually happens when plans are put into action. Clear links are shown between physical activity, language and mathematics. The learning bays together offer the whole curriculum with each bay emphasising some areas of learning more than others.

Food	Personal, social, emotional	Communication, language and literacy	Mathematics	Knowledge and understanding of the world	Creative	Physical
Imaginative – pizza delivery, shop inside or out	Cooperation, being approachable, working as a team, encourage girls to use bikes, encourage less forceful children	Lots of child-led conversations. Writing, and reading orders, maps, addresses, giving clear instructions	Money, writing numbers, totalling, spatial awareness, bike numbers, bike number plates	Locations, distances, routes, maps	Designing, making salt dough junk pizzas, garlic bread, designing and making logos and labels	Moving around area on bikes, writing skills, arranging food in boxes
Construction – setting up homes for delivery – simple and complex	Encourage 'having a go' approach, emphasis on safe building, encouraging reticent children, all children supporting this	Clear discussions, being able to visualise construction and describe	House numbers	Science – sand tray, different size and weight of balls dropping from different heights to see impact re jumping	For some thinking about the aesthetics of the design, drawing out initial plan	Emphasis on lifting properly, notdragging. Using trucks to move things in. When using fiddly things – bands, pegs, etc – encourage children to do this themselves
Small motor – jumping	Helping each other improve movements, and discussing how to improve	Jumping onto associated words – jump, high, low, up, down, bounce, spring, pounce, kangaroo, hare, leap, wallaby, skip, gravity, hopscotch. Using the words as children move	Maths lang		Thinking through	Bending knees, jumping from one foot to other, skipping on own and with others, feet together and apart, hopscotch – older children

Figure 7.1 (Continued)

Gymnasium – balance, chosen groups of children set up arrangements	Concentration, perseverance, giving time to achieve balance, not giving up, controlling environment, leadership					Concentrating on improving balancing techniques – not wobbling, hands aloft, looking ahead, posture
Gardening – put in carrot seeds, onion sets	Cooperation, thinking about what needs doing	Drill, depth, space, length, hole, furrow, dig, cover	Depth of holes, distances in planting	Weather, possible frosts, possible pests – carrot fly		Careful work, use trowels and spades with thought, piling up earth next to hole
Science, environmental – observational drawings – bluebells, purple spouting broccoli	Celebrate and appreciate different styles of drawing				Own work, celebrate diversity of styles, link to story writing about flowers and vegetables and flower/veg fairies	
Quiet – books and tapes of stories and songs to do with food, making own jigsaws from postcards, writing stories about flowers and flower fairies	Confidence in getting to know songs and stories and so tell/sing to others, give confidence for those less sure about own writing and creating skills, telling stories into tape recorder	Story procedure, rhyme, communicating ideas	Shape – rectangle, creating other shapes when making postcard, fitting together only one way possible	Food from around the world – postcards, usefulness of tape recorders		Scissor control
Other						

Figure 7.1 (Continued)

It may be that staff consider it important that children set up their own play and so, although the equipment will be provided, it will not be laid out, allowing children to do this from scratch. The fashion of setting up every area with some activity is a rather modern approach, but one which can be limiting. The planning, therefore, does not necessarily have to state what will be provided but could suggest possible questions to ask the children. Or it could evaluate what has happened in a day and where the learning will go the next day based on the current interests of the children.

Some schools use themes to support the planning and curriculum. This is fine as long as the theme does not restrict learning and staff feel they have to fit absolutely every activity to the theme. Themes should be there to support, not act as a straitjacket! The beauty of setting up the curriculum across the space – through learning bays or experiences – is that one has already made sure that as a whole the activities are covering the complete curriculum. The activities themselves need to demonstrate a progression across time. For example in the planning sheet (Figure 7.1) the gymnasium area is about developing balance and the small apparatus area about developing the skill of jumping. This will then be changed to another aspect of movement and motor control, but incorporating other curriculum areas where necessary. The horticultural or gardening bay has a theme all of its own and does not need any addition of a false one. This is called the seasons! This learning experience is a real experience and one that children can properly contribute to. It enables children to be involved in a worthwhile and authentic activity and enables them to really investigate something. In this way they can follow their own interests and the teachers can ensure this is incorporated into their planning. Katz argues that children need real experiences and investigation is a natural way for them to learn; 'children are born natural scientists and social scientists' (1995: 40). See the account of Sue Humphries' work in Chapter 2.

Planning can only act as a guide: the ongoing assessment and the evaluation at the end of a day gives the more complete picture. Some staff record general observations as the session progresses, others spend time after the session in recording observations (see Figure 7.2). It is always important to note how the weather has affected play, either in a positive or negative way, and whether there are any problems with the two areas working together. One nursery, for example, found that the small blockplay area positioned outdoors was not being played with in a sustained fashion and children tended to flit in and out of the area. The reason for this could not be found, but staff moved the area to just inside the door and the behaviour became much more consistent.

There are processes within play and outcomes of play; both need to be looked at to see the value of play. Wood and Attfield, having looked at the relationship between play, learning and development, suggest there are critical questions to ask: 'What actually happens inside children's heads when they play? How do they become 'master players' and successful learners? What are children doing which is of value and interest to them in the immediate term, and may be of relevance in the longer term? (1996: 125). These questions are expecting practitioners to analyse play generally and also analyse each child's play. This then leads to looking at the outcomes of play. Again Wood and Attfield suggest 'the outcomes can be enjoyment, peer group affiliation or status, rehearsal and

Imaginative	High quality play. PSE – cooperation, lengthy concentration span, groups 1–9 children, negotiation. Lang – copy writing, children reading own writing, emergent. Maths-lang – distance, time, size, space. Fun rearrangement of furniture. Planning – keep available alongside map work, KUW – link to technology inside. Lang – develop reading own writing, copy and emergent-offering written instructions in play, more numbered lists to complete.
Construction	Saima and Em more confident, went alone for 10 mins. PSE – good concentration. Maths – children surprised by quantity to fill large cube, realised needed to be systematic, if thrown in, packed in less. Was naturally extended to making 3-d filled in construction. Planning – Maths – go onto 2-d space, large horizontal surface area to fill, link to drawing (Creative, KUW).
Gymnasium	PSE – lot of unsure children, need adult input. Physical – effective strengthening of arm muscles. Planning – challenges to older children (physical), stretching lang – stretch, pull, straight, taut.
Small apparatus	Very effective for boys, quality learning. Lang – very keen to be right, therefore concentration went up. Planning – lang-use words and phrases from imaginative work – how many, upright, forward, back, push, up, down, more. Physical – challenges to some children. PSE – involve particular girls.
Science	Final termers – Lang – worked well, they fed information back to all children during review time, very logical when explaining. PSE – Jagdeep and Junser argued re what they had found, but sorted differences through compromise. Lang – Josh and Josh wanted to be involved in recording. Good spoken lang – reasons given for wet and and covered – insects frightened (PSE), 'animals dry out', no water to drink (KUW).
Gardening	KUW and PSE – Nakita very interested – therapeutic. Maths – M, R, J, E – estimating depth and length. Planning – Maths – use rulers, children decided to leave forward planning, concluded (KUW) not much to do. Wait till Wednesday to check, they have put notice on board (Lang).
Other activities	Planning – not enough creative work. Move table outside for painting – possible stimulus – painting favourite houses, designing. KUW – painting large boxes, use wallpaper on wooden cubes for decorating. Lang – children to tell about their play scenes, adults to act as scribes. Jo, Esther, Ryan, Rachel, Josh to retell in review time. More written number work needed.

Figure 7.2 Evaluation of the week

repetition leading to mastery and control, or just fun and relaxation' (1996: 125). Chapter 2 looks at the play continuum, play assessment and play spiral.

Assessment of children is about observing them, writing down the information and finally making judgements. When making observations of children it needs to involve:

- watching and listening to children while they are playing with other children, adults and alone

- talking to children about their play and work
- combining observations of children outside and in
- taking photographs of children playing
- discussing observations with parents and carers.

Given that some children will behave quite differently inside and out (Chapter 1 and 6), observations of them in both areas will give a more complete picture of their personality, their level of understanding and where they need help. A dated running record (see Figure 7.3) for each child is probably the simplest and most effective way of writing down observations and within this making comments about strengths, weaknesses and what help is needed. Looking at the two examples given in Figure 7.3 it is quite staggering how much information has been gleaned about each child over a period of seven weeks. This type of written work is read by the staff and they use the records to help plan the curriculum.

When making observations of children it is important to appreciate the significance of non-verbal indicators. Looking to the research by Whitebread as discussed at the beginning of Chapter 6 into self-regulation, one of the signs of the ability to self-regulate is shown through behaviour and gestures, but not dialogue. These involve the planning, monitoring, control and evaluation of oneself but we cannot assess that children are capable of this unless we analyse their actions. Behaviours that indicated planning included 'making a decision on a task and seeking and collecting necessary resources'. Monitoring behaviours included noticing an error, and checking on performance through gaze, pause or gesture. Control behaviours, which were easily the most numerous, included using gesture as a strategy to support cognitive activity, repeating a strategy to check for accuracy and changing from one strategy to another on task. 'Evaluation behaviours included careful observation of the child's own performance and testing the effectiveness of a strategy in achieving a goal' (Whitebread *et al.* 2007: 84). All of these actions can be watched and so give a clearer picture of the child's ability.

The Early Childhood Environment Rating Scale (ECERS-E) would be a useful place to make an in-depth analysis of practice. This is used to analyse practice in the Effective Pre-School Education Project, a longitudinal study of what makes good practice. The assessment scale and how to use it is detailed in an accessible booklet by Sylva *et al.* (2006). It can be used to look at practice both inside and out, detailing language, mathematical and science understanding but also diversity including gender and race. But as it recommends this cannot be done half heatedly but carefully and with lots of initial research and discussions.

'Fine-tuning'

Planning cannot be static and, as McLean (1991) demonstrates through the description of one teacher, there has to be constant 'fine-tuning' of the environment to fit the needs of the children's play. 'Fine-tuning' seems a particularly useful description for the

Boy 5 years, third term in the nursery class

4.5 A lot of time playing solitary and watching what others were doing (sand). Does not talk a lot to other children. Talking to himself during imaginative play in house, pretending to peel an orange. Played with J in house pretending to be asleep. Loved playing with big bricks (with G and J), not a lot of talking though. Talked to me, pointed out correctly the colours of the bricks (R, Y, B, G) without being asked about it.

10.5 Needs language extension in English. Very immature syntax, usually only using nouns and verbs. Look at books with him 1:1. Drawing: did a very 'interesting' drawing of Mrs P. head separate from the eyes. Circle with bumps (photocopy).

11.5 Initiated several verbal exchanges with me. Needs a lot more basic vocab.

11.5 Same as above, played at the water tray for a long time, filling containers until they overflowed. Very pleased with it. Asked me to come and look.

13.5 Outside; very careful and attentive with C on the slide. Helped her up and also coaxed her down. Very gentle with her. 'Painted' the shed for a long time. Did not volunteer any observations verbally. Trying to talk to adults, but very limited vocabulary and syntax. Keeps nodding when adults talk to him, not sure how much he understands. Will talk to Mum and Dad.

14.5 Definitely does not understand 'again'. Finds it difficult to understand basic instructions. Should really be seen by a home-language teacher to assess if his understanding in Urdu is any different.

24.5 Knows numbers up to 5, count and recognise.

7.6 Did milk today, knows who every label belongs to and who is in.

11.6 Cutting and gluing – problems with both. Needs lots more practice in this area.

15.6 Outside: clay work: stayed for a long time, making rolls for walls. Then proceeded to represent house in 2-d fashion, using rolls like pencil marks. Made a home with roof and 4 rooms. Then went on to put little bits of clay all on top of it. Said they were 'openings'. Outside: ice balloons: very interested, stayed with the activity for a long time. Had to introduce word 'ice'. No concept of melting. Very surprised by it. Had difficulty with pronouncing words. Painted first picture of person with body, arms, legs, hair and 'willy'. Very pleased with himself. Emergent writing: used A to sign his name.
Drew self-portrait. Looked at himself and chose colours carefully.

21.6 Told milk label story today, volunteered to do it. Made a real effort to say sentences. He did extremely well, very pleased with himself. After milk told a whole long story to everybody – what he, his dad, and his sister had done in the park.

Figure 7.3 Running records   (cont'd)

(cont'd)

In a period of 7 weeks not only had this child progressed but also the staff had learnt a great deal about him and there is clear evidence of how the staff were supporting this child's development. The child in this period went from being quiet to being able to recount to the whole group an event in his life. He demonstrates clear empathy with other children, is willing to have a go at a range of activities and is learning from those experiences. His representational skills had developed so that he was able to actually draw himself and make a 3-d house. These are really significant developments over such a short period of time. However, much of what staff do in schools can be lost if it is not written down.

2. Boy, four-and-a-half-years old, 2nd term in nursery class
7.5 Played a lot with A in the hospital outside. He and A in leading roles, other children following. Needed to be reminded to look out for other children and not to run several times. Spent quite a long time at the drawing table with I, both looking at the 'Goldilocks' book. He then did some drawing but not associated with the book.

10.5 Very willing to come and help with the brick house. Worked on the roof, overlapping tiles. Finished it all by himself. Remarked that it needed a chimney pot. When asked where, pointed out appropriate spot and stuck it on from behind. Was very pleased with the result. Very precise about his work with good, appropriate language: 'I need another layer'.

11.5 Spent quite a time with splatter painting outside. Really seems to enjoy art activities. Very concentrated play with big bricks outside. Was only one who really understood 'bond' and overlapping bricks. Very careful work. Then into imaginative play: 'This is Humpty Dumpty's wall'. Electricity: had fine motor problems. Needed a lot of help with crocodile clips. Persevered though and understood principle.

11.6 Electricity: investigated further, again needed help because of fine motor problems. Cutting: does not hold scissors properly. Cuts upside down. Needs help and practice.

15.6 Spent quite a while at the clay table, rolling clay out flat, imprinting, making patterns. Commented on the 'cold' feel of clay.

17.6 Remembered really well what we had already said about Inuits, and Igloos. Was able to show on the globe where England and North Pole are. Knew that water freezes in the cold.

Again, this running record tells a great deal about this child and his learning. Although his overall development in the same period of time is not as obvious as the previous example, it does pick up on his personality and where he needs help. For example, he has good passive and active vocabulary and remembers information easily. It would be easy to let this child coast, however, he has fine motor difficulties, which need addressing and his interest in art to be seriously encouraged.

Figure 7.3 (Continued)

minute-by-minute management of the space; it relies on the ability to scan the area and constantly watch the progress of children's engagement. It is about interacting with children, furthering the play situations, stimulating and feeding ideas to the children. Some children will need plenty of time to learn how to actually play and they will need adult support for this. Staff will need to spend time with children to make sure that play flows well.

Fine-tuning is about adding resources which children may need, or simply pointing children in the direction of resources which might fit their needs. It is about making sure one group of children's play does not encroach on another's, that some children do not dominate, and supporting children who are reticent. It is about making sure children all have enough choices, so that if two children move into role as painters and six other children want to join in, either more equipment is found for all of them, or some children are moved into another role. Fine-tuning is about pre-empting problems before they occur; it involves encouraging children to try out new skills and ideas, for example, the skill of climbing higher, or the skill of clearer negotiation. Children need to learn to think, to be confident in solving problems and to come to appreciate the useful effects of sharing, collaboration and negotiation. All these abilities need practice.

Fine-tuning also has to involve tidying up. The Gura (1992) research found that often blockplay was over by 10 a.m. because the area had been used and was in such a mess to be unusable. Staff need to discuss and agree at what point materials become too untidy. This will have to rely on the observation of the staff member at the time, and from the reaction of the children it will be possible to ascertain whether play has gone off-track and whether resources need to be sorted out. Staff need to check whether constructions have been finished with and, if not, they should be left in situ or, if this is not possible, moved to a safe spot. Sometimes children wish to have their constructions displayed for everyone to see (see Figure 2.5, page 57, regarding the adult role).

Fine-tuning is, therefore, a crucial part of our interaction with children. The ongoing assessment ensures we react to children's interests, difficulties and needs at the time and then help teach children or assist in their learning when appropriate.

Knowing what to look for

If we look to Bee and Boyd (2006), Gallahue (1989), Gallahue and Ozmun (2005) and Sheridan (2008), all argue that although to an extent some development does just happen, physical development cannot be left to chance. We the adults can fundamentally affect children's development to its detriment or to good effect. Looking more closely at motor development, which refers to the ability of a person to perform any physical activities, much of the activity involves space and space is something which is available outside. The Gallahue and Ozmun study (2005) indicate that children go through certain phases of motor development – namely reflexive, rudimentary, fundamental and specialised.

The **reflexive movement phase** is from four months to a year and in the uterus to about 4 months. A child is acquiring the skills of grasping, pulling up, crawling, swimming, stepping and sucking reflexes. The movements are mostly about nourishment, protection and information gathering; they are involuntary reactions to various forms of external stimulation.

The **rudimentary movement phase** is from birth to two years and has a reflex inhibition and precontrol stage. A child learns to make voluntary movements and this movement phase is about stability (such as gaining control over the head, neck and trunk muscles), manipulation (such as reaching, grasping and releasing) and locomotor movements (creeping, crawling and walking). This phase is very dependent on others making the environment safe, supporting the desires and needs of the child and biological factors such as diet.

The **fundamental movement phase** from two to seven years is divided into three stages; as children pass through each stage they gain increasing control of their movements:

- The initial stage is from two to three years, during which children make their first attempts to use movement patterns.
- The elementary stage is from four to five years, during which children's performance of movement improves.
- The mature stage is from six to seven years, during which children's movements are well coordinated and purposeful, resembling those of a skilled adult in terms of control and quality.

The **specialised movement phase** includes the transitional stage (seven to ten years), the application stage (eleven to thirteen) and lifelong utilisation stage (fourteen years and older). This spans from rope jumping activities and dancing, to walking on a rope bridge and playing kick ball to choosing activities to specialise in such as playing in teams or at track events and developing skills and applying strategies. It is all leading to life-long daily living use, recreational use and possibly competitive use.

Significant to our work is that the reflexive and rudimentary phases pretty much just happen, children tend to sit, stand, walk, run, and children need us to be there and arrange the environment so it is safe. With regard to the fundamental stage our role is hugely significant and we need to teach, encourage, help and support so children move forward in their abilities and skills. 'Most children must have some combination of opportunities for practice, encouragement, and instruction in an ecologically sound environment' (Gallahue and Ozmun 2005: 56). The skills children are acquiring at this phase are many and varied – there is a wealth of difference between hitting a moving ball and hitting a stationary one – we have to help children become proficient, we cannot leave it to chance or assume it will automatically happen, it will not. Therefore, we cannot allow outdoor play to happen periodically or as we drink a coffee. If we look at Figure 7.4 this shows the developmental phases but also how these relate to the function of the movement whether it be stability (balance), locomotor (transportation) or manipulation (force).

It is necessary for us to be aware of the skills and the range of skills children need. Figure 7.5 demonstrates how many physical skills children have to master. We need to ensure children can do all those skills listed, whether it be gross motor development such

	Intended Function of the Movement Task		
Phases of Motor Development	**Stability** (emphasis is on body balance in static and dynamic movement situations)	**Locomotion** (emphasis is on body transportation from point to point)	**Manipulation** (emphasis is on imparting force to or receiving force from an object)
Reflexive Movement Phase: Involuntary subcortically controlled movement abilities in utero and early infancy	• Labyrinthine righting reflex • Neck righting reflex • Body righting reflex	• Crawling reflex • Primary stepping reflex • Swimming reflex	• Palmer grasp reflex • Plantar grasp reflex • Pull-up reflex
Rudimentary Movement Phase: The maturationally influenced movement abilities of infancy	• Control of head and neck • Control of trunk • Unsupported sitting • Standing	• Crawling • Creeping • Upright gait	• Reaching • Grasping • Releasing
Fundamental Movement Phase: The basic movement skills of childhood	• Balancing on one foot • Walking on a low beam • Axial movements	• Walking • Running • Jumping • Hopping	• Throwing • Catching • Kicking • Striking
Specialized Movement Phase: The complex skills of later childhood and beyond	• Performing a balance beam routine in gymnastics • Defending a goal kick in football	• Running the 100-metre dash or hurdles event in track • Walking on a crowded street	• Performing a goal kick in football • Striking a pitched ball

Figure 7.4 Gallahue's two-dimensional model for classifying movement with examples provided

Source: David Gallahue & John Ozmun (2005) *Understanding Motor Development: Infants, Children, Adolescents, Adults.* (6th edn). © The McGraw-Hill Companies Inc. Reproduced with permission of McGraw-Hill Companies Inc.

as running, or non-locomotive which is about balancing or fine motor skills such as holding a pencil in drawing. We need to be aware that the ability to be stable is the most
important aspect of learning to move (Gallahue and Ozmun 2005: 194). In terms of
range within each skill, if we just take one for example, jumping, there are many types
of jumping: jumping from side to side, jumping backwards, jumping forwards, jumping
on the spot, jumping down, jumping up onto something, jumping across, jumping using
two feet or one foot, jumping over something and so on, jumping and using arms in a star
shape for example, jumping from a squat position, jumping into or from something
moving. We have to know that children can achieve all these skills before we blindly
suggest they are physically able. We do not have the right to stunt children's development because we do not want to be physically active inside or outside ourselves.
Gallahue and Ozmun argue that 'Under the proper circumstances, children are capable
of performing at the mature stage in the vast majority of fundamental movements patterns
by age 6' (2005: 59). Gallahue also argues that by age 7 all the fundamental movements
should be in place and if they are not they may never be. As it makes obvious at the
mature stage children's movements are 'well coordinated and purposeful, resembling
those of a skilled adult in terms of control and quality' (1993: 111).

It is not enough to have a 'sense' about what constitutes movement, it is necessary
to know exactly what it is and its component parts (Davies 1995). Davies classifies movement as being about the body (action, articulation, design, fluency and shape), about
dynamics (weight, space (qualitative), time and flow), about space (size, extension, zone,
level and direction) and about relationships (between parts of the body, with objects
and with people) (1995: 1–2). Just as adults will have a repertoire of ideas, for example,
to help children to learn to read, they also need a repertoire of ideas to teach movement
skills. Davies details the stages of development, such as the change in throwing

Motor skills
• **Locomotor** development or gross motor is about moving through the environment, which involves large movement patterns, such as: walking, running, jumping, hopping, skipping, sliding, leaping, climbing, crawling, standing, sitting.
• Non-locomotor development, or **stabilising** maintaining equilibrium, is about balancing – such as: bending, stretching, twisting, pivoting, swinging, rolling, landing, stopping, dodging, balancing, inverted supports (upside down)
• **Manipulative** or fine motor skills and hand–eye and foot–eye coordination skills is about imparting force on objects such as: throwing, catching, kicking, trapping, striking, volleying, bouncing, rolling, pulling, pushing, punting, grasping, reaching, gripping, holding, (including the skills of sewing, cutting, typing, writing, drawing and painting).

Figure 7.5 Motor skills
Source: Gallahue, D. L. and Donnelly, F. C. (2003) *Developmental Physical Education for All
Children*. Champaign IL: HumanKinestics, 54 Figure 3.1. Reproduced with permission from
Human Kinetics

technique, from age 18 months (1995: 25). With this type of knowledge teachers can really help children to move on in their skill acquisition.

Maude (2008) helps us to appreciate the significance of young children's movements and how these are linked to the three PE fields – dance, games and gymnastics. She describes how the fantasy play of young children will eventually lead to dance. Children might twirl and leap and pause in their fantasy play, these are all skills necessary for the dance curriculum. Games of chase and hide and seek, ball games that involve either batting or kicking lead to the games curriculum of organised sport. When young children roll, jump, swing and climb, these are leading to the gymnastics curriculum. If we want children to be successful we need to make sure they are skilled and confident.

Sheridan (2008) indicates the general milestones in a child's life to age five and in less detail to age seven; this book serves as a very useful reference when working with young children, to support one's diagnosis and suggestions. For example, she notes that at age five most children can 'walk easily on a narrow line. Runs lightly on toes. Active and skilful in climbing, sliding, digging and doing various "stunts". Skips on alternate feet' (2008: 47). We need to know the stages, not to impede development but to know when we need to be concerned. She also references 'markers that indicate abnormality' (2008: 60) all of which are to do with motor coordination and demonstrate the centrality of our understanding of child development. So much of this can be noticed when children are outside. This is worth having as a reference book for staff and parents.

Adult behaviour and gender

The majority of early years staff are female but unfortunately outdoors is not necessarily a natural environment for many of them. They are, more often than not, keener to be involved in sedentary activities, which usually take place indoors. As a general rule, men tend to do the heavy, active, manual work and play games such as football. All of this type of work occurs outside. This stereotype is reflected in the Foundation Stage setting, with many women preferring to work indoors at the creative activities and not wanting to venture into the outdoor play area. Tizard et al. (1977) found that there were significant differences in the way staff worked indoors, to outdoors. In nine centres where there were significant observations there was a trend for lower cognitive content in the staff behaviour outdoors, in seven cases the staff talked less to children in the garden, used more negative controls ('Don't do that') and in eight cases the amount of minimal supervision outdoors was greater compared with indoors. There can be more DIY-type jobs in the outdoor area which many women are not confident about (Gilkes 1987). Paley (1984) acknowledges that she prefers the girls' play which tends to be quieter, more work-oriented, more 'let's-sit-round-mother-in-the-kitchen' type activity. She also admits that she appreciates the boys more when they are not playing boys' games or fantasy games but when they are being more like the girls! It is likely that many women working in early years may feel the same. However, as Paley further argues, it is important for staff to appreciate and understand boys' play, as males make up around half of the population.

Boys are often engaged in activities that do not have a classic end product, such as painting or drawing. If staff do not rate this type of experience or work with children in these spaces then they are oblivious to the learning. Constructions are often broken up at the end of the session; this to me seems a ludicrous waste. Constructions tell a story, a story which likely cannot be written down by the maker but which is in their head. This can be told and written down by the adult. We underestimate the relevance of constructions whether they be from Lego or boxes and blocks outside. As children construct they are thinking and creating in a logical fashion. They need the opportunities to describe what they have made, how they have made it and how they might improve it another time. In this way we can support children in their skills of language – of learning to be clear, succinct and logical. Writing down what they say (scribe writing) we can demonstrate to them what great narrators they are! This can only develop their confidence and their drive to go forward and confidently write formally. Simply put, construction supports literacy (Pahl 1999 and Smith 1982 as cited in Holland 2003).

'Teacher presence and modelling is an extremely powerful factor determining children's play activities' (Whyte 1983: 52). It is therefore not only important that staff use the outdoors effectively but also work with all children regardless of gender or experience. Girls and boys can be treated differently by staff. Skelton and Francis talk about girls facing a 'double bind' (2003: 49): being required to be good because that is what girls are but also being required to be good at mathematics. But in the research it was found that girls good at mathematics were described by some teachers more disparagingly than their male counterparts. The girls good at mathematics were described as 'hard workers, plodders, capable, neat, conscientious and helpful' (Skelton and Francis 2003: 49 describing the research of Walden and Walkerdine 1986). However, these adjectives do not describe mathematical talent, but approach. Other research (Walkerdine and Lucey 1989) found boys who were not as able mathematically as some of the girls and caused behavioural problems in the classroom, were described as 'bright' and having 'flair' although the evidence for this was not apparent. This is simply not right or fair and does not offer equality of opportunity. We have to be wary of ourselves.

Holland, looking at war, weapon and Superhero play, demonstrates that much of the staff's time can be taken up with 'dealing' with boys and their active play. But those same staff can tend to ignore the girls who are being sedentary and unprepossessing. 'Do we focus equally on the quiet, passive, domestically orientated play that occupies so much time for so many young girls? Do we feel concern about the impact on their physical development of an excess of sedentary activity?' (2003: 21). From her research it is clear more needs to be done to support girls and that staff need to ensure they interact with children who are demanding attention through their behaviour but also interact with those who do not demand attention. The zero tolerance approach to Superhero and gun play militated against males and females playing together. By allowing Superhero and gun play, children naturally mixed across gender. The girls were able to see that it was okay to be boisterous and lively and to be so with boys and girls (Holland 2003).

Thorne (2002) argues, having looked extensively at children's lives in school, there is much teachers can do to help boys and girls see themselves as people not as separate groups.

Teachers should:
- avoid dividing a group/class of children by gender
- refrain from talking about boys and girls, but use the term 'class'
- praise girl/boy interactions
- group children themselves, don't ask children to do it
- watch for one gender taking control or the majority of access to a resource/piece of equipment
- teach new non-gender-specific games
- sometimes openly deal with social divisions, which means talking to children about what is happening, for example if a girl feels pushed out of a game outside or a boy in the home corner
- discuss ideas such as a girl can't be a doctor or a boy a nurse by arguing these are 'old fashioned'.

Figure 7.6 Supporting boys and girls
Source: Thorne (2002)

(My only misgiving about her work is the term she uses for children: 'kids', which is a baby goat). See Figure 7.6 for a list of suggestions to improve gender relations and gender attitudes.

Likewise Benjamin (2003), looking into SEN and gender (see Chapter 6), suggests that improvements can be made so that all children succeed. Her research points to the notion that SEN is not a simplistic case of boys' underachievement but looks more keenly at what is happening in classrooms. She discusses how children set themselves up in positions of what they view as masculine or feminine. She cites two schools which have a high proportion of children with SEN, who are both considered high achievers in terms of national tests. The success of the schools lies in their ability to ensure children see the school:

- as a collective where everyone helps everyone
- as somewhere that giving and receiving help is the norm
- as somewhere help and helping does not have a gender tag
- as somewhere gaining help does not mean one has to become an overly vulnerable female or giving help is not seen as macho.

Interestingly this fits with Whitebread's self-regulated regime where children are able to become independent and therefore more able.

Jago, as we saw in the previous chapter, found girls were less active than boys in the playground, and argues that we need to ensure we have a balance of activities and games available outside so girls and boys become physically involved, not just the boys. He argues there needs to be enough playground stimulus, space and time available, that there needs to be the dissemination of knowledge to children, staff and parents about the why and how of activity and that there needs to be 'gender sensitive' games available (2002: 188) to ensure all children benefit.

Teacher presence will raise the status of the activities. Children know which are the 'status activities' by the presence of the staff (Anning 1994). Children need to see female staff playing football, helping with pulling a truck full of children or playing with cars. Tizard et al. (1976a) found that preschool centres are markedly female-orientated, not only by virtue of the sex of the majority of the staff but also because of the amount of equipment that they have that is preferred by girls. The authors argue that the mismatch between the interests of boys and teachers starts early and that if staff want to reach out to boys then they need to interact more with boys and their interests, such as cars, garages, football and large construction. Likewise all children need to see female staff digging in the wild area, using the woodwork tools and playing Superhero roles.

In reading, children tend to follow behaviour along gender lines, with girls showing interest in their mothers' reading material and boys in their fathers', which tend to be more action- and sport-orientated (Millard 1997). Reference books, magazines and comic strips are read more frequently by men and there has been a growth in magazines for men, such as GQ. Therefore, at school where most staff are women, a concerted effort needs to be made to offer appropriate reading matter to boys. Staff need to show an interest in all reading material, not just their own preference. The skill required for reading non-fiction has to be valued as much as reading a book from cover to cover. Within the outdoor area there are many experiences which will support non-fiction reading, such as gardening or mini-beast observations. Likewise, children need to see men sitting reading stories or helping with a piece of collage work. Such behaviour means that children, regardless of gender, will be accepted and supported and that any activity children decide to do now or in the future is supported. The differences between people have to be recognised; men and women are different, they do take on different roles, but no one is better than another by virtue of gender.

Joining in with children's play

Being part of children's play is probably the most difficult job we have to do, because to get it right requires a lot of effort. The adult involved has to be thinking all the time about how to help the play and learning along. But it is essential to be part of children's play otherwise:

> children left alone to play do not develop imaginatively; after a time much of their play becomes repetitive and lacking in progression … Without the help of a teacher setting the environment and providing the suggestions, children reach stalemate and their play becomes intellectually aimless.
>
> (Manning and Sharp 1977: 15)

This was true 32 years ago and is still true. I would add that it does not necessaryily need to be an adult, just an older child can ensure play does not reach stalemate. Holland (2003) beautifully describes how we can get involved in children's play alluding to the adult being a sculptor and going with the grain of the wood not against it. She further suggests that children's behaviour is not set in stone and can be altered/transformed/modified by sensitive adults. Stephenson noted in her study that outside, staff felt they were more able than in to dip in and out of children's play. Staff considered children were more engrossed in what they were doing and so were not so disturbed by staff joining or leaving their play. Play outside enabled children to get very absorbed, more able to 'extend themselves, set challenges for themselves' (2002: 36). It seemed when staff joined children's play inside there was more chance they would expect the adult to become the leader and so this disturbed the play.

Cullen (1993) found that the quality of play in the outdoor sandpit area was very low level in terms of physical, creative, social and cognitive dimensions. She argues that adults need to intervene by questioning, adding resources and joining in the play. The Hutt et al. (1989) study found that at the collage table, where an adult was in almost permanent attendance, the play was high quality and included wide-ranging conversations, but at the sand and water area there was no adult present and the play was low quality and repetitive. Kostelnik et al. (1986) suggest that quality collaborative play can occur with the intervention of an observant teacher. They also suggest how adults can enhance Superhero play into complex socio-dramatic play episodes and still involve physical activity. Intervention therefore can stop the rather meaningless Superhero play that sometimes occurs. Blatchford's (1989) study of children during the primary playtime similarly suggests that adult involvement in the play could improve the play quite considerably.

The impact on behaviour when teachers are not involved in play is even more apparent where boys are involved. Davies (1991) and Davies and Brember (1994), looking into children's adjustment to nursery class, found that boys' adjustment to nursery was not as successful as that of girls. They argue that as staff are not visiting those areas where boys tend to play, then there is little chance of developing their positive learning attitudes. If staff spend more time inside with the creative or quiet activities, then it will be the girls who benefit from the interaction and not the boys. Staff do need to ensure that all areas within the class and outdoor space get equality of input from the staff. Davies suggests that staff should check whether the time planned actually matches the time spent on various activities, in order to ensure the equality of adult participation and intervention in all areas of the setting.

Sometimes it is appropriate to become involved in children's play to defuse confrontational situations which children cannot sort out themselves. Without this support the play can disintegrate or end in unresolved stand-offs. In role, children can either be led into a sidetrack of the play or into a new play situation, if staying in the present one may cause arguments over the direction of play, the use of resources, or over who is playing which role. In the McLean study, Nan, one of the teachers observed, was very keen to create a good environment for the children to play in. She made sure they had a lot of space and resources to work with, but she was also involved in attracting 'particular children to specific areas, to aid in the formation of the desired peer groups, to extend children's play and avoid potential peer conflicts' (1991: 101). Most of her strategies were very subtle, so children were unaware of her role.

Some staff are reticent about joining in with children's play, arguing that they are concerned that children will be interrupted and that their play is a private affair. This is a valid point and children, whatever they are doing, should be credited with some degree of privacy. Paley, talking about joining in with children's play, says, 'often I drift around the edge of their knowing without finding a place to land' (1986: 131). However, this concern does somewhat contradict how children can behave. One of the wonderful, yet quite difficult, traits of young children is their ability to tell you when to go away. They will walk away when they have had enough of you, they will say 'Bye' in the middle of your talk; they will say 'No thanks' when you offer them what you think is the most stimulating activity going. So children will say, in the right environment, whether they want you or not. Sometimes it is appropriate to say, 'Can I join you?' At other times it may be appropriate to get into role as you approach. It is important to assess why you are joining in and how this will help the children involved.

Staff also need to be involved in children's play to offer support. This is a crucial component of children's play and one which ensures the continuation of quality play. Dunn and Morgan (1987), looking into play patterns in nursery and infant classes, found that children's play at school was actually helping to reinforce stereotyped role models and behaviours. Studies such as those of Halliday *et al.* (1985) show that stereotypical play choice is reduced when staff get involved in children's play. Actually being part of children's play, and thereby challenging prejudice as it arises, has to be part of the whole package of prejudice removal from the Foundation Stage, in effecting a change in children's attitudes. But equally, children need to work through stereotypical ideas through their play (Bruce 2005), again a sentiment echoed in the research by Holland (2003) in which she found that by outlawing Superhero and gun play, ideas were locked into children's heads which needed to be aired and gently countered, such as sexism and racism. How prejudice is challenged has to be considered. Becoming the heavy-handed adult may have little effect, but challenging prejudice when in role as part of imaginative play may have more impact. Sometimes classes use drama to show what sort of behaviour is and is not acceptable and report that this has a lasting effect on the children.

Morgan and Dunn (1990) found that some resources had 'high status' and these gave rise to disputes about access, to unwillingness to share and, in almost all cases, the winners in the disputes were the boys. A classic example of this is bikes. Bikes seem to inherit a status level all of their own! No one says that 'bikes are best', no one says 'the red bike is the best of all', but this is what happens. What then follows is that some children, mostly boys, will race to get the bikes, to get the 'best' bike. These children will do just about anything to achieve their aim, and this may include harming other children and damaging equipment. They will then do anything to stay on the bike for as long as possible. The reasoning behind this behaviour is that a perceived high status toy gives high status to the owner, therefore the child's self-esteem goes up. When the child has to give up the bike their self-esteem goes down, and they feel unimportant and often lost – their only direction is to seek out the high status toy again. In classes where staff plan and get involved with children's play this does not happen and children show much less interest in bikes as a means to raise their self-esteem. Morgan and Dunn (1990) found that the 'invisible' children in the class tended to be girls and the 'visible', and those demanding most teacher attention, were the boys. Again, unless adults interact with children and have observation at the heart of their work, they will be unlikely to pick out those children who are fading into the background and those who are taking over.

It may be that a child needs support because they are unsure in the situation of play outdoors or within one particular learning bay. With an adult there, a child can enter a play situation without feeling threatened and can find out about the potential of an activity with the help of an adult. Holland (2003) found that adult presence encouraged the girls to join in with 'war, weapon and Superhero play'. This regular adult presence finally enabled the girls to partake of this type of play absent of adults. An example from a play situation may help to demonstrate the importance of adult presence (see Figure 7.7). The teacher's role in this situation seems crucial and makes the job of fine-tuning very apparent. She made herself available to the children and was someone they could play with. She played with Emily and protected her from children wishing to dominate the scene. She steered other children away to a new scene, and steered Emily on the first day to construct a new building, so making sure the boys' play was not disturbed. She stayed quiet when Timothy had made a door and allowed Emily to deal with the situation. Given time and adult input, Emily should be able to discover the joys of a new resource, play with boys and gain in confidence through being in charge. However, the length of time an adult needs to stay to encourage a reticent child to work without adult support will vary. The results from the Halliday et al. (1985) study into influencing children's choice of activities at kindergarten through teacher participation found that girls stayed at the blockplay while the adult was there but moved away once the adult left. The authors argue that teachers do influence play choice by their presence and involvement, but they also need to stay long enough, and on enough occasions, for children to

Two boys, confident when working outside, had elicited the help of the teacher in building a house, using crates, planks and boxes. Emily entered the scene saying she wanted to make a house. The teacher did not want to disturb the play situation of the boys by taking some of the crates, so suggested that Emily and she build a house using barrels, ladders and large plastic cubes, which they did. Emily continued to watch the boys. Two other girls joined Emily. The next day, Emily approached the teacher and asked if they could make a house using crates. The teacher and Emily filled a truck with crates and set off to build a house. Manmit, Gurjit (the boys who had built the house the day before) and Timothy came over and wanted to build the house, and they immediately assumed positions of control. The teacher said no, and suggested another play situation for them. Emily described what she was doing – 'building a back door, a front door, two seats'. Timothy had wandered back by this time and had arranged two barrels at the side of Emily's house. He said, 'This is the back door.' Emily disagreed but then said, 'Alright, let's have two doors.' Two other girls entered the scene and helped Emily. When they had finished, the three sat down and Emily, with much pleasure said, 'Look at this building we have done.' Timothy continued to stay on the side lines. The teacher was called away but Emily's game continued. She stayed in charge and Timothy stayed on the periphery.

(Bilton 1989: 63)

Figure 7.7 A girl building with blocks

discover or come into contact with enough satisfying aspects of the play, so that they will wish to return to it with a friend or alone.

Skill teaching

Rather than merely participating in outdoor activities children need to be taught specific skills, just as children need to be taught specific skills with regard to, say, reading. Skills are generally taught in a PE or movement lesson but often, when staff move outdoors, they do not see it as their duty to teach motor skills. Practice, encouragement and instruction are crucial for the development of mature patterns of movement (Gallahue 1989). In the Stephenson (2002) study, staff saw their role outside as teacher, using more directive strategies, such as teaching specific 'sport' skills and more so than inside. In the outside space staff would be happy to demonstrate an action, such as dribbling the ball, but would not have been happy to show a child how to draw a circle inside. So skill teaching was seen as a crucial part of the adult role outside.

In a study by Miller (1978) it was found that three- to five-year-olds, when given a structured movement programme, improved their fundamental movement patterns beyond those children who had not been given a programme and had been left to themselves. Wetton (1983) was concerned as to why four-year-olds used a climbing frame less than the three-year-olds. She concluded that the four-year-olds had been given no help or challenge in developing their skills beyond what they could find out themselves: the adults had not been helping the children to gain new skills.

Cullen (1993) argues that preschool children will not achieve physical objectives or gain skills if they only have a free play programme. But she also issues a warning about the planned supervised obstacle course, which, although it addressed the need for skill improvement, created problems as children spent a great deal of time waiting for their turn. Wetton (1998) highlights the centrality of observation and assessment in a structured play environment. She argues that sometimes children can become 'wanderers' even in a well-set-up environment; these are the children who are unable to access this type of free choice environment. There are also the children who do not have suitable clothing or footwear, who lack the necessary negotiation skills or have immature motor development, who will also be excluded from many of the activities. This demonstrates the need to actually observe, assess and then teach children the necessary skills, to be instrumental in supporting them in their efforts and making sure practical matters such as clothing do not stop them having equality of access. A balance, therefore, needs to be achieved between free choice and intervention (Boorman 1988). Direct teaching is best for teaching the best way to move, refining and combining skills, and indirect teaching encourages exploration, discovery and combining of movements (Gallahue 1989).

Cullen (1993) suggests that staff tend to be vague about physical development and talk in general rather than in specific terms. Staff need to be skilled in the systematic evaluation of motor skills in order to help children develop. Not only should the skills and activities be part of the planning, but staff need to note down what skills they are

186

hoping specific children should be learning next. Some children, for example, may not know that they need to bring their hands into their body when catching a ball, some children may be ready to throw high and accurately, to throw to someone else; most children need to be shown that a ball will go further if kicked from a run rather than from standing still. Likewise, with movement on the apparatus, children need ideas on how to move around, for example, stepping up a ladder, balancing without holding on or hanging and moving under monkey bars. Wetton (1988) offers a useful source of games to be played with nursery and infant children.

But equally, children need to learn the skills of getting on with others, of being able to negotiate with someone so that both parties feel they have succeeded. Through imaginative play and construction where children are working toward a common goal, children need to refine their skills of collaboration. Staff need to point out to children the consequences of their actions and if they continue, say, to argue, the tower, tunnel or whatever, will not get built. Children can be given pointers as to how to cooperate, such as talking about what they all anticipate the final product might look like, or actually stopping an imaginative scene, moving children out of role to discuss what has happened so far in the play and where children want it to go next. The children can then go back into the play scene and hopefully carry on with more success. Sometimes they need to be left to sort out difficulties themselves, thereby consolidating learning and developing their understanding.

Costello (2000) argues that there is a direct relationship between thinking and behaving and thinking well and behaving well. An educated adult is one with knowledge and skills in a number of areas but is also one who thinks critically and carefully about beliefs, attitudes and values and acts in morally appropriate ways (2000: 102). Part of our role is to help children think. The debate about thinking skills has been raised again with the introduction of citizenship education in schools. But to understand citizenship one has to be able to think for oneself first. Helping children to think critically means not teaching a body of knowledge but providing an environment, in which children are able to debate issues, evaluate arguments, question evidence, formulate theories. Stories and videos can be one way to open up debates, but, equally, as we work and play alongside children, our questioning of how and why things happen and are done in a particular way will raise children's desire to question. Margy Whalley describes how one local teacher calls the children from her nursery as having 'the Pen Green Syndrome' (1997: 171) – it strikes me these children have simply been taught to think!

Talking and listening to children

Thinking back to the work of Whitebread and Katz in the previous chapter we need to consider what the findings mean for how the adult in the educational setting talks to children. Katz and Chard discuss the need for teachers to ensure children take on the dispositions for learning, such as persistence, concentration, a 'can do' approach. Equally Whitebread is arguing for classrooms which encourage children to be independent, who are confident to take up the challenge and have a go, to understand they have options and choices. It means the adult:

- needs to take the lead from the children sometimes
- supports children in their endeavours, not shower them with praise, reward and stickers
- encourages children to be proactive in their learning, not constantly be told what to do
- needs to be a good role model and show that they are interested in learning
- should give helpful useful feedback so children can consider what they are doing and improve it
- asks questions which are thought provoking (see Figure 6.3, page 150)
- encourages children to ask questions (see Figure 6.4, page 150)
- ensures children have time to devote to their interests, projects and explorations.

Most of these approaches involve talking to and listening to children and we need to do this with a great dollop of caution. We can do more damage the moment we open our mouths and sometimes it is better just to stay quiet. We need to remember that just because we are teachers not all our words are 'words of wisdom'. The Leverhulme Project involving Ted Wragg (Wragg and Brown 2001a, 2001b) found that the greatest confusion to children is caused when teachers ask questions during an explanation. In the research the average wait time after a question was three seconds. When the wait time was increased to ten seconds, more children responded and more of those responses were of a high level. This would make sense – not all of us can think on our feet, it does not make us stupid, it just means we need a little more time to think the ideas through. The research found that a lot of the questions asked by teachers were closed or, as Katz and Chard (1989: 29) describe them, 'interrogatory': 'What colour is grass?' 'How many buttons are there?' 'What are you doing?' The problem with these types of questions is that they are not how we talk when outside school. Normal conversation is like a game of tennis; back and forth we go, asking things we do not necessarily know the answer to. The interrogatory style of communication can make children feel intimidated and confused. If you know grass is green and then someone asks you, there is a tendency to assume that it may not be green otherwise why would the expert (the teacher) be asking such a daft question. So children stay silent. The need for an open approach to dialogue is a theme which has been aired over time and is picked up once again with the findings of the Effective Provision of Pre-School Education (EPPE) Project and the idea of 'sustained shared thinking' (Sylva et al. 2004). This approach is supported by:

- tuning in
- sharing genuine interest
- respecting children's own decisions and choices
- inviting children to elaborate
- recapping

- offering one's own experiences
- clarifying ideas
- waiting for a response
- not hurrying children (Siraj-Blatchford 2007).

Katz and Chard (1989), looking to research, indicate that how we respond to children can impact on their interest level. If children are rewarded for doing something that they are intrinsically interested in, the reward will lessen the interest. Intrinsic interest is a reward in itself and to be rewarded means you are being given something to encourage you to do something you do not necessarily like. So we have to be very careful we do not offer rewards whether they be actual or verbal. To tell a child 'well done' for playing something they like doing is likely to lessen that interest. Second, Katz and Chard refer to research which indicates where children are rewarded they can then assume the effort is not down to them but to something outside of them. Third, Katz and Chard found that giving rewards after something else has been done is likely to make them consider the thing they have to do is less appealing. So if you offer play/golden time/free choice, etc as a reward for something the teacher requires you to do, such as completing a work-sheet or say reading a book, this can unwittingly put down the value of the required work. This is the very opposite reaction to what the teacher is hoping for. So outdoor play should never be used as a reward for more important things to be done.

We then need to analyse the depth of feedback. Again Katz and Chard refer to research which indicates that when we offer positive but general feedback the productivity rises but the interest lessens. When that general feedback is withdrawn motivation drops. This depth of feedback is called an 'inducement'. So we need to be specific about the feedback we are giving – and this is called a 'tribute' (1989: 34). So we need to be thoughtful as we open our mouth and consider before we do so what it is we are trying to achieve. If we want the interest to continue, then discussing an aspect of whatever the child is doing adds to the interest, or 'I didn't know that' style of question. It could be you say nothing but the next day bring a book in regarding something the child was talking about and without any conversation you are saying 'you are really interested in this and so am I and here is something which might further that interest'. Finally, Katz and Chard discuss the need for children to be engaged in 'sustained effort and involvement' (1989: 35) in projects over a period of time of days and weeks. Twenty years on the EPPE project discusses the success of 'sustained shared thinking' in helping children develop.

So outdoor play cannot be a twenty minute a day runabout where adults ignore children. Adults need to be having plenty of conversations with children about shared interests not be interrogating them.

Deployment of staff

When indoors and outdoors are available simultaneously, it is preferable to have one member of staff indoors and one outdoors. Any more adults can then be assigned to areas as agreed by the staff group. The rota will be flexible so that staff can react to the children's needs and although initially assigned to one particular area, can then move between play scenes both indoors and outdoors as needs arise. In some situations where the play is so intricately wound up with a particular member of staff it may be necessary for that member to go indoors if the group of children want to and have a member of staff from indoors swap with them. Where there are only two adults available, one indoors and one outdoors, this swapping can still occur. It may be that children move indoors and outdoors a lot, for example, when using the writing equipment to make signs or constructing something from reclaimed material to use in the play situation outdoors, and they can move between the two areas on their own. It may be in some circumstances that staff can have a quick conversation and pass on any relevant information about the play and how the adult has been involved.

If there is only one member of staff for two areas, such as an infant class, then it is important to discuss procedures with the head teacher and to seek extra help. White-hurst, looking into her own practice with reception children, concluded that the inner courtyard just outside the classroom could be utilised by the children and without adult presence all the time. In fact this would help further promote children's independence (2001: 62). We need to learn to trust children and not assume they are going to get hurt every time they are out of sight. There are always solutions to problems. The Cleave and Brown (1991) study highlights one school which joined three classes of children together for the afternoon and then used one of the classrooms and the adjacent outdoor area for children to simultaneously use indoors and outdoors. Two teachers stayed outdoors and one indoors and, when an extra adult was available, children were able to use the wheeled toys on the school's playground.

Setting up and tidying away

A classroom is like a home and needs to have a safe feeling. Likewise a home has useful resources such as scissors, pens and paper and a place for everything. This is all that a class and garden need. Sometimes in a home we create games and activities for children and give them new experiences, we would also expect this in a class. But children do not need a completely ready-made environment where staff have run ragged setting it up. Otherwise children are not given opportunities to think and create for themselves and this is a thread which has been running throughout this book and is one of the guiding principles. So yes, the environment does need a degree of daily setting up but it is more crucial to have created a workshop environment where children can collect and combine resources and know that actually the staff are a resource.

Some setting-up is about giving children ideas, posing questions, teaching a specific skill, offering ideas by laying out books alongside resources. Photographs of children in imaginative play scenes, taken at the nursery, can act as an ideas bank for children. The mere presence of an adult alongside some resources may start a scene off. Sometimes children will use these ideas, or they may ignore them and start with their own. As long as children are secure in the knowledge that they have control over their environment then quality learning will occur.

One way of helping children to get started in a play scene or to develop their play is through storying, and this is a means by which adults can get involved in children's play. Children will use stories from the television, partly because these are stories that they know. Staff can add to a child's repertoire by telling stories beforehand and gathering the necessary resources. However, whatever the story, it has to be well resourced and it has to be available but not exclusively. I have seen a set-up of three bowls, three stools and three beds and nothing else. What happens if the child does not want to play that story? What happens if I want to adapt the story and add a visit to the moon? Many stories can be used; for example, in one school a teacher based the whole curriculum around the story of *Watership Down* and activities in the nursery incorporated themes from the story (Meadows and Cashdan 1988). Stories such as *The Enormous Crocodile, The Town Mouse and the Country Mouse, The Animals of Farthing Wood* and *The Enormous Turnip* are possibilities; some stories would obviously be told over a period of time. The Suzanne Gretz stories are quite detailed and complicated and yet the stories are actually reasonably short. These stories have lots of potential for acting out a variety of themes. Fiction is also highly relevant and many children may prefer to be told the story of the river, or the building and become a captain or a designer. Some children would relish the stimulus, others would not want to follow such a theme. Some children, who have little experience of play and need help in how to play, would find such a stimulus very helpful. The involvement of staff would of course be based on the children's needs. This approach may also benefit some children who are not used to the forms and meanings of narrative; the acting out of the story would mean they could use the familiar vehicle of conversation to interpret the story. This would reflect the approach of the teacher in the Dombey (1993) study who was able to introduce children to the narrative processes by using the familiar conversational approach during storytime.

Everyday the space is going to need tidying up. Sometimes as play goes along areas need to be tidied otherwise no one can play with the equipment and then at the end of the session it will need a complete tidy. But this is not the job of staff, this has to be a shared occupation (Chapter 2 looks at the rationale for this in more detail). First, there needs to be an ethos of caring and sharing so everyone does their bit and second, children need to know how to tidy up. Children who are taught how to do so can carry planks, stack crates, blocks and bricks, arrange equipment in labelled trolleys, fold material and the like. They need to be taught the correct methods and they need to be given time to become proficient. Older children will support and help the younger ones once the system is established. It is wasteful of staff and children's time to tidy up for them and it is simply wrong. We are not children's slaves. Through tidying up children learn to respect each other and their school environment, to cooperate, to be responsible ('now this needs tidying up'), to match shapes and sizes, to problem solve, to read signs and labels, to think ahead ('if I do this, this will happen, therefore I'd better stop'). It initially takes more effort from the staff to get tidying up running well, but once in place it is far easier and more useful than doing it for the children. This is the work component of the children's day as described in Chapter 2.

Children can also be involved in the daily and seasonal clearing. For example, children enjoy and learn from sweeping up leaves. The actual skill of wielding a brush is difficult – one has to learn to be aware of both the brush end and the pole end so one does not knock anyone. Arm muscles are strengthened through the motion of sweeping. Children will need to work together and cooperate to get the leaves into piles, into bags, onto the compost heap. Finally children are filled with a sense of pride at their achievement. I was amazed recently to see a parent sweeping and weeding in a nursery class garden – what a waste for the children. Social and emotional development can be fostered through clearing, cleaning, sweeping, weeding, sorting and throwing out. In this way children get a sense of ownership and so pride and they are then keen to look after the environment.

Parents

Parents need to see the purpose and benefit of what is done in the early years. This is very pertinent to outdoor play, as it is quite alien to many people. Staff want parents and carers to support what they are doing, so it is their responsibility to convey its relevance. Margaret McMillan felt that if parents could watch their children at play and staff could interpret the play, then parents would be able to see the reasons for it. Talking to parents about the work in the setting, having regular parent meetings focusing on aspects of the work, encouraging parents to come in, or better still, having somewhere that parents could watch and not be seen, are all helpful in enabling parents to see the relevance of early years education. A school in Hartlepool asked a group of parents to be the leading participants in a project to make a video of the nursery in action. One of the difficulties with such activities as parenting classes is that they can appear to be patronising. However, this project, by asking the parents to actually do the work of making the video, did not patronise anyone and parents' self-esteem and understanding of the preschool curriculum were increased. They felt more involved with the education of their children. Parents clearly took ownership of their own children's education as a result of their participation in the project (Robson and Hunt 1999).

Staff must make sure they make a relationship with all parents, even the ones who do not appear to want it! A part of this partnership is conveying to every parent, on a regular basis, the achievements of their child. Bartholomew talks about parents being 'partners in observation', and that this sharing between parents and teachers plays a central role in supporting children in their learning (1996: 54). Talking to a parent about something the child has done, which they have enjoyed and learned from, will not only help to raise the self-esteem of parent and child, but also convey more vividly the work of the early years and the reasons for working in a particular way. This has to be done systematically to ensure each parent is spoken to within, say, a one- or two-week period. If you only talk to those parents who approach you then you will not form a relationship with all parents.

Staff find some parents easier to talk to than others, some parents make themselves more available and are more confident than others. Just as there are children who take up more of the staff's time and there are children who fade into the background, so too are there such parents. But all have a right to celebrate their child. A comment could be along the lines of: 'Darren did a superb picture today, did you see it?' which can then be followed by a comment about why it was good, and a discussion about the level of concentration, the detail in the picture, the deliberation over colour mixing and matching. And it can be a comment on children playing outside: 'Erin worked really hard outside today, when she was playing at being a post lady'. This could involve a discussion about an interaction between two children and how they cooperated, how they sorted out difficulties together and how long they concentrated. In this way the parent is finding out that through play children learn to cooperate and negotiate and that outdoor play has a purpose to learning and understanding. It does not have to be put into 'education-speak', but does need to be positive. Comments about children at work and play celebrate the child and the methods by which they learn. The parent will then hopefully feel confident to talk about their child, their needs and concerns. Having a secure relationship means parents will be willing to share information about the child, themselves and the family. This can all help paint a clear picture of the child for the staff.

Photographs of children at work and play can support discussions with parents and can be the focus of a discussion. They can be displayed with written information and transcripts of what the children were saying for parents and carers to view at their leisure. This is the approach adopted by the Emilio Reggio schools in Italy. A school in Berkshire continually takes photographs of children and staff at work as a record for parents, to support displays, but also to go onto the school website. Children can access them to use in their work, concerning what they will be doing, what they have done and so on. As they say, a picture can paint a thousand words! Books can support verbal discussions and photographic evidence. A shelf with books and magazines for carers to borrow is a useful addition to any early years class. In terms of play an accessible book for carers could be something like Christine Macintyre's *Enhancing Learning through Play* (2001).

Supportive learning environments, more than just health and safety

See Chapter 1 and particularly Figure 1.4 for more discussion on health and safety.

Staff have to consider the issue of safety, whether the environment is indoors or outdoors. It has to be considered particularly closely outdoors as children are more active and will be moving around on equipment. In recent times, safety in the outdoor area has centred around the need to have safety surfaces. However, safety in school is about much more than this. It is about making sure that equipment and resources are not dangerous and that staff and children do not behave dangerously. The adult has responsibility with regard to design, installation, maintenance and supervision. Children need to see good role models in adults and to learn alongside them about being safe. Rather than stopping children doing things we need to see how we can support them. Chapter 1 discusses the centrality of learning through movement: children need to do things for themselves. For example, some staff can act as though stairs are dangerous. They are if a young child is left on them alone! But children need to learn about stairs and practise going up and down. It is far better to let an 18-month-old practise going up and down the stairs with the adult there, than never allow them near them. Sometimes there are steps outside and staff get anxious about them and then spend all the time telling children to get off them. Better to let children on the steps with a watchful adult so they get used to them. The adult might hold the child's hand(s) as they go up and down, sit on the steps and be close and watchful. This is an ongoing and daily responsibility. Many safety issues are tied up with common sense. However, it is worth looking at evidence as to what causes accidents. Avery and Jackson (1993) found that the majority of accidents occurred when differing age groups were together, when children attempted something beyond their capabilities and when the equipment had been poorly maintained. The most common accidents were on swings, slides and climbing frames. Tina Bruce (1987 and 2005) argues that having equipment out infrequently can cause accidents. For example, if the climbing frame comes out say once a week, children can be so desperate to use it that they may do things they would not normally, such as pushing others, getting on too quickly, not thinking before they make a move and then accidents happen.

Staff need to check on a daily basis that equipment is safe, free from splinters and that nothing is broken. Metal equipment needs to be wiped after rain because it can be slippery when wet, equipment can get dangerously hot, so needs covering up until the children use it. When setting up the equipment staff need to check it has been put together properly and is secure. When assessing the safety of equipment it is important to get down at the child's level, to see if it is safe at their height and that there are no dangerous bits, particularly at their head level. As staff work and play with children it is most important to keep a careful eye on safety and check that children are behaving safely. In this way staff can anticipate problems and avert them. They need to keep an eye on those children whom they know probably have not yet reached an appropriate level of understanding of the potential dangers of the situations that are provided for them, and on those who are simply not used to the equipment or the level of freedom given in the Foundation Stage setting.

Teaching children to use equipment safely will greatly help in reducing accidents (Avery and Jackson 1993), and is another aspect of the common-sense strategy to ensuring safety. Children need to be safety conscious and they can be asked about issues to do with safety in their class and be part of the discussion process. When they are using equipment children need to know that they should only do what they feel safe doing. The moment a child feels unsure is when they will wobble, fall and hurt themselves. So although staff will set challenges and children will set challenges for themselves, they need to be told to go only as far as they feel safe. And children will be able to know when they have reached that point.

The accident study found that, where children were of different ages, accidents were more likely to occur. Children, therefore, need to know that just because someone else can do something does not mean they have to have a go. More confident children must be aware of children who are less confident, so guidelines about no pushing or pulling on any apparatus, especially climbing apparatus, will have to be made clear to all the children. They also need to be told that vehicles cannot be put under climbing frames, that they cannot climb with heeled or loose footwear, and they cannot climb in long clothing. If there are parts of the garden where it is not possible to see round a corner, children need to know to take it wide, or staff may need to put up a barrier so that children have to go round wide of the corner.

Equipment has to be used so it fits the needs to the children. Rubber tyres are heavy and when rolled can easily knock a two-year-old over. Therefore, if they are to be rolled the children need to be older. A hoop can be used for rolling purposes instead. Milk crates are very useful for loading into trucks, making into buildings and constructions, for blocking in an area. They are not safe for climbing on, but if a piece of wood is attached to the underneath surfaces and then turned over they can be made into level stepping stones. Parents will also need to be involved in making sure children come in footwear and clothing which enables them to move easily. Where staff are able to demonstrate the benefits of their work, parents are more able to see the reasons for requests such as sending children in shoes which they can climb, jump and run in. A box of spare shoes is always handy in case children do not have safe footwear.

Schools do need to make an assessment of the safety of their establishment, both indoors and outdoors. This is known as a risk assessment and focuses on the safety of materials. This can include not only whether a piece of equipment is safe, but also whether its positioning is safe. Equipment put close to a doorway can create a real safety hazard, equally a cluttered space can be a safety problem. So when making a risk assessment everything has to be looked at: resources, equipment, amount of space, positioning and use of equipment. A safety document written by the staff group makes safety issues clear to other visiting staff and parents and can be reassessed and updated periodically. The safety representative and the PE adviser from your local authority will of course be able to give advice.

Esbensen (1987) argues that when purchasing outdoor equipment, staff should have a good knowledge of child development and anthropometrical data, so only equipment which is right for the age group and height of the age group is bought. Companies who sell equipment need to be told what your needs are and not dictate their requirements. Staff must take responsibility for equipment they buy and ensure it is age specific. We cannot hide behind manufacturers if we buy equipment which is not appropriate for the age. If a company cannot tailor-make equipment then go to another company that can. Equipment needs to be robust and strong enough to withstand use by many children and the effects of the weather. Wood is the preferred material, then wood and metal and then metal on its own. Most quality wooden material is expensive, such as that made by Community Playthings, but it will last (see Chapter 10). So in the long run, it will be more cost effective to buy the more expensive, well-made products.

The worst injury a child can sustain is that of falling from a height and hitting their head. Shock-absorbent surfaces can be put in to make sure that if a child does fall they will not be permanently injured. However, it needs to be clear that a safety surface will not keep anyone completely safe and children can still get broken arms and the like.

A safety surface is safer but nothing more. And there is evidence that safety surfaces can give a false sense of security to both children and adults. People will behave more rashly because they think they are safe; this is called risk compensation. So the worry is that increasing the safety will actually cause accidents (Ball 2004). Gill (2007) describes the installation of public playgrounds using moveable equipment such as logs, boulders, plants, sand and natural land features in the German city of Freiburg. The deputy director of parks comments that within the more natural play spaces children generally take more care and accidents have not increased.

The important consideration is what is called the critical fall height. The maximum safety surface will take a critical fall height of 2.5 metres, in other words, if a child falls from this height onto the maximum safety surface, they will not sustain a permanent head injury. The European standards which dictate the need for a safety surface with climbing apparatus only applies to fixed equipment. Movable equipment such as A-frames, planks, ladders, crates, etc. do not need safety surfaces. This type of equipment can be placed anywhere. Walsh (1991) suggests that no fixed structure should be higher than 1.5 metres and no platform should be higher than 1.3 metres.

Staff need to consider space as a safety issue (see Chapter 8). Figure 8.1 details the optimum size of outdoor play spaces for Queensland in Australia. England has no such guidance but needs it. 'Larger numbers of children need not only a larger total square footage, but they also appear to need a large proportion of open space' (Kritchensky et al. 1977). So each setting needs to decide what the optimum number of children are for the space and not to put too much gear into that space.

Although safety is very much a case of common sense, staff groups have to be aware of liability and need to make a thorough risk assessment so that they can categorically say that safety issues have been addressed. Most important is the attitude of the staff. The manic, let-off-steam behaviour that one can see in some early years settings is caused by children not having enough to do, who are bored and have not had their play channelled or their ideas engaged. In this atmosphere accidents are many. A well-resourced, well-managed and cared for environment, with children and staff working together, will have very few accidents. As the day progresses staff do need to keep a watchful eye, observing, scanning, anticipating problems, knowing who may need what help, but at the same time giving children a degree of privacy.

Analysis of practice

Sometimes it is helpful to look systematically at your practice to check whether what you think is happening is the true state of affairs. Davies (1991) argues, for example, (in connection with which areas of the class are used and which are not), that 'time planned' does not always match up to 'time spent'. In the course of a week it would be quite simple for each member of staff to take a notebook and jot down which areas they work in and for how long. In this way it will be quite apparent whether some areas of the classroom and outdoor space are getting a lot of adult intervention and whether others

Activity	5 mins	5 mins	5 mins	5 mins	5 mins	5 mins

Figure 7.8 Involvement analysis

are getting little. The situation can easily be rectified, the observation schedule in the study by Dunne and Bennett (1990) clarifies what demands, and the number of demands, that are being made on a teacher. This type of schedule could be used in the outdoor setting to look at whether best use is being made of staff time. Figure 7.8 can be used to analyse who is working where, for how long and which adults are present. All experiences need to be listed in the left-hand column and then whoever is making the observations checks every 5 minutes to see who is working where, putting the child's initials in the box relating to that experience. This can also be done for staff members. The more observations done and compared over a few weeks, the better the findings. In this way you can find out:

- who is moving about a lot
- who is staying at certain activities for a long time
- who and with what staff are working
- which experiences are not being visited.

Once this information is gleaned it needs to be analysed. If a two-year-old is flitting, I would be happy, but if a five-year-old was, I would be concerned. If a child is staying at an activity for a good deal of time I would want to check how much they are learning and achieving and if there are aspects of the curriculum they are missing. If yes and they are learning little I would want to help move them to other experiences or bring those experiences to their comfort zone. If no one is visiting an experience/activity then I would want to know why. If adults are not visiting certain experiences again I would want to be questioning this. One cannot have an experience which staff never visit. This often is the case for sand and water and the book corner. So in this easy way one can learn a great deal about what is going on in the environment and then move to improve it.

A similar grid could be devised for analysing outdoor play, looking at interaction between children and children, and staff and children. The interactions of interest could include demands for staff to get involved in play, demands to sort out disputes over resources, demands to find a resource, or demands of a routine nature (those concerning going to the toilet or getting a coat) (see Figure 7.9). These demands could be noted down in a 20-minute period. It may be that, for example, many of the demands concern disputes over bikes and that these take up a lot of staff time. It will then be necessary to analyse

Type of demand	Number of demands in 20 minutes
Play	
Disagreements	
Find resource	
Fix something	
Routine – e.g. toilet	
Talk	

Figure 7.9 Demand schedule

why this is happening. Staff will need to look at the organisation and management issues raised in Chapter 2, and consider the number of resources, whether there is a culture of high-and low-status toys or whether the children are not able to negotiate. Once there are some explanations then solutions can be found. Staff may want to go further and analyse who is making particular demands; it may be that the demands are about children wanting staff to play with them. It may be worth checking to see if only certain children are asking for this and others are not getting as much adult input. There may be organisational problems, or it may be something more subtle, involving the expectations within the class and that children are not expected to be autonomous and think through their own ideas. They then simply access equipment which does not involve much input from them. By making changes to what is available in the outdoor area, by working more closely with groups of children, these demands could be lessened and in this way staff can use their valuable time better.

Another method of recording that could be used is the Effective Early Learning's three types of 'engagement' to analyse practice with children. This describes:

- sensitivity to children
- stimulation of children
- giving some autonomy to children about what they want to learn

as three types of interaction an adult may have with a child (Pascal et al. 1997). They found that staff were able to react sensitively to children, but there was a lack in the other two types of engagement. However, practitioners showed greater sensitivity, stimulation and autonomy after taking part in the EEL project. Children were measured in terms of their level of 'involvement', which was demonstrated through creativity, persistence, energy, precision and concentration. There were five levels, from low involvement to high. It would be helpful to use these to look at one's own practice to see how one reacts to children. The methods of observing adults and children are based on the work of Professor Ferre Laevers of Leuven University, Belgium.

Discussion

The way adults behave does affect children and their learning. Staff need to join in with children's play and all activities. Sometimes the adult may need to support reticent children in their play, sometimes they may need to help children use negotiation to solve problems, sometimes they may need to challenge stereotypical play. Their mere presence at an activity raises its status and enhances the self-esteem of the children involved in the activity. Staff need to be sensitive to all children, not just react to those who make demands. Staff need to be aware they have both boys and girls in their settings and what their respective needs are. Analysis of one's work helps to make sure that the whole environment is working in the best way for all children. Children need to be in a safe but not risk-free environment and adults need to be cognisant that one can never have a totally safe space just as it can 'never be a totally safe life' (Walsh 1991: 34).

Questions

1. Do you focus equally on the quiet, passive, domestically orientated play that occupies so much time for so many young girls? Do you feel concern about the impact on their physical development of an excess of sedentary activity? (from Holland 2003).
2. Take Figures 7.8 and 7.9 and use the forms to make detailed observations in the setting. What do you find out? What can be improved and how?
3. List all the tidying-up activities in the setting. Make the list child friendly with words and pictures. Decide which children would be best to tackle which jobs, for example the older tackling the more complicated jobs. Over the course of a week or two, ensure all the children get to understand how the various pieces of equipment should be carried, tidied, washed. Talk to the children about how you would like everyone to help at tidy-up time and discuss the fairness of all helping. Then put the system into operation. Be prepared for chaos initially! If the whole group is very young, one can still start to instil a view of helping, even if they move one brick into a box.
4. Looking back to Chapter 2 Moyles argues that some things need to be explicitly taught and some things can be left to experimentation. As a staff group, list what skills need to be taught. These might include cutting, gluing, woodwork, ball and bat skills. Even very specific things need to be taught such as angling the paper to the left if the child is left handed.
5. What can be defined as safe? What impact does this safety have on children and their play? (taken from Walsh 1991: 34).

Section 3 Making changes

A successful playground is often a deceptively simple affair, a natural playscape which is, however, full of subtle stimuli and sensory experiences. It will suggest but not dictate a wide range of responses and usage, allowing children flexibility to experiment with things and ideas in their own time and at their own pace.

(Walsh 1991: 9)

Developing outdoor provision

Summary

We never stand still in education, we are always reflecting, always attempting to improve whatever we do. So this chapter is about developing outdoor provision whatever stage you are at, whether at the beginning with the idea to build a nursery, or with an established garden which needs a re-look. See the Contacts and resources section for many of the ideas suggested here.

Size and layout

Rooms and gardens can be too big or too small, and both can create specific difficulties. In the outdoor area which is too small, children can simply be knocking into each other, ball activities are almost impossible to organise, running and spatial awareness hard to cater for. Lack of space can also affect behaviour. Bates (1996) made a study of children in a playgroup, systematically observing them over a three-month period and found that children's behaviour did change as the number of children increased and so the space available decreased. More crowding led to more aggressive behaviour. Hutt (1972) came to the same conclusions more than 30 years ago when studying three- to eight-year-olds, playing in different group sizes. The larger the group, the more aggressive the behaviour towards people and equipment. We therefore need not only to make sure the space is available but that the area is of a generous size. On the other hand, in too large a garden children can feel lost and staff can spend most of the time checking up where everyone is, as opposed to playing with the children. It would be ideal if all outdoor areas were of an optimum size so that children were able to move around freely, without fear of crashing into things or people, and big enough to hold the variety of activities that should be available in the garden but not too spread out. Walsh, looking at Australian provision, details specific amounts of space for early years outdoor settings (ECA 2004) (see Figure 8.1). Unfortunately our government is not as farsighted. With the introduction of the Foundation Stage, new outdoor areas are being built and sensibly some schools are taking time to really plan out what they want. Where schools are being dictated to by architects and builders, unnecessary problems are being created for staff and children.

75 place centre: 15 sq m per place
40 place centre: 20 sq m per place
25 place centre: 25 sq m per place

Minimum 9.3 sq m per place
Veranda or transitional area: minimum width 4m, 2.5 sq m per place and/or
around 10% of the total site

Figure 8.1 Size of outdoor space and veranda
Source: ECA (2004)

The shape of the outdoor area needs to be compact, simply a continuation from the building wall; not long and narrow, a view echoed in an Australian policy document (ECA 2004). If the garden is all around the building, staff can feel obliged to supervise as opposed to play with children. If there are various spaces dotted about the outdoor space or if the garden is all around the building staff need to trust the children and allow them to exist sometimes out of sight.

A small space

An outdoor play area can be very small, but when viewed in conjunction with the indoor area, can become a reasonably-sized space. In the Bilton (1993) study, it was found that the difficulties created by a garden being too small for 26 children to work in at once were immediately overcome by accepting one of the principles of outdoor play (see Chapter 4) that indoors and outdoors are a combined environment and that both are available at the same time. So a small outdoor space can be made much more useful and manageable if available in conjunction with indoors. It is highly unlikely that all children will want to go outdoors at once, but will pass from activity to activity, moving from indoors to outdoors as need arises. In nurseries which have small outdoor areas, but where staff consider outdoors and indoors together, it is indeed rare for one area to become full with children. If the garden does reach saturation point then children will have to be asked to come back later. They are very accepting when told a maximum of 'four children at the water tray', so they can accept 'only x number of children in the garden'. It is obviously not an ideal situation.

What about the garden which is so small that it is impossible to have a balance of activities going on at the same time? Starting from the premise that one cannot provide all activities as the space is too small will mean that the space constraints dictate the curriculum; starting with the needs of the children and then working out how best to provide for them will ensure that the teacher, and not the space, is in charge of the curriculum. If you are trying to offer a balanced curriculum then you need to offer it despite the restrictions. Many nursery schools do not have a school hall; this does not mean, however, that music and movement is abandoned; instead, ways of providing for it have to be found. It is a case of allocating different time or space to accommodate the relevant activities; furniture and equipment may well have to be moved out of the way for the session and replaced when the movement lesson has finished.

Young children are physically active, and where a classroom and outdoor area are small, children still have a right to be physically active. In order to maximise space, it may be necessary to remove superfluous furniture from indoors and outdoors. The primary playground can be utilised when the older children are not using it for the practice of fine motor skills. All the children may have to go into the area and practise together and this is not the best approach, but it may be the only option available.

If imaginative play is seen as essential, then it may be possible to use the outdoor area exclusively for this and other activities such as gross motor may have to be timetabled inside daily, similar to a timetabled PE lesson. Or again, it could be that the primary playground is used for the vigorous activity with one member of staff inside, one member of staff with the children in the outdoor area and one in the primary playground. Bikes can create problems in a small outdoor play area and it may be best simply to dispense with them. The skills involved in bike riding can be catered for to a degree, through climbing and running games, and it may be better to encourage group rather than solitary play by having a truck in the garden which children can use together. If seen as an essential experience, bikes could be provided at a separate time or again in the primary playground. Gardening work may have to be organised on a rotational basis, with one group of children at a time doing the work. Tubs, plant pots and boxes can all be used for seeds, bulbs and plants if there is no garden space.

A large space

When a garden space is large it is important to consider carefully how children and staff will respond to it, bearing in mind studies such as Sylva et al. (1980) and Smith and Connelly (1981) which concluded that children found it harder to settle and play in large open spaces and in larger groups. Neill (1982) found that, in large open space, adults tended to oversee a range of activities rather than become involved with specific children. This view was highlighted by a teacher in the Bennett et al. (1997) studies who felt too much space was difficult to manage without additional help.

The larger nursery garden is often associated with the nursery/Foundation Stage school setting which may have a number of classes accessing one garden. It may be worth considering dividing the area so that each class has a designated piece of garden, an extension of their classroom, with the rest of the space as free access to all children. This can often be seen in nurseries built prior to, or during, the Second World War with the outdoor space immediately outside the classroom possessing not only a veranda but also dividing walls between the classes. In this way children can play in or out in their specific class and garden and then later can use the whole space. In this way children have the opportunity to feel secure in their home base but also have the opportunity to branch out and meet a wider group of people.

One concern with a large and totally open space is that it can become similar to an infant/junior playground. Children can feel lost in such a large space, play can become somewhat frantic and less developed and it is very difficult from the staff's point of view not only to evaluate children at work, but also to play with and teach them. It is rare to find actual classrooms for 60 or 80 plus children, because it is felt children need smaller numbers in order to feel secure. Even in an open-plan situation, where children might be working in fairly large groups, children usually have a home base, a smaller known area, which is theirs.

Outside needs to be viewed in the same light and in some spaces it may be worth considering breaking up a large outdoor area, which is accessed by a large number of children, and creating home bays outside. It may be appropriate to divide the whole garden so that each class has its own garden area with a repeat of all or some of the activities and equipment within each area, although of course this may be restricted by cost. Where a school does have a large outdoor space accessible by children from all classes, staff need to be very attentive in their observations of the children and be able to talk easily as a staff group.

Fixed equipment

More and more nurseries have purchased large play structures and playhouses similar to those found in playgrounds in public parks. In part, this may have occurred as staff, unsure about outdoor play, have seen such fixtures as filling the void of insecurity. It is often considered a good way of bringing parents together for a very evident fund-raising scheme. This type of permanent fixture is rarely apparent in the class inside. Although they may be of use in the public park it is doubtful whether they are of much use for the learning of young children in the early years setting. The study by Brown and Burger (1984) found that the playground with the most fixed equipment and which looked very pleasing had in fact the lower rating of play. The difficulty with the fixed play structure was that only a finite number of movements were possible and children had no opportunities to change it. What the children had in the playground with the highest play rating was equipment which they could manoeuvre, which had a number of approaches, and a variety of differing areas. Playgrounds which encouraged good quality play had features such as linkages of equipment, flexible material – those which can be changed, manipulated or combined, graduated challenges and a variety of possible experiences (Johnson et al. 1987).

Blatchford (1989), looking into playgrounds in the primary school, argues that the 'contemporary' playground equipment can do little to help children develop and may even do less than the 'traditional' equipment. A study by Walsh (1993), looking at outdoor play in Australia, and referring to research both there and in the USA, argues that fixed playground equipment is of little use with young children. She points to research which shows that children prefer creative playgrounds; action-orientated equipment over fixed equipment, because the resources can be adapted to suit the children's play ideas. In this study, the fixed equipment was used for less time and in less complex ways. Frost and Campbell (1985) found primary-aged children preferred movable and complex equipment which had a number of options and could be used in a variety of ways. This was because children could change it rather than have to adapt their play to the limitation of static equipment. The beautifully designed and costly climbing apparatus stretches the designer's imagination, but does little to stretch the child's. Sometimes it is possible to do too much, to build something too perfect, so the child has little to do. Blocks may not look good or real, but the possibilities for their use are endless. Equipment needs to be simple, natural, unlimiting, interpretable, moveable and adaptable (Miller 1972).

Barbour (1999) made a study of two school playgrounds in Texas for use by children during their break time. One playground was what is described as traditional and had such things as see-saws, jungle gyms, slides, all of which were simply for exercise. The other playground had much more variety of equipment and included a play structure with lots of parts – tunnels, bridge, rings, wide platform, steering wheel, overhead ladder – plus various loose parts – building blocks, wooden planks, plastic spools, tools, chairs, containers and sandpit, playhouses, garden area. The equipment in this playground was often designed for more than one child. The author looked at the children with both high and low physical competence and concluded that the playground that emphasised physical play tended to segregate children and stopped some children being able to socialise. Competitive play rather than cooperative play was being encouraged in the traditional playground with fixed equipment. She argues that playgrounds that support a range of play types help 'foster the social involvement of all children regardless of (their) level of motor proficiency' (Barbour 1999: 95). This study found that the equipment provided actually affected social development and as a consequence must have been affecting personal and emotional development. It seems fairly obvious really, but if we want all children to attempt to work together we need to provide them with equipment that helps that, not just equipment that some children can use confidently. She further argues that playgrounds that focus on physical skill are giving high status to those who can achieve this and low status to those who cannot. Although this study is dealing with primary playgrounds, the findings are relevant to the Foundation Stage as it deals with fixed equipment versus movable.

For fixed equipment to be of use to young children it needs to have loose parts which children can attach themselves and thereby change the structure (Walsh 1993, Pellegrini 1991). The old-fashioned, smaller, non-permanent fixed climbing frame has this potential. Complexity has to be the key to sustaining a child's interest, enjoyment and development and needs to be built into play provision (Frost 1986). Enabling children to incorporate planks, ladders and resources so that they can make spaceships, boats, homes, building sites, and so on, may be one way round the problem. Sometimes this is not possible as the bars on the fixed play structure are too wide and homemade planks and ladders will have to be made. Likewise, playhouses can look good, but often be quite small inside and very expensive. These fixed houses can be poorly used as there are few resources provided. Just as with any role-play area children need to be inspired by a focus and need good resources to play with. So, for example, the house could be a fairy-tale castle, a home, a florist, a railway station waiting room, with all the necessary paraphernalia associated with that particular setting. A florist could have flowers, large vases, paper, sticky tape, till, money, ribbon and scissors. This play could then flow into the rest of outdoors and indoors. Bikes could have baskets or boxes attached to the front bars to hold flowers for delivery. If staff show interest in an area, by resourcing it and working in it, children will do also. If a house has one table, one chair and a broken bed it says to children 'we do not care, so why should you'. Even sand and water pits need to have accessible loose parts, not what the staff decide to throw in. A fantastic example of versatile water play is in the Walsh (1991) book and includes a water course, where the water can be dammed and bridged and played in. The creation of a water course would be much more useful than some fixed climbing frame.

A fixed structure can mean that staff feel obliged to include it in the planning, and then list what activities it might be used for. Unfortunately, in such a situation it is the equipment which is controlling the curriculum. It would be more effective to list the learning bays or areas of learning and then see how such permanent structures can be incorporated into the various bays or areas. However, it may be necessary to actually get rid of such items, if they are taking up too much valuable space.

Blatchford (1989) issues a word of warning about purchasing fixed equipment. He suggests that the purchase of costly outdoor equipment is often not based on clear research, as the purchase of indoor equipment generally is. Instead it is more likely to be a hit-and-miss affair, with a hope that the children will like it. For the class or school it can be not only costly but can also take up a major part of the outdoor area. Young children need space and this can be greatly affected by the fixing of a huge play structure. The only well-used piece of fixed equipment is monkey bars. A school that has both climbing frame and monkey bars found the latter was still used after many years but not the former. Another school found children initially keen to use a newly installed climbing frame but two years later no interest was shown in this costly item. The purchase of fixed equipment needs to be considered from the point of view of children's learning, not the needs of parents to fundraise or the head to show off to visitors.

Slopes

A very versatile addition to a Foundation Stage outdoor area is a slope. A steep grassed slope can be used to manoeuvre oneself or objects up and down. Its shape lends itself to encouraging cooperative play, for example when pushing a truck up the hill. It is safe and can offer a major challenge with little chance of danger. It can give as much a thrill to be at the top of a steep slope as being at the top of a climbing frame. A rope can be securely fixed into the ground at the top, to aid with moving up and down. If there is potential to have a slope then it would be beneficial to fundraise for one.

The weather

The most unpredictable component of working outside is undoubtedly the weather! However, it has to be worked with so that children do not miss out. In terms of design and layout it is important to take into consideration all possible permutations of weather, including rain, sun, wind, extreme heat and extreme cold. Obviously with the latter two types of weather, protection can be offered in the form of clothing and creams. But the space also needs the protection afforded by trees and shrubs. When building a new class or redesigning an old one it is necessary to consider which part of the school grounds is most protected from the wind, sun and cold. Strong and persistent wind or continual shade can impinge on play and concentration and such an environment is not conducive to learning. The outdoor area needs to be protected from the wind either by buildings, fencing, trees and shrubs or a combination of these. Although a south-facing area is lovely it needs a great deal of protection with good shade, otherwise it will be too hot. Nurseries in Frankfurt are always built so the garden is south facing, but then shade is created (Bergard 1995). Ideally then, an outdoor area which receives some sun and some shade is the best. When considering the needs of part-time children, both sessions need to benefit from the sun and shade. The ground needs to be checked to see how the drainage is. There is no point creating a lovely place which then collects the rain for 9 months of the year. (Learning through Landscapes offer information about such issues, see Chapter 10.)

The weather also affects inside. You need to make sure that the fresh air comes into the class everyday, but also that the space inside does not get too hot nor cold. Chapter 1 details research about how lack of oxygen and overheated classrooms affect children's ability to work well. So the doors and windows need to be open daily, but do not have to stay open all the time, but can be opened and closed as the need arises. However, the door to the outside area may need to be kept open continuously. This can be a problem in the cold weather as it can make the room too cold. Consider purchasing a see-through plastic door similar to those seen in the butcher's freezer (see Chapter 10). This is a perfect way to ensuring the heat stays in but children can see who is coming towards the door so no one crashes into each other.

Covered areas

In an ideal world there would be a veranda/covered way/transition terrace, so that children can be outside whatever the weather. The nursery pioneers considered the veranda an essential component of the nursery. Many nurseries built years ago also had sliding doors so that one side of the nursery could open out completely. In Australia it is the norm to have a veranda: 'In common with many Australian preschool buildings, there was no firm distinction between indoors and out. Sliding doors created an easy flow from playroom to patio to playground' (McLean 1991: 71). If money is available or if the parent group wishes to have a specific item to raise funds for, a veranda or covered way would be ideal. A cheaper option could be a shop awning which can be pulled out when needed.

Pergolas are another way of offering protection in the outdoor area. These can either be attached to the class outside or built as a separate fixture in the garden. The siting needs careful consideration as it should not take over the garden. Climbing plants trained up the sides can soon give an enclosed feel to the pergola and if trained across the top can offer some protection from the elements. A thick canvas or bamboo sheeting across the top can be used to offer greater protection from the rain, wind and sun. Children can incorporate such a structure into their play, and use blocks and crates to make a hidey-hole.

Trees are not as useful for offering protection from the rain but do offer good shade from the sun. Whether taking over a class or setting up a new one it is important to have trees planted as soon as possible. The longer the delay, the longer it will take to get the shelter benefits. A reasonably-sized tree purchased from a garden centre should be offering protection within three years.

It is always possible to rig up makeshift protection outside, whether there is already permanent protection in the area or not. For example, a sheet of canvas can be strung up attached to a fence, tree, shrub or wall close at hand. Climbing frames, A-frames or even ladders attached horizontally can be draped with fabric to offer shade. Another possibility is a large umbrella, such as those found on the beach. These can offer shade from the sun and in winter some degree of shelter and can act as rest spots for children for imaginative play purposes, games or simple quiet reflection.

Surfaces

It is preferable to have different surfaces in the outdoor area, just as there are different surfaces within the class. With different surfaces different activities can be offered. A hard surface is probably the best type of flooring for the area in front of the class or access point, so that children can always go out and use the area even if the grass is like a quagmire.

A hard surface is better for manoeuvring wheeled vehicles on. Naylor (1985) looked at various studies which reveal that children prefer hard surfaces because they can use wheeled toys easily on such a surface. It can be easier to build on a hard surface. The grass is a better surface for climbing and for actually sitting on, as it is softer! Imaginative play works well on either surface. If there is only a hard surface and no earth, then plants and shrubs can be planted in pots, tubs or any container which will hold soil. Where there is no grass, it is necessary to provide carpet squares or pieces of thick material for children to sit on and to use as gathering spots. Long term, it is preferable to get a hard surface if there is none and similarly a grassed or a soil area if none exists already.

Some settings have had a shock-absorbent surface built which can then be used for any piece of equipment, not just for one fixed climbing frame. In this way the safety surface is more flexible and the staff can use it as they wish. If there is mostly grass outside, in the long term some of it needs to be taken up and replaced with a hard surface. In the meantime children can wear Wellingtons boots when it is very muddy and wet outside. Children soon learn to wash down boots in a bowl of water with a long-handled scrubbing brush. Children will only find out about muddy areas and how to walk on them if they are allowed to experience them. Viewing each day separately and deciding whether children can go on the grass or need boots will ensure that the outdoor area is used as much as possible. Blanket rules about 'no one on the grass in winter' mean a valuable resource is lost.

Seating

One of the noticeable differences about some outdoor areas in comparison to others is the distinct lack of seating. It is, therefore, not surprising that some staff find it tiring working in the outdoor area and some children find it daunting when there is no seating. Having somewhere to sit has a significant and immediate impact on the play within the outdoor area; it also helps staff feel happier about working out there. Chairs from inside can be used outside, or child chairs can be purchased specifically for use outside. Crates with planks balanced across can act as a seat, so too can a large tyre. Seating which is movable is much more useful as it is versatile. A proper garden seat can be added, but in some areas it may have to be fixed to the ground so it cannot be stolen.

The look of the place

One needs to make the space into a place (Tovey 2007) that children can have owner-ship of, and feel proud of it. But the outdoor area is not a suburban garden, with its carefully tended rose beds, nor is it a play park with a wooden play structure. It is a working environment for young children and as such it needs to look stimulating and full of possibilities. It needs to be exciting, and in order for this to be so, it needs to have resources and equipment which have unlimited possibilities.

Obviously it is important to make the outdoor class look as attractive as possible so that children and staff want to go into the environment and feel tranquil in the setting. This can be achieved with the planting of shrubs and trees, the use of good quality equip-ment and the careful laying out of the resources and equipment. Gilkes discusses how what she describes as 'one of the most sterile and unattractive play areas one could imag-ine' was transformed (1987: 73). She is realistic and discusses how much harder it is to effect change in the outdoor area, but with a good deal of time, effort, money, staff and parental involvement plus help from other adults, the area was changed and made a more interesting and appealing area. Shrubs and trees do make such a difference and as Walsh (1991: 21) argues: 'ideally, plants should be the most dominant feature of the playground'. With shrubs and trees it is easy to create a space where children can go and get away from adults. Figure 8.2 lists a number of easily grown trees and shrubs. The Royal Horticultural Society and *BBC Gardening* both have websites where you can explore the huge range of plants for any space (see Chapter 10). ECA (1994) argue that

Alder
Birch
Buddleia
Clematis (*montana*)
Coronilla
Cornus
Flowering quince (*Chaenomeles speciosa*)
Forsythia
Hebe
Jew's Mallow (*Kerria*)
Juniper (*Juniperus*)
Lavender (*Lavandula angustifolia*)
Mexican orange blossom (*Choisya ternata*)
Oak
Rosemary (*Rosmarinus officinalis*)
Tree mallow (*Lavatera*)
Weigela
Willow
If three trees are put in the same hole and the leaders taken out, this will quite quickly give good coverage.
See Cooper and Johnson (1991) for a list of poisonous plants.

Figure 8.2 Easy trees and shrubs

the space beyond and outside the garden is important to consider. Attention needs to be given to 'views, vistas, attractive natural features' for those arriving at the setting and those actually in the setting.

Plastic and coloured equipment, resources or furniture must be avoided. This is essential. A place cannot be made aesthetically pleasing with coloured pencils for fencing, plastic red mushrooms or those horrid multi-coloured plastic bobble cars. These are an insult to children and of no use. The outdoor space should consist of as much natural material as possible and if wood is being used it must not be painted. The world is abundant in beautiful natural materials.

Storage

Outdoor equipment can be big, bulky and cumbersome and consequently needs considerable space for storage. Both the Gilkes (1987) and Bilton (1993) studies highlighted staff concerns about moving outdoor equipment; this is made doubly difficult if there is no shed. In this case it can mean staff are required to move equipment long distances and around awkward spaces. The lack of a shed can be a hindrance to the use of the outdoor play area, as the movement of equipment can be difficult, while the use of indoor areas to store equipment can decrease the amount of usable space inside.

Without a shed it is worth looking at the present equipment and considering what is not used much, what is perhaps not very versatile and so can be dispensed with. This can then be replaced by more versatile and less cumbersome equipment, such as imaginative play resources and bricks. In this way the lack of a shed is not so problematic in terms of moving equipment about, as the reduced amount and size of equipment is easier to handle. If the area is not prone to vandalism, things made of plastic, aluminium and coated metal can be left outside, but would need periodic cleaning and checking.

If it is possible to have a shed this should be organised to maximise the space available, with shelves, hooks and labels. Staff need to view the shed as any other storage space, which children can access. Without 26 bikes the shed can become a very useable space, that children know they can access as the equipment has been safely stored. There are a whole range of sheds now. A cycle shed bought from a local DIY store can be used to house blocks, or sand equipment or even imaginative play scenarios (Bilton 2002). If there is the potential for arson then metal sheds are much better than wood. In one setting they have the back part of a container truck as the shed, this is so solid that vandals cannot destroy it, but they do have lots of garden space for it. Sand can be stored in a small wooden box similar to an old coal shed. In this way it can be used about the garden rather than in one place, but care does have to be taken as sand on a hard surface can get very slippery. Large ice-cream tubs can be used to hold shells, bottle tops, cones and the like. But one can also simply keep equipment in place and attach quality thick tarpaulin and cover when it rains or at the end of the day (see Figure 8.3). Children's clothing, hats, gloves, coats and Wellington boots can be stored either in boxes or on racks (see Figure 8.4, see Chapter 10).

Figure 8.3 Covering equipment in tarpaulin

Figure 8.4 Rack for Wellington boots, De Bohun Primary School

Tap

An outside tap and hose attachment makes life very much easier and ensures children and staff can:

- collect water for use in their play and scientific experimentation
- water plants
- wash down areas if they have become dirty
- create puddles and rain for experimentation
- fill paddling pools/water trays/mud holes.

Designers

Designers and planners need to listen to teachers when they have the privilege of designing an outdoor space for children (Walsh 1991). Just because they know about landscape architecture does not mean they know anything about children's gardens. If a landscape architect has a lovely time designing a garden it is likely it will not be much use to children. It may look stunning but perceived by children to be owed by adults not them. If they do not have ownership they will not feel able to work to their true level. This type of environment cannot be adapted, changed or modified just as a fixed climbing frame cannot. Landscape architects need to concern themselves with creating secret areas, similar to a forest space, where children can drape fabric over branches and dig in the mud. They need to concern themselves with creating shade, a slope and a covered way, but not much more than this. If they create wavy paths, willow structures and sails then what do children do? If we go back to the Introduction and consider what games were played by adults when they were children they didn't have ready-made environments. The environment has to be one that can develop over time and that is the beauty of a true 'place'. Inside and out need to be planned together so 'they complement and flow from one to another' (Walsh 1991: 9).

Primary playtime

I have made it crystal clear that primary or for that matter secondary playtime is not how true outdoor learning should be organised, but some of the lessons learned about the early years' outdoor space can be used in the playtime setting.

It would appear that the playtime break has been part of the school system for a long time and although some have ventured the need for improvements, little has changed in the playground. Seaborne (cited in Visser and Greenwood 2005) looks at the development of the school playground and offers examples of those since the 1600s who suggest the playground needs a covered way and equipment needs to be provided. More recently, Pellegrini and Blatchford have both been pivotal in researching playground activity. If we think of playtime as roughly an hour at lunch and one fifteen-minute morning break this accounts for just under one-fifth of the school day. It seems staggering that so little attention has been paid to it and, as Blatchford argues, almost every other aspect of education has been tampered with but playtime, which 'could lay claim to being the forgotten part of the school day' (1989: 4).

In 2006 the government produced a pamphlet entitled 'Learning Outside the Classroom Manifesto', urging people to pledge support for learning outdoors by signing online. 'Outside' for the government is basically any experience away from the classroom, including learning outside in the school grounds, school visits to parks, participation in outdoor adventure, fieldwork studies, visits to environmental centres, theatres, museums and residential trips. Sadly the government has managed to misunderstand that playtime is also an experience away from the classroom, where children spend on average one-quarter to one-fifth of their time every single school day. 'Learning outside the classroom is about raising achievement through an organised approach to learning in which direct experience is of prime importance. This is not only about what we learn but importantly how and where we learn' (DfES 2006: 3). So in fact for the government a visit to a place inside would constitute learning outside the classroom, but not to the playground at playtime!

Research has suggested high levels of bullying in playgrounds (Whitney and Smith 1993, Berger 2007), children not wishing to venture out at playtime (Mooney et al. 1990) and unfair opportunities in terms of age, race, ethnicity and gender (Blatchford 1998). The response of government and many schools has been to shorten or even remove break times. This seems an irresponsible response, given break is a time when children can learn so much. They are freer to pursue friendships, to learn how to cooperate and get on with others and to be physically active (Blatchford 1998, Tovey 2007, Yilmaz and Bulut 2007). Looking to the Opies (1969) playtime was a central place for practising and improving language and learning about the social skills of life. But negative lessons can also be learned.

Primary playtime whether it be at lunchtime or break-time can have many of the problems discussed in this book and many of those issues can be solved by using the strategies discussed here. For example primary playtime involves a large number of children going into a large and open space with little for the children to do. They are joined by untrained adults who are often unable to wield any power because: 'you're not a teacher, so I do not need to take notice of you'. Children can be hurt physically and mentally. After the break and before lessons can resume teachers may be dealing with the resolution of a range of issues, which have occurred in the break.

If we look at this chapter regarding a 'large space' it suggests that children can feel lost and do not necessarily settle in a large outdoor space. To help the situation and lessen the confrontations and the accidents it is important to give children things to do. But this does not necessarily mean providing expensive climbing apparatus (see the section on fixed equipment above). It does mean providing spaces and places (see Chapter 5), space which gives opportunities for a variety of activities and also places which children can call their own. The space will of course need to be sufficient to play games such as football, or basketball or racket ball. Spaces where children can play 'it', 'stuck in the mud'. Spaces where children can skip and play clapping games. Places where children can go and play with the leaves, the twigs, the mud, the moss, the stones; where they can create imaginary scenes whatever they may be. Places where they can just sit and be and chat without the adults watching. Places where they do not feel part of a huge crowd but part of a small group of friends.

Playgrounds need to be divided up so that children have a number of micro-environments (see Chapter 5). This can easily be done with the planting of trees and shrubs. It does not take much to create an enclosed area of buddleia, kerria, agapanthus. Although these will not create the undergrowth of leaves, moss, and twigs that are a by-product of a wooded area made up of trees, they at least create a hidden place. Long term, one would want to create an area made of trees and shrubs, with log seating and some kind of natural path through it.

By making improvements there is no guarantee that everything will be perfect in the garden. The study by Visser and Greenwood (2005) did change the ethos of the playground and demonstrates that adding playground games and activities lessened the incidence of minor altercations, but did not lessen the number of severe disputes. Staff in the study indicated that they were dealing with fewer disputes and the atmosphere was far pleasanter on the games days than on non-games days. But as the authors indicate severe, possibly long-standing and maybe deeply entrenched incidents, concerning for example sexism, racism or religious differences which led to severe disputes, were not lessened with the introduction of games. More needed to be done to improve this.

As aired in Chapter 6, Connolly (2003) discusses the issues of girls and boys at playtime and how girls in particular can be put into a position of subjugation and in the same text Benjamin argues that the ability to excel in sport and in particular football 'is one of the foremost sites for the production of masculinities in English primary schools' (2003: 102). Further, Benjamin cites research that emphasises success at football and success in school and for those with additional needs the desire to reach success on the football pitch as they do not have success elsewhere in the school system. In terms of girls Benjamin suggests that there may not be as many girls as boys identified as SEN, as they do not set themselves up as such and actually get support from others to succeed sufficiently, whereas the boys are unable to help themselves. Connolly makes suggestions for improvements to playtime in the light of his study which should help improve playgrounds for both sexes, namely:

- there needs to be a whole-school policy approach and understanding of the playground
- playgrounds need to be divided and offer a range of play opportunities, to help stop the segregation by gender
- staff need to watch what is going on and if activities and games become gendered, staff need to intervene to stop this
- staff need to recognise the power of gender in shaping young children's identities and become involved in talking to children about what is happening
- staff need to involve the children in deciding about their playground
- staff need to be aware that schools differ in what happens in the playground therefore relationships are quite context bound in the culture of the area (Connolly 2003: 128–9).

Jago, as we saw in the Chapter 6, found girls were less active than boys in the playground, and argued that we need to ensure we have a balance of activities and games available outside so boys and girls become physically involved. He found that there were attitudinal (staff and parents), structural (lack of time, space or equipment) and functional (lack of knowledge on behalf of children, staff and parents) barriers to ensuring play was successful at playtime. He argues that there needs to be enough playground stimulus, space and time available; that there needs to be the dissemination of knowledge to children, staff and parents about the why and how of activity and that there needs to be 'gender sensitive' games available (2002: 188) to ensure all children benefit from the games outside (see Figure 8.5). This activity can make a significant contribution to the Health Education Authority's recommendation for children to have one hour per day of exercise. He also noted that the structural changes had the most impact on making change but that the impetus needed to be kept up to ensure the children stayed more active. It is not a case of having a skipping workshop and thinking everything is going to be good in the playground or adding some balls and bats. Making improvements

> Structural provision
> - playground stimulus
> - space
> - time.
>
> Gender-sensitive provision
> - differences in male and female activity
> - gender-specific interventions.
>
> Educational provision
> - knowledge of why to be active
> - knowledge of how to be active.

Figure 8.5 The Jago (2002) play activity provision model for optimising break time physical activity

is much more involved and ongoing. The suggestion that the children should be involved in making changes and having real impact, not consultation without any chance of affecting change, is summed up by a child in the Milligan research: 'we could say all the games we like and agree on some games that we could play together' (2008: 28).

It may be time to change the focus of the adults outside, rather than dinner ladies or lunchtime controllers, who smack of supervision and control. In the past there were always teachers in the playground whose presence helped to create calm. With the change in the workload model, teachers stopped going into the playground. Some schools are now taking on play leaders as opposed to controllers. Although we do need to guard against the take-over of the playground by adults as this would be completely counterproductive. Whatever the title of the adults outside at playtime, they need training as they could be creating half the problems which occur. Looking to Chapter 2, the discussion about play fighting needs to be understood by all that venture into a primary playground. Adults need to know the difference between play fighting and real fighting, as they could be halting perfectly functional and useful play, misunderstanding rough and tumble as real aggression and not picking up on the children who do not know the difference. The adults need to take on board the work of Whitebread (referenced in Chapter 6) which argues for children to become more self-regulatory and demonstrates that those who are will go on to be more able as they grow older. Adults need to learn when to step back and when to intervene. Adults need to know about gender segregation and control. It is much more than just standing around in the playground chatting.

Making playtime work for children and staff

One infant school in Maidenhead and one particular teacher whom I have had the pleasure to work with has over many years endeavoured to develop playtime practice and has been successful in helping children. In 2003, due to the poor

Three distinct activities for children to partake of:

- playground challenge
- huff and puff equipment
- elite challenge.

The playground challenge consists of five physical activities, developing different muscle groups using the existing climbing equipment. The five activities are to:

1. climb along a wall using foot and arm holds
2. skip 10 times with the large skipping rope
3. balance along the chains
4. play hopscotch
5. swing along the monkey bars without dropping down.

The huff and puff equipment is materials which became available for schools and training was given to teachers and teaching assistants (www.qca.org.uk). A shed was purchased to separate out this specialist equipment from the standard PE equipment to give it more prominence and the equipment is topped up yearly with the supermarket vouchers.

The elite challenge was created by the demand of children who had achieved the playground challenge and wanted to go further. It involves five more challenges:

1. walking on stilts
2. balancing along the log trail
3. skipping rhymes
4. achieving the lo-lo ball
5. climbing the scramble net.

Figure 8.6 Improving the playground

behaviour at break time that was then impacting on the learning sessions after, the school decided to make changes to the playground routines. This involved three distinct improvements:

- playground challenge
- huff and puff equipment
- elite challenge (see Figure 8.6).

For the project to be successful and sustainable over time (this project started in 2003 and is still going strong) there were a number of actions that needed to be taken:

1 A dedicated member of staff willing to oversee it, to keep the project going, to keep staff and children enthusiastic about the project.
2 Manageable activities, sufficiently challenging but which were achievable for all children.

3 Clear procedures, rules and regulations, written down on laminated cards so they keep looking presentable. For example a game like hopscotch or a skipping game has to have agreed rules which everyone knows and then adheres to.

4 Involves the whole staff group, including the lunchtime staff. Having dedicated meetings about the project and how the project is going and how to improve it.

5 Real school council meetings where children actually see their ideas put into action, such as the elite challenge, which was suggested by the children.

6 A visible reward system, so each child has a card to be completed with a record as each achievement is gained. The school then offers a certificate for achieving the first lot of challenges and a metal badge for the elite challenge.

7 The launching of the challenge, for every new intake of children. The school actually made a video which can then be used by any member of staff to introduce the challenge.

8 A display of the features of the challenge, photographs of children performing the tasks, drawings and writing about the challenge and so on.

The success of the project lies with the changes in children. Porter shares the following outcomes from the project:

- children playing happily
- a drop in the number of children in trouble after play
- a decrease in the number wandering aimlessly
- playtime becoming more organised and controllable
- children getting more exercise
- a greater understanding of how and what to play
- increased self-esteem
- a more positive attitude of the lunch time staff (2005: 36).

This project puts into practice the guiding principles of this book, as seen in Chapter 4. So although much of this book is about early years' education, the principles apply across all ages. The playground is not left as an empty space but is seen as a learning environment, having maybe not an equal status with indoors, but at least having a much raised status. The space is divided into areas and staff value it. The space is seen as part of a whole-school approach and one which needs revisiting regularly. One could argue that children should not have this level of control in a space which they view as their own and where many feel we should not be imposing our will at all. Having seen this playground in action, children are still doing their own thing, there are still all sorts of other games going on whether it be chase games, imaginary scenarios, or simply chatting. The three activities did not appear to have deprived the children of their freedom, but they have given a focus, which at times all children need. The school has not stood still and has now provided a table for writing and drawing, with crayons, paper, colouring books and comics freely available. This was in response to children's demand.

The planned primary curriculum and outside

It is an April morning as I write this section. The weather is glorious. There is a cloudless sky, it is bright and sunny, but with a slight nip in the air, so jumpers and/or coats and, for some, gloves are needed. The air smells clean and fresh. And yet how many children in this nation are outside? I suspect few and as I stand outside I cannot hear any sound of children. We go on about children being outside, of using the outside to deliver the curriculum, to understand the curriculum and yet schools make very few opportunities for children to do so. And yet when you read these two accounts from two PGCE Primary students (see Figure 8.7), one working with children aged four and one working with children aged ten and eleven, outside is a highly significant place in which children can learn. Both accounts demonstrate that this is a place where some children can only function properly. In the first account children wrote who did not normally and in the second a child displaying challenging behaviour inside did not outside. It is, as these two students demonstrate, quite simple to get children outside working and learning. Fabian, wishing to make improvements for children moving from Foundation Stage to Key Stage 1 created 'SPACE time', when each class in the school had a designated time to use the outdoor areas for a learning activity, such as music and dance. She concluded that the Year 1 children enjoyed this time, which was freer and more creative (2005: 7). This is something schools could quite easily introduce.

Foundation Stage:
'Just a quick email to let you know that I finally got them outside! Sadly it wasn't a planned event. The children were brilliant: they were enthusiastic and I got some great evidence for my profile children. I also managed to get three children who are very reluctant to write inside to write outside. They saw me writing on my stickies and were intrigued and wanted to "make important university observations" too. So we sat on benches and made important observations together.'

Year 6:
'The children were doing some quick revision of the topic (parallel and perpendicular lines) on the Smartboard using a PowerPoint I had made, this lasted about 10–15 minutes. The main part of the lesson happened in the playground and involved going outside to find "real life" examples of parallel and perpendicular lines. The children (a low ability year 6 maths group) really gained a lot from it. One boy with behavioural issues really shone and came back with so many good examples which we talked about in the plenary. What I was particularly pleased about was that hardly any of the children knew what perpendicular lines were at the start of the lesson, but by the end, all of them were really eager to show me their examples of what they had found outside. What I also liked was that the children really had control of their learning in the playground. I didn't tell them areas to go, they did this for themselves. I also found that by taking them outside, their behaviour was brilliant, probably because they were very focused. I also think the 'real life' element helped – much more beneficial than working on lines – (which, let's face it, has the potential to be a very boring topic) from a worksheet or textbook.'

Figure 8.7 Two accounts of impromptu activities outside

Discussion

Layout, size, equipment, positioning, seating, the look, the weather will all impact on the outdoor learning space and the level of education to be offered. As Barbour argues, 'playground design influences children's physical competence, play behaviors, and ultimately their peer relationships' (1999: 96) and Frost (1992) contends that some outdoor learning environments more effectively support children's growth and development than others. The evidence in Chapter 2 supports this view. At the planning stage a basic reasonably large space with tarmac and grass needs to be created. Secret and hideaway places, shade and shelter must be created using shrubs and trees. A covered way is an essential. Designers and planners need to be considerate and humble towards children and teachers and listen to what is really needed. It is the children's imaginations which need stretching, not those of the adults. The space must not be created overnight: this is an organic thing and it will develop and change over the coming years.

Questions

1. Thinking about the children in your setting, and the age at which they leave you, what do you want them to look like in terms of skills, values, attitudes, knowledge and understanding? And what do you want them to be able to do when they leave, on different pieces of equipment, toys or resources. This has to be an average but you have to have an idea of what a three-year-old as opposed to a five- or seven-year-old looks like when playing for example with sand. If you do not then the children are likely to be still only pouring at age 7 when there is pouring but so much more to do with sand or water. I would want my five- to six-year-olds to be able to build effective tunnels in sand. But I would not want this with my two-year-olds. (Look back at Chapter 7 for a discussion on this.)

9

Epilogue

I will always remember one warm Monday morning in Hackney when Darren's mum rushed in and said, 'Darren writted his name. You didn't teach him, I didn't teach him!' I took this as a compliment. Darren and his friend Jason played almost exclusively in the garden, but used the indoors when they needed resources for their outdoor play. Darren had used the outdoor area in the way described in this book and he managed to 'writ' his name at four and a half years of age. His Mum had seen me play and work with Darren in a learning and teaching environment, so she did not consider I had formally taught him.

Indoors, and outdoors, together make a complete nursery learning and teaching environment. By the time Darren left to go to infant school his mum knew the power of outdoor play.

Making changes to practice has to be about taking small steps, many of which this book covers, but with such small steps, big leaps can be made.

Section 4 Further information

Contacts and resources

Local contacts for resources

Your local authority will have a contact person with regard to safety issues. Some local authorities may have a contact person for the Countryside Management Service, who can offer advice about improving the school grounds and possible sources of funding. Sawmills, country parks, forestry departments, etc. may be able to help with providing log sections and wooden boxes.

Royal Society for the Prevention of Accidents (RoSPA)

The Royal Society for the Prevention of Accidents has useful publications regarding safety, risk assessment, standards, but be aware not all directly relate to educational settings.

Edgbaston Park, 353 Bristol Road, Birmingham, B5 7ST Tel: 0121 248 2000 Fax: 0121 248 2000 Email: help@rospa.com Website: www.rospa.com

Playground office: 3 Earning Street, Godmanchester, Cambs, PE29 2JD Tel: 01480 411384 Website: www.rospaplaysafety.co.uk

Community Playthings

A supplier of extremely well-made and long-lasting equipment for all aspects of play – imaginative, physical, constructive. They are also very friendly and helpful. The blocks (unit and hollow, large and small) and wheelbarrows are a must in any early years' setting. They also sell a two-wheeler bike called a tweeler, scooters, pushcarts, child-sized stool, hideaway cubes. 'I made a unicorn' is a very useful booklet about play and is available from Community Playthings for trainers.

Robertsbridge, East Sussex, TN32 5DR Tel: 0800 387457 Website: www.community playthings.co.uk.

Sheds

Different types of storage are needed outside, so think laterally. Shedstore have a useful bike storage shed which can easily house things such as blocks, sand and water equipment and it is accessible for the children.

Shedstore LLP, Unit 1, Southview Park , Caversham, Reading, RG4 5AF. Tel: 0844 8500 710, Fax: 0844 8500 720. Website: www.shedstore.co.uk

Woodwork

Children can use woodwork tools as long as they are taught how to. The website www.tool-up.com has a decent bench and the height can be adjusted by cutting the legs down.

A-frames/trestles

It is hard to find A-frames or trestles with only specialist PE companies dealing with them now. Olympic Gymnasium Services sell a pack of two galvanised steel A-frames and two plastic-coated ladders. They also sell thick PE mats and wooden planks.

Olympic Gymnasium Services, Greatworth Park, Greatworth, Banbury, Oxfordshire, OX17 2HB. Tel: 01295 760 192 Fax: 01295 768 092 Email: sales@olympicgymnasium. com Website: www.olympicgymnasium.com

Creative Cascade

Storage for Wellington boots which can be left out all the time and supports for guttering for water play can both be bought from Creative Cascade UK Ltd. (see Figure 10.1).

1 Walnut Tree Cottage, Whempstead Rd, Benington, Herts SG2 7DH. Tel: 01438 869 788 Fax 0118 900 7804. Email: enquiries@creativecascade.co.uk Website: www.creative cascade.co.uk

Educational suppliers

NES Arnold, Hyde Buildings, Ashton Road, Hyde, Cheshire, SK14 4SH Tel: 08451204525 Fax: 0800 328 0001 Email: enquiries@nesarnold.co.uk Website: www.nesarnold.co.uk

Suppliers of foldaway climbing frames, 4-wheel carts, push chairs, gym equipment including A-frames/nests, benches, balls, bats, hoops, ropes and junior gardening equipment.

Figure 10.1 Water cascade

WESCO, Unit 20 Manvers Business Park, High Hazles Raod, Cotgrove, Nottingham NG12 3GZ Tel: 0115 989 9765 Fax: 0115 989 2401 Email: sales@wescouk.co.uk Website: www.wesco-group.co.uk

Ropes, balancing ropes, motor education kits, balls, mats, hoops, bean bags, PE benches, skipping ropes and pulling ropes made from hemp, bats, large hour glasses.

Other resources

Learning Outside in the EYFS: A Guide for Practitioners – this accessible DVD and book-let from Buckinghamshire County Council illustrates how the whole EYFS curriculum can be enhanced through the outdoor environment. Orders: Early Years and Childcare Service, Buckinghamshire County Council, The Friary, Rickfords Hill, Aylesbury, Bucks, HP20 2RT. Tel: 0845 3708090.

A Place to Learn – this is such a useful and practical document full of ideas about how to set up the environment for learning. A must in any setting. Orders: LEARN (Lewisham Early Years Advice and Resources Network) Forster Park School, Boundfield Road, London SE6 1PQ Tel: 0208 695 9806.

BBC Gardening (http://www.bbc.co.uk/gardening/) – a useful site for selecting plants, planning the gardening year, garden tools, organic gardening, patio gardens, pruning, soil, lawns, growing flowers and vegetables, watering, house plants, garden structures. Another useful site is www.bbc.co.uk/digin, which very simply explains all that needs to be done when growing things like tomatoes, lettuce, carrots and squash.

Natural England (www.naturalengland.org.uk/) – Natural England is here to conserve and enhance the natural environment, for its intrinsic value, the wellbeing and enjoyment of people and the economic prosperity that it brings. It provides information for students and teachers including places that schools can visit, resources for lessons, and contacts for other relevant information. Head Office: Natural England, 1 East Parade, Sheffield, S1 2ET. Tel: 0845 600 3078. Fax: 0300 060 1622.

Heads, Teachers and Industry – this is an organisation which is attempting to link up schools and business. One of their projects is Go4it. Go4it is a leading national award for schools which demonstrate a culture of creativity, innovation and adventure for learning with a positive attitude towards risk. Go4it Manager Tracey Maude. Tel: 024 7669 8513. Email: t.maude@hti.org.uk Website: www.hti.org.uk

Learning through Landscapes (LTL) – this is the national school grounds charity and it will give help, advice and information on any aspect of the school grounds. They can offer information about good practice and possible sources of funding. They also provide legal and technical advice as well as training, and they produce books and pamphlets. This charity's work deals with all schools. Third Floor, Southside Offices, The Law Courts, Winchester, SO23 9DL. Tel: 01962 845 811. Email: member@ltl.org.uk

Health and Safety Executive – 'HSE's job is to protect people against risks to health or safety arising out of work activities'. But it is not about closing down challenge and risk. Every month there is a myth of the month to demonstrate what the health and safety executive is and is not about. Tel: 0845 345 0055. Fax: 0845 408 9566. E-mail: hse.infoline@connaught.plc.uk. Website: www.hse.gov.uk

Reading International Solidarity Centre (RISC) – they work with schools, trainers and community groups to raise the profile of global issues and promote action for sustainable development, human rights and social justice. They offer training and advice to school staff and children, in house or at the school, have a huge range of artefacts and teaching materials available on loan, a database of over 9,000 books and teaching materials and a sustainable garden to inform schools about how to set up their own garden. 35–39 London Street, Reading, UK, RG1 4PS. Tel: 0118 9586 692. Website: www.risc.org.uk.

Freecycle – the Freecycle group is open to all who want to 'reuse' their clutter rather than throwing them away. Freecycle groups match people who have things they want to get rid of with people who can use them. Their goal is to keep usable items out of landfills and to encourage community involvement in the process. The beauty of freecycle is that it is local so you don't have to travel far. It is a good source of free materials. Website: www.freecycle.org

Met Office Education – this is a useful site to help with the study of the weather, to set up experiments which demonstrate weather features, and to help children become meteorologists. Website: www.metoffice.gov.uk/education/kids/weather_station.html

Royal Horticultural Society – this is the UK's leading gardening charity advancing horticulture and promoting good gardening. They want to inform and inspire. They have a very useful website, with a wealth of information in which one can find shrubs, trees and plants for any space and an within a whole range of limitations. They have four gardens to visit in Yorkshire, Essex, Devon and Surrey (free to schools). They have publications, books and an online sale of plants. There are often campaigns to join and competitions to enter. 80 Vincent Square, London, SW1P 2PE. Tel: 0845 260 5000. Website: www.rhs.org.uk/

Plastic door strip curtain – these lightweight plastic strip curtain partitions are commonly designed to slide open and for you to move through and are very useful when wanting to keep the heat in. Available from: http://www.pvc-strip-curtain-warehouse-plastic.co.uk/

Bibliography

Aasen, W. and Waters, J. (2006) 'The New Curriculum in Wales: a new view of the child?' *Education 3–13*. 34 (2), 123–9.

Adams, S., Alexander, E., Drummond, M. J. and Moyles, J. (2004) *Inside the Foundation Stage: Recreating the Reception Year*. London: ATL.

Anning, A. (1994) 'Play and legislated curriculum. Back to basics: an alternative view', in Moyles, J.R. (ed.) *The Excellence of Play*. Buckingham: Open University Press, 67–75.

Armstrong, N. and Bray, S. (1991) 'Physical activity patterns defined by heart rate monitoring', *Archives of Disease in Childhood* 66, 245–7.

Athey, C. (2007) *Extending Thought in Young Children. A Parent–Teacher Partnership* (2nd edn) London: Sage Publications.

Avery, J. G. and Jackson, R. H. (1993) *Children and Their Accidents*. London: Edward Arnold.

Bako-Biro, Zs., Kochhar, N., Clements-Croome, D. J., Awbi, H. B., and Williams, M. (2008) *Ventilation rates in schools and pupil performance using computerised assessment tests. Indoor Air*, Paper ID: 880, Copenhagen, Denmark.

Ball, C. (1994) *Start Right: The Importance of Early Learning*. London: The Royal Society for the Encouragement of Arts, Manufactures and Commerce.

Ball, D. (2004) 'Policy issues and risk benefit trade-offs of "safer surfacing" for children's playgrounds' in Accident Analysis and Prevention. 36, 661–70.

Barbour, A. (1999) 'The impact of playground design on the play behaviors of children with differing levels of physical competence', *Early Childhood Research Quarterly* 14(1), 75–98.

Barrett, G. (1986) *Starting School: An Evaluation of the Experience*. London: Assistant Masters and Mistresses Association.

Bartholomew, L. (1996) 'Working in a team', in Robson, S. and Smedley, S. (eds) *Education in Early Childhood*, 47–55. London: David Fulton Publishers.

Bates, B. (1996) 'Like rats in a rage', *The Times Educational Supplement* 2, 20 September, 11.

Bayley, R. and Broadbent, L. (2008) 'Child-initiated learning and developing children's talk', in Featherstone, S. and Featherstone, P. *Like Bees, not Butterflies: Child-initiated Learning in the Early Years*. London: A and C Black Publishers Limited.

BBC (2009) http://www.bbc.co.uk/digin (accessed 28.1.09).

Bee, H. and Boyd, D. (2006) *The Developing Child* (11th edn). New Jersey: Pearson Education.

Benjamin, S. (2003) 'Gender and special educational needs', in Skelton, C. and Francis, F. *Boys and Girls in the Primary Classroom*. Maidenhead: Open University Press, 98–122.

Bennett, N. and Kell, J. (1989) *A good start? Four year olds in infants schools*. London: Simon & Schuster Education.

Bennett, N., Wood, L. and Rogers, S. (1997) *Teaching Through Play. Teachers' Thinking and Classroom Practice*. Buckingham: Open University Press.

Berger, K. S. (2007) 'Update on bullying at school', *Developmental Review*, 27, 90–126.

Bergard, R. (1995) *Building for Children: The Frankfurt Nursery Building Programme*. Lecture given at the Royal Institute of British Architects, 4 December.

Betram, T. and Pascal, C. (2002) *Early Years Education: An International Perspective*. London: QCA and NFER.

Bilton, H. (1989) *The Development and Significance of the Nursery Garden and Outdoor Play*. Unpublished MA dissertation, University of Surrey.

Bilton, H. (1993) 'The nursery class garden – problems associated with working in the outdoor environment and their possible solutions', *Early Child Development and Care*, 93, 15–33.

Bilton, H. (1994) 'The nursery class garden: designing and building an outdoor environment for young children', *Early Years* 14(2), 34–7.

Bilton, H. (2002) *Outdoor Play in the Early Years*. London: David Fulton Publishers.

Bilton, H (2004a) *Physical Development. Study Topic 12*. Buckingham: The Open University.

Bilton, H. (2004b) *Playing Outside. Activities, Ideas and Inspiration for the Early Years*. London: David Fulton Publishers.

Bilton, H. (2004c) 'Movement as a vehicle for learning', in Miller, L. and Devereux, J. (eds) *Supporting Children's Learning in the Early Years*. London: David Fulton Publishers.

Bilton, H., James, K., Marsh, J., Wilson, A. and Woonton, M. (2005) *Learning Outdoors. Improving the Quality of Young Children's Play Spaces*. London: David Fulton Publishers.

Bird, W. (2009) 'Natural Health Service', in *The National Trust Magazine*, Spring. London: The National Trust, 20–3.

Blackstone, T. (1971) *A Fair Start. The Provision of Pre-School Education*. London: Allen Lane The Penguin Press.

Blair, S. N. and Connelly, J. C. (1996) 'How much physical activity should we do? The case for moderate amounts and intensities of physical activity', *Research Quarterly for Exercise and Sport*, 67(2), 196–205.

Blakemore, S. J. and Frith, U. (2005) *The Learning Brain. Lessons for Education*. Oxford: Blackwell Publishing.

Blatchford, P. (1989) *Playtime in the Primary School. Problems and Improvements*. Windsor: NFER-Nelson.

Blatchford, P. (1998) 'The state of play in schools', *Child Psychology and Psychiatry Review*, 3, 2, 58–67.

Blenkin, G. M. and Whitehead, M. (1988) 'Creating a context for development', in Blenkin, G. M. and Kelly, A. V. (eds) *Early Childhood Education. A Developmental Curriculum*. London: Paul Chapman Publishing, 32–60.

Blurton-Jones, N. (1967) 'An ethological study of some aspects of social behaviour of children in nursery school', in Morris, D., *Primate Ethology*. London: Weidenfeld and Nicolson, 347–68.

BMA (British Medical Association) (2005) *Preventing Childhood Obesity. A Report from the BMA Board of Science*. London: British Medical Association.

Board of Education (1905) *Reports on Children Under Five Years of Age in Public Elementary Schools by Women Inspectors of the Board of Education*. London: HMSO.

Board of Education (1912) *Statistics*. London: HMSO, Table 3(b).

Board of Education (1936) *Nursery Schools and Nursery Classes*. London: HMSO.

Boorman, P. (1988) 'The contributions of physical activity to development in the early years', in Blenkin, G. M. and Kelly, A. V. (eds) *Early Childhood Education. A Developmental Curriculum*. London: Paul Chapman Publishing, 231–50.

Booth, R. (2008) 'How we loved the open-air school', *Flashback* Issue 180, July 28, 3.

Boulton, M. (1992) 'Participating in playground activities', *Educational Research* 34, (3) 167–82.

Bradburn, E. (1976) *Margaret McMillan. Framework and Expansion of Nursery Education*. Redhill: Denholm House Press.

Brearley, M. (ed.) (1969) *Fundamentals in the First School*. Oxford: Blackwell.

Brown, J. G. and Burger, C. (1984) 'Playground designs and preschool children's behaviors', *Environment and Behavior* 16(5), 599–626.

Bruce, T. (1987) *Early Childhood Education*. London: Hodder & Stoughton.

Bruce, T. (2005) *Early Childhood Education* (3rd edn). London: Hodder Arnold.

Building Bulletin 101 (2006) *Ventilation of School Buildings. Regulations, Standards, Design Guidance*, 2006 July, ISBN 011-2711642.

Burstall, E. (1997) 'Unappreciated and underpaid', *Times Educational Supplement* 2, 14 February, 13.

Calfas, K. J. and Taylor, W. C. (1994) 'Effect of physical activity on psychological variables in adolescents', *Paediatric Exercise Science* 6, 406–23.

Campbell, J. and Neill, S. R. St J. (1992) *Teacher Time and Curriculum Manageability at KS1*. London: AMMA.

Carruthers, E. (2007) 'Children's outdoor experiences. A sense of adventure', in Moyles, J., *Early Years Foundations Meeting the Challenge*. Maidenhead: McGraw-Hill Education.

Children's Play Council (2003) 'Grumpy grown ups stop children play reveals Playday research', news story, 7 August 2003, http://www.ncb.org.uk/cpc/news_story.asp?id=116.

Clark, M. M. (1988) *Children Under Five: Educational Research and Evidence*. London: Gordon and Breach.

Cleave, S. and Brown, S. (1989) *Four Year Olds in School. Meeting their Needs*. Slough: National Foundation for Educational Research.

Cleave, S. and Brown, S. (1991) *Early to School. Four Year Olds in Infant Classes*. Windsor: NFERNELSON Publishing.

Clements-Croome, D. J. (2008) http://www.reading.ac.uk/about/newsandevents/releases/PR18842.asp (accessed 27.12.08).

Clements-Croome, D. J., Awbi, H. B., Bako-Biro, Zs., Kochhar, N. and Williams, M. (2008) 'Ventilation rates in schools', *Building and Environment The International Journal of Building Science and its Applications* 43, 3, 362–7.

Cohen, D. (1993) *The Development of Play* (2nd edn). London: Croom Helm.

Cole, E. S. (1990) 'An experience in Froebel's garden', *Childhood Education* 67(1), 18–21.

Connolly, P. (2003) 'Gendered and gendering spaces. Playgrounds in the early years', in Skelton, C. and Francis, B., *Boys and Girls in the Primary Classroom*. Maidenhead: Open University Press, 113–33.

Connor, K. (1989) 'Aggression: is it in the eye of the beholder?', *Play and Culture* 2, 213–17.

Cook, B. and Heseltine, P. (1999) *Assessing Risk on Children's Playgrounds* (2nd edn). Birmingham: RoSPA.

Cooper, M. and Johnson, A. (1991) *Poisonous Plants and Fungi – An Illustrated Guide*. London: HMSO.

Costello, P. J. M. (2000) *Thinking Skills and Early Childhood Education*. London: David Fulton Publishers.

Cowgate (2008) http://www.cowgateunder5s.co.uk (accessed 30.12.08).

Cratty, B. J. (1986) *Perceptual and Motor Development in Infants and Children* (3rd edn). New Jersey: Prentice Hall.

Cullen, J. (1993) 'Preschool children's use and perceptions of outdoor play areas', *Early Child Development and Care* 89, 45–56.

Cunningham, H. (2006) *The Invention of Childhood*. London: BBC Books.

Cusden, P. E. (1938) *The English Nursery School*. London: Kegan Paul, Trench, Trubner.

Darling, J. (1994) *Child-centred Education and their Critics*. London: Paul Chapman.

Davies, J. (1991) 'Children's adjustment to nursery class: how to equalise opportunities for a successful experience', *School Organisation* 11(3), 255–62.

Davies, J. and Brember, I. (1994) 'Morning and afternoon nursery sessions: can they be equally effective in giving children a positive start to school?', *International Journal of Early Years Education* 2(2), 43–53.

Davies, M. (1995) *Helping Children to Learn Through a Movement Perspective*. London: Hodder & Stoughton.

Davies, M. (1997) 'The teacher's role in outdoor play. Preschool teachers' beliefs and practices', *Journal of Australian Research in Early Childhood Education*, 110–20.

de Lissa, L. (1939) *Life in the Nursery School*. London: Longmans, Green and Co.

Department for Transport (2002) *National Travel Survey:1999–2001 Update*. London: Transport Statistics, Department for Transport.

Department for Transport (2006) *National Travel Survey: 2005*. London: Transport Statistics, Department for Transport.

DES (Department of Education and Science) (1989) *Aspects of Primary Education. The Education of Children Under Five. Her Majesty's Inspectorate*. London: HMSO.

DfCSF (Department for Children, Schools and Families) (2008) (May revised) *The Early Years Foundation Stage*. Nottingham: DfCSF Publications.

DfCSF (2009) *Independent Review of the Primary Curriculum: Final Report*. Nottingham: DfCSF Publications.

DfEE (Department for Education and Employment) (1996) *Schools' Environmental Assessment Method (SEAM)*. London: The Stationery Office.

DfES (Department for Education and Skills) (2004) *Every Child Matters: Change for Children*. London: DfES.

DfES (2006) *Learning Outside the Classroom Manifesto*. Nottingham: DfES Publications.

Dillon, J., Rickinson, M., Teamey, K., Morris, M., Choi, M. Y., Sanders, D. and Benefield, P. (2006) 'The value of outdoor learning: evidence from research in the UK and elsewhere', *School Science Review*, March, 87 (320), 107–11.

Dockrell, J.D. (2009) *The Learning Environment. How Classroom Acoustics Affect Learning and Attainment*. Lecture: University of Reading, Institute of Education 30.4.09.

Dombey, H. (1993) ' "And, they went, they lived there after": making written narrative accessible in the nursery class to children whose cultures do not embrace it', *Changing Education* 1(1), 141–53.

Donaldson, M. (1978) *Children's Minds*. London: Collins/Fontana.

Dowling, M. (1992) *Education 3–5* (2nd edn). London: Paul Chapman Publishing.

Dudek, M. (1996) *Kindergarten Architecture*. London: Chapman and Hall.

Dunn, J. and Hughes, C. (2001) ' "I got some swords and you're dead": violent, fantasy, antisocial behaviour, friendship, and moral sensibility in young children', *Child Development*, 72(2) 491–505.

Dunn, S. and Morgan, V. (1987) 'Nursery and infant school play patterns: sex-related differences', *British Educational Research Journal* 13(3), 271–81.

Dunne, E. and Bennett, N. (1990) *Talking and Learning in Groups*. London: Routledge.

Dyson, J. (2009) 'Battling for design', http://www.dyson.co.il/nav/inpageframe.asp?id=DYSON/HIST/BATTLE (accessed 7.5.09).

ECA (1994) *Planning the Location of Centre-based Early Childhood Services*. Queensland: ECA (QLD Branch).

ECA (2004) *Physical Environments for Centre-based Early Childhood Services*. Queensland: Early Childhood Association (Queensland Branch).

Eccles, R. (2002) 'An explanation for the seasonality of acute upper respiratory tract viral infections', *Acta Otolaryngologica* (Stockholm) 122: 183–91, http://www.cardiff.ac.uk/biosi/subsites/cold/commoncold.html (accessed 27.12.08).

Eccles, R. (2008) *General Common Cold Information*, http://www.cardiff.ac.uk/biosi/subsites/cold/commoncold.html (accessed 27.12.08).

Edgington, M. (2003) *The Great Outdoors. Developing Children's Learning through Outdoor Provision* (2nd edn). London: British Association for Early Childhood Education.

Edgington, M (2004) *The Foundation Stage Teacher in Action. Teaching 3, 4 and 5 year olds*. London; Paul Chapman Publishing.

Edwards, L. (1992) 'Osteoporosis: the fight for recognition', *Nestlé Worldview* 1(1), 8.

Endocrine Society, The (2008) 'OR46-4: Adequate vitamin D may help us live longer', http://www.endo-society.org/media/ENDO-07/research/Adequate-vitamin-D.cfm (accessed 28.12.08).

Esbensen, S. B. (1987) *The Early Childhood Playground. An Outdoor Classroom*. Ypsilanti, MI: The High/Scope Press.

Evans, J. (1989) *Children at Play Life in the School Playground*. Victoria: Deaken University Press.

Fabian, H. (2005) 'Outdoor learning environments: easing the transition from the Foundation Stage to Key Stage 1', *Education 3–13*, June, 4–8.

Fagen, R. (1981) *Animal Play Behaviour*. Oxford: Oxford University Press.

Fisher, J. (1996) *Starting from the Child?* Buckingham: Open University Press.

Fletcher, V. (2008) 'Sunshine Key to Long Life', *Daily Express* (24.6.08). London: Daily Express.

Forest Schools (2009) 'What are forest schools?', http://www.forestschools.com/what-are-forest-schools.php (accessed 17.5.09).

Formby, L. (2007) *Go4it Today's Pupils Tomorrow's Innovators*. Coventry: Heads, Teachers and Industry. (HTI).

Fox, K. (1996) 'Physical activity promotion and the active school', in Armstrong, N. (ed.) *New Directions in Physical Education. Change and Innovation*. London: Cassell, 94–109.

Francis, B. (1998) *Power Plays: Primary School Children's Construction of Gender, Power and Adult Work*. Stoke-on-Trent: Trentham Books.

Frost, J. L. (1986) 'Children's playgrounds', in Fein, G. and Rivkin, M. (eds) *The Young Child at Play – Reviews of Research*, Vol. 4. Washington, DC: National Association for the Education of Young Children.

Frost, J. L. (1992) 'Reflections on research and practice in outdoor play environments', *Dimensions* 20(3), 6–10.

Frost, J. L. and Campbell, S. D. (1985) 'Equipment choices of primary aged children on conventional and creative playgrounds', in Frost, J. L. and Sunderlin, S. (eds) *When Children Play. Proceedings of the International Conference on Play and Play Environments*. Wheaton, MD: Association for Childhood Education International, 89–101.

Gallahue, D. L. (1989) *Understanding Motor Development. Infants, Children, Adolescents* (2nd edn). Indianapolis: Benchmark Press.

Gallahue, D. L. (1993) *Developmental Physical Education for Today's Children*. IA: Wm. C. Brown Communications, Inc.

Gallahue, D. L. and Donnelly, F. C. (2003) *Developmental Physical Education for All Children*. IL. Champaign: HumanKinestics.

Gallahue, D. L. and Ozmun, J. C. (2005) *Understanding Motor Development: Infants, Children, Adolescents, Adults* (6th edn). New York: McGraw-Hill Companies.

Galton, M., Simon, B., Croll, P. (1980) *Inside the Primary Classroom*. London: Routledge and Kegan Paul.

Gater, M. (2009) 'A case study of the impact of the outdoor learning environment on pupil involvement in the foundation stage', dissertation in part fulfillment of the MA in Teaching Learning, University of Reading.

Gilkes, J. (1987) *Developing Nursery Education*. Milton Keynes: Open University Press.

Gill, T. (2007) *No Fear. Growing Up in a Risk Averse Society*. London: Calouste Gulbenkian Foundation.

Goddard-Blyth, S. (2000) 'First steps to the most important ABC', *Times Educational Supplement*, 7 January, 23.

Goldstein, J. H. (1994) *Toys and Play and Child Development*. Cambridge: Cambridge University Press.

Great Britain. House of Commons, Education, Science and Arts Committee (1988) *Educational Provision for the Under Fives: First Report from the Education, Science and Arts Committee, session 1988–9, II*. London: HMSO.

Gruber, J. J. (1986) 'Physical activity and self-esteem development in children: a meta analysis', *American Academy of Physical Education Papers* 19, 30–48.

Guldberg, H. (2009) *Reclaiming Childhood Freedom and Play in an Age of Fear*. London: Routledge.

Gura, P. (1992) *Exploring Learning: Young Children and Blockplay*. London: Paul Chapman.

Gwaltney J. M., Moskalski P .B., and Hendley J. O. (1980) 'Interruption of experimental rhinovirus transmission', *The Journal of Infectious Diseases* 142, 811–15.

Haines, J. S. (2000) 'What's in the garden? A comparative study of philosophies in English and Danish nursery settings and their influence on the use of the outside environment'. Unpublished Advanced Diploma, Homerton College.

Hall, N. and Abbott, L. (1992) *Play in the Primary Curriculum*. London: Hodder Arnold.

Halliday, J., McNaughton, S., Glynn, T. (1985) 'Influencing children's choice of play activities at kindergarten through teacher participation', *New Zealand Journal of Educational Studies* 20(1), 48–58.

Hanks, P. (ed.)(1986) *The Collins English Dictionary*. London: Collins.

Harris, P (2000) *The Work of the Imagination*. Oxford: Blackwell.

Hart, R. (1978) 'Sex differences in the use of outdoor space', in Sprung, B. (ed.) *Perspectives on Non-Sexist Early Childhood Education*, 101–9. New York: Teachers' College Press.

Hartley, D. (1993) *Understanding the Nursery School*. London: Cassell.

Hastings, N. and Wood, C. K. (2001) *Re-organising Primary Classroom Learning*. Buckingham: Open University Press.

Health Education Authority (HEA) (1998) *Young and Active?* London: Health Education Authority.

Health and Safety Executive (2009) http://www.hse.gov.uk/myth/index.htm (accessed 06.03.09).

Henniger, M. L. (1985) 'Preschool children's play behaviors in an indoor and outdoor environment', in Frost, J. L. and Sunderlin, S. (eds) *When Children Play. Proceedings of the International Conference on Play and Play Environments*. Wheaton, MD: Association for Childhood Education International, 145–9.

Henniger, M. L. (1993/4) 'Enriching the outdoor play experience', *Childhood Education* V, 87–90.

Heschong, L., Elzeyadi, I. and Knecht, C. (2002) Re-Analysis Report: Daylighting in Schools, Additional Analysis. Task 2.2.1 through 2.2.5. Sacramento: California Energy Commission, http://www.newbuildings.rog.pier (accessed 14.02.02).

Hetherington, E. M. (ed) *Handbook of Child Psychology. Vol IV Socialization, Personality and Social Development*. New York: Wiley, 693–77.

Hill, P. (1978) *Play Spaces for Preschoolers: Design Guidelines for the Development of Preschool Play Spaces in Residential Environments*. Ottawa, Canada: Central Mortage and Housing Corporation, National Office.

Hillman, M., Adams, J. and Whitelegg, J. (1990) *'One False Move ...' A Study of Children's Independent Mobility*. London: PSI Publishing.

Hilsum, S. and Cane, B. S. (1971) *The Teacher's Day*. Slough: National Foundation for Educational Research.

Holland, P. (2003) *We Do Not Play With Guns Here: War, Weapon and Superhero Play in the Early Years*. Maidenhead: Open University Press.

Holmes, B. M. and Davies, M. G. (1937) *Organized Play in the Infant and Nursery School*. London: University of London Press.

HTI Heads, teachers and industry (2009) *Go4it Information Pack*. Coventry: HTI, http://www.hti. org.uk/pdfs/go/300909%20version_WEB.pdf (accessed 25.1.10).

Hutt, C. (1972) *Males and Females*. Harmondsworth: Penguin Education.

Hutt, S. J., Tyler, S., Hutt, C. and Christopherson, H. (1989) *Play, Exploration and Learning: A Natural History of the Pre-School*. London: Routledge.

IOTF (International Obesity Taskforce) (2002) *Obesity in Europe: The Case for Action*. London: International Obesity Taskforce.

Isaacs, S. (1932) *The Nursery Years*. London: Routledge and Kegan Paul.

Isaacs, S. (1954) *The Educational Value of the Nursery School*. London: The Nursery School Association.

Jago, R. (2002) 'Testing a model for the promotion of pre-pubescent children's physical activity: the effects of school based interventions'. PhD University of Reading.

Johnson, J. E., Christie, J. F. and Yawkey, T. D. (1987) *Play and Early Childhood Development*. Glenview, IL: Scott Foresman, and Company.

Jones, C. (1996) 'Physical education at Key Stage 1', in Armstrong, N. (ed.) *New Directions in Physical Education. Change and Innovation*. London: Cassell, 48–61.

Jones, D. (2007) 'Cotton wool kids: releasing the potential for children to take risks and innovate', *HTI Issues 7*. Coventry: HTI.

Jordan, E. (1995) 'Fighting boys and fantasy play: the construction of masculinity in the early years of school', *Gender and Education 7*(1), 69–86.

Katz, L. G. and Chard, S. C. (1989) *Engaging Children's Minds: The Project Approach*. New Jersey: Ablex Publishing.

Katz, L. G. (1995) *Talks with Teachers of Young Children*. New Jersey: Ablex Publishing Corporation.

Kitson, N. (1994) ' "Please Miss Alexander, will you be the robber?" Fantasy play: a case for adult intervention', in Moyles, J. R. (ed.) *The Excellence of Play*. Buckingham: Open University Press, 88–98.

Klein, R. (1997) 'Let the children decide', *The Times Educational Supplement* 2, 31 October, 12.

Kostelnik, M. J., Whiten, A. P., Stein, L. C. (1986) 'Living with he-man: managing Superhero fantasy play', *Young Children* 41(4), 3–9.

Kounin, J. S. (1970) *Discipline and Group Management in Classrooms*. New York: Holt, Rinehart and Wilson.

Kritchensky, S., Prescott, E. and Walling, L. (1977) *Planning Environments for Young Children: Physical Space*. Washington DC: National Association for the Education of young children.

Lally, M. (1991) *The Nursery Teacher in Action*. London: Paul Chapman Publishing.

Lally, M. and Hurst, V. (1992) 'Assessment in nursery education: a review of approaches', in Blenkin, G. M. and Kelly, A. V. (eds) *Assessment in Early Childhood Education*. London: Paul Chapman Publishing, 69–92.

Lancy, D. F. (2007) 'Accounting for variability in mother-child play', *American Anthropologist*. 109 (2): 273–84.

Lasenby, M. (1990) *The Early Years. A Curriculum for Young Children. Outdoor Play*. London: Harcourt Brace Jovanovich.

Lepkowska, D. (2008) 'In your own time' (Stealth Learning), *Guardian* (17.06.08), 1.

Lindberg, L. and Swedlow, R. (1985) *Young Children: Exploring and Learning*. Boston, MA: Allyn and Bacon.

Lindon, J. (1997) *Working with Young Children* (3rd edn). London: Hodder and Stoughton.

Macintyre, C. (2001) *Enhancing Learning through Play*. London: David Fulton Publishers.

Mackett, R., Brown, B., Gong, Y., Kitazawa, K. and Paskins, J. (2007) 'Setting children free: children's independent movement in the local environment', *UCL Working Papers Series*. University College London Centre for Advanced Spatial Analysis. Paper 118-March: 1–13.

Manning, K. and Sharp, A. (1977) *Structuring Play in the Early Years at School*. London: Ward Lock Educational.

Martin, C. (1974) *The Edwardians*. London: Wayland Publishers Limited.

Matthews, J. (1988) 'The young child's early representation and drawing', in Blenkin, G. M. and Kelly, A. V. (eds) *Early Childhood Education. A Developmental Curriculum*. London: Paul Chapman Publishing, 162–183.

Matthews, J. (1994) *Helping Children to Draw and Paint in Early Childhood*. London: Hodder and Stoughton.

Matthews, J. (2003) *Drawing and Painting Children and Visual Representation*. London: Paul Chapman Publishing.

Maude. P. (2008) ' "How do I do this better?" From movement development to physical education', in D. Whitebread and P. Coltman, *Teaching and Learning in the Early Years* (3rd edn), London: Routledge, 251–68.

Maynard, T. and Waters, J. (2006) *Learning in the Outdoor Environment: A Missed Opportunity?* Paper presented at the 16th EECERA conference, Reykjavik, Iceland.

McAuley, H. and Jackson, P. (1992) *Educating Young Children. A Structural Approach*. London: David Fulton Publishers.

Mcintyre, C. (2001) *Enhancing Learning Through Play*. London: David Fulton.

McLean, S. V. (1991) *The Human Encounter: Teachers and Children Living Together in Preschools*. London: Falmer Press.

McMillan, M. (1919) 'Nursery schools', *The Times Educational Supplement*, 13 February, 81.

McMillan, M. (1930) *The Nursery School*. London: Dent and Sons.

MacNaughton, G. (1999) 'Even pink tents have glass ceilings: crossing the gender boundaries in pretend play', in Dau, E. (ed) *Child's Play: Revisiting Play in Early Childhood Settings*. Sydney: Maclennan and Petty.

McNee, D. (1984) 'Outdoor play in the nursery – a neglected area?', *Early Years* 4(2), 16–25.

Meadows, S. and Cashdan, A. (1988) *Helping Children Learn. Contributions to a Cognitive Curriculum*. London: David Fulton Publishers.

Mercogliano, C. (2007) *In Defense of Childhood: Protecting Kids' Inner Wildness*. Boston MA: Beacon Press.

Millard, E. (1997) *Differently Literate: Boys, Girls and the Schooling of Literacy*. London: Falmer Press.

Miller, P. (1972) *Creative Outdoor Play Areas*. New Jersey: Prentice Hall.

Miller, S. (1978) 'The facilitation of fundamental motor skill learning in young children'. Unpublished doctoral dissertation. Michigan State University.

Milligan, E. (2008) 'To what extent are there gender differences in the school playground?' MA Dissertation, University of Reading.

Mohr, S. B., Garland, C. F., Gorham, E. D., Grant, W. B., and Garland, F. C. (2008) 'Could ultraviolet B irradiance and vitamin D be associated with lower incidence rates of lung cancer?' *Journal of Epidemiology and Community Health*, Jan 2008; 62: 69–74.

Mooney, A., Creeser, R. and Mooney, A. (1990) 'Children's view on teasing and fighting in junior schools', *Educational Research* 33, (2): 103–12.

Morgan, V. and Dunn, S. (1990) 'Management strategies and gender differences in nursery and infant classrooms', *Research in Education* 44, 81–91.

Moser, T. and Foyn-Bruun, E. (2006) 'Small children condemned to freeze? The pedagogical foundations of Nature and Outdoor Kindergartens in Norway', paper presented at the 16th EECERA conference, Reykjavik, Iceland.

Moss, G., Jewitt, C., Levaaic, R,. Armstrong, V., Cardini, A., and Castle, F. (2007) *The Interactive Whiteboards, Pedagogy and Pupil Performance Evaluation: an Evaluation of the Schools Whiteboard Expansion (SWE) Project: London Challenge (Research Report RR 816)*. London: DfES.

Mostofsky, D. L. and Zaichkowsky, L. D. (2006) *Medical and Psychological Aspects of Sport and Exercise*. WV US: Inc Fitness Information Technology.

Moyles, J. (1989) *Just Playing? The Role and Status of Play in Early Childhood Education*. Milton Keynes: Open University Press.

Moyles, J. R. (1992) *Organizing for Learning in the Primary Classroom*. Buckingham: Open University Press.

Moyles, J. (2008) 'Empowering children and adults: play and child-initiated learning', in Featherstone, S. and Featherstone, P. *Like Bees, not Butterflies: Child-initiated Learning in the Early Years*. London: A and C Black Publishers Limited.

Murphy, P. (2002) 'Gendered learning and achievement', in Pollard, A (ed.) *Readings for Reflective Teaching*. London: Continuum, 323–6.

Nash, B. (1981) 'The effects of classroom spatial organisation on four- and five-year-old children's learning', *British Journal of Educational Psychology* 51,144–55.

Naylor, H. (1985) 'Outdoor play and play equipment', *Early Child Development and Care* 19, 109–30.

Neill, S. (1982) 'Open plan or divided space in pre-school', *Education* 3–13 10, Autumn, 45–8.

Neumark, V. (1997) 'Father and son reunion', *The Times Educational Supplement* 2, 13 June, 6.

Noble, C., Brown, J. and Murphy, J. (2001) *How to Raise Boys' Achievement*. London: David Fulton Publishers.

OMEP UK (World Organisation for Early Childhood Education) (2001) *Playing to Learn – the Foundation Stage*. Wolverhampton: OMEP UK.

Opie, I. and Opie, P. (1969) *Children's Games in Street and Playground*. Oxford: Claredon Press.

O'Sullivan, J. (1997) 'A bad way to educate boys', *The Independent, Education+*, 3 April, 8–9.

Ouvry, M. (2003) *Exercising Muscles and Minds: Outdoor Play and the Early Years Curriculum*. London: The National Early Years Network.

Overholser, K. M. and Pellerin, D. M. (1980) *An In-service Program in the Area of Children's Outdoor Gross Motor Playground Considerations, Design and Apparati, for the National Association for the Education of Young Children's 1980 Conference Attendees*. Conference paper,

Annual meeting of the National Association for the Education of Young Children, San Francisco, 21–4 November.

Owen, G. (1928, rev. edn.) *Nursery School Education*. London: Methuen.

Owens, P. (2004) 'Researching the development of children's environmental values in the early school years', *Researching Primary Geography* 1, August, 64–76.

Pahl, K. (1999) *Transformations: Meaning Making in Nursery Education*. Stoke on Trent: Trentham Books.

Paley, V. G. (1984) *Boys and Girls: Superheroes in the Doll Corner*. Chicago: The University of Chicago Press.

Paley, V. G. (1986) 'On listening to what children say', *Harvard Educational Review* 56(2), 122–31.

Palmer, S. (2006) *Toxic Childhood. How the Modern World is Damaging Our Children and What We Can Do About It*. London: Orion.

Parker, C. (2008) ' "This is the best day of my life! And I'm not leaving here until it's time to go home!" The outdoor learning environment', in Whitebread, D. and Coltman, P. *Teaching and Learning in the Early Years*. Abingdon: Routledge.

Parkin, J. (1997) 'Boys and girls come out to play', *The Times Educational Supplement*, Extra,13 June, VI.

Pascal, C., Bertram. T. and Ramsden, F. (1997) 'The effective early learning research project: reflections upon the action during phase 1', *Early Years* 17(2), 40–7.

Pellegrini, A. (1988) 'Elementary-school children's rough-and-tumble play and social competence', *Developmental Psychology* 24 (6): 802–6.

Pellegrini, A. D. (1991) *Applied Child Study*. New Jersey: Lawrence Erlbaum Associates.

Pellegrini, A. D. (2005) *Recess: Its Role in Education and Development*. Mahwah NJ: Erlbaum.

Pellegrini, A. D. and Smith, P. K. (1998) 'Physical activity play: the nature and function of a neglected aspect of play and social competence', *Developmental Psychology* 69 (3) 577–98.

Plaisted, L. (1909) *The Early Education of Children*. Oxford: Oxford University at the Clarendon Press.

Ploughman, N. (2008) 'Exercise is brain food: the effects of physical activity on cognitive function', Developmental Neurohabilitation, July–September, 11(3), 236–40.

Pollard, A. (2008) *Reflective Teaching*. London: Continuum International Publishing Group.

Pollard, A. and Tann, S. (1987) *Reflective Teaching in the Primary School*. London: Cassell.

Porter, H. (2005) 'Take the playground challenge', *Child Education*. London: Scholastic Publications. September, 33–6.

Postman, N. (1982) *The Disappearance of Childhood*. London: Allen.

Pound, L. (1987) 'The nursery tradition', *Early Child Development and Care* 28, 79–88.

Pugh, A. (2005) *Climbing Higher. The Welsh Assembly Government Strategy for Sport and Physical Activity*. Cardiff: Sports Policy Unit.

QCA (2000) *Curriculum Guidance for the Foundation Stage*. London: Qualifications and Curriculum Authority.

Ranzoni, P. (1973) *Considerations in Developing an Outside Area for Schools/Centers for Young Children*. Orano: University of Maine.

Richards, R. (1983) 'Learning through science', in Blenkin, G. M. and Kelly, A. V. (eds) *The Primary Curriculum in Action*. London: Harper and Row.

Roberts, R. (1980) *Out to Play: The Middle Years of Childhood*. Aberdeen: Aberdeen University Press.

Robson, M. and Hunt, K. (1999) 'An innovative approach to involving parents in the education of their early years children', *International Journal of Early Years Education* 7(2), 185–93.

Robson, S. (1996) 'The physical environment', in Robson, S. and Smedley, S. (eds) *Education in Early Childhood*. London: David Fulton Publishers, 153–71.

Rogers, S. and Evans, J. (2008) *Inside Role-Play in Early Childhood Education. Researching Young Children's Perspectives*. Abingdon: Routledge.

Ross, C. and Ryan, A. (1990) *'Can I stay in today, Miss?' Improving the School Playground*. Stoke on Trent: Trentham Books.

Rubin, K., Fein, G. and Vandenberg, B. (1983) 'Play', in Hetherington, E. M. (ed.) *Handbook of Child Psychology. Vol IV Social Development*. New York: Wiley, 693–774.

Salmon, M. (2009) 'Brainsex – a new way of learning for girls and boys', *Headteacher Update Magazine* May, summer 1, 17–18.

Sammons, P., Sylva, K., Melhuish, E. C., Siraj-Blatchford, I., Taggart, B. and Elliot, K. (2004) *Measuring the Impact of Pre-school on Children's Progress over the Pre-school Period. (The Effective Provision of Pre-School Education (EPPE) Project, Technical Paper)*. London: Institute of Education.

Seaborne, M. (1971) *The English School: Its Architecture and Organisation 1370–1870*. London: Routledge.

Schafer, M. and Smith, P. K. (1996) 'Teachers' perception of play fighting and real fighting in primary school', *Educational Research* 38 (2) 173–81.

Shackell, A., Butler, N., Doyle, P. and Ball, D. (2008) *Design for Play: A Guide to Creating Successful Play Spaces*. Nottingham: DfCSF.

Sheridan, M. D. (2008) *From Birth to Five Years Children's Developmental Progress* (3rd edn). Abingdon: Routledge.

Shield, B. M. and Dockrell, J. E. (2008) 'The effects of environmental and classroom noise on the academic attainments of primary school children', *The Journal of Acoustical Society of America* Vol 123, 1, 133–44.

Singer, D. and Singer, J. (1990) *The House of Make-Believe: Play and the Developing Imagination*. Cambridge, MA: Harvard University Press.

Siraj-Blatchford, I. (1999) 'Early childhood pedagogy: practice, principles and research', in Mortimore, P. (ed) *Understanding Pedagogy: and its Impact on Learning*. London: Paul Chapman.

Siraj-Blatchford, I. (2007) 'Looking closely at teaching. Promoting adult pedagogy and child learning in the EYFS'. *The Early Years Foundation Stage: Views from near and far*. Conference 23.1.07. Oxford University Department of Education.

Siraj-Blatchford, I. and Sylva, K. (2004) 'Researching pedagogy in English pre-schools'. 30 (5) 713–30.

Skelton, C. and Francis, F. (2003) *Boys and Girls in the Primary Classroom*. Maidenhead: Open University Press.

Smilansky, S. and Shefatya, L. (1990) *Facilitating Play: A Medium for Promoting Cognitive, Socio-Emotional and Academic Development in Young Children*. Gaithersburg, MD: Psychosocial and Educational Publications.

Smith, F. (1982) *Writing and the Writer*. London: Heinemann Educational Books.

Smith, P. K. and Connelly, K. J. (1981) *The Ecology of Pre-School Behaviour*. Cambridge: Cambridge University Press.

Sports Council (1992) *Allied Dunbar National Fitness Survey. A Summary*. London: The Sports Council and the Health Education Authority.

Steedman, C. (1990) *Childhood, Culture and Class in Britain: Margaret McMillan, 1860–1931*. London: Virago.

Stephenson, A. (2002) 'Opening up the outdoors: exploring the relationship between the indoor and outdoor environments of a centre', *European Early Childhood Research Journal,* 10, 1, 29–38.

Stevenson, C. (1987) 'The young four year old in nursery and infant classes: challenges and constraints', in *Four Year Olds in School. Policy and Practice.* Slough: NFER/SCDC, 34–43.

Stewart, D. (1989) 'Forward role', *The Times Educational Supplement,* 21 April, B2.

Stine, S. (1997) *Landscapes for Learning: Creating Outdoor Environments for Children and Youth.* New York: Wiley.

Stratton, G. (1999) 'A preliminary study of children's physical activity in one urban primary school playground. Differences by sex and season', *Journal of Sport Pedagogy* 5 (2), 71–81.

Sugden, D. and Wright, H. (1996) 'Curricular entitlement and implementation for all children', in Armstrong, N. (ed.) *New Directions in Physical Education. Change and Innovation.* London: Cassell, 110–30.

Sylva, K., Roy, C., Painter, M. (1980) *Child Watching at Playgroup and Nursery School.* London: Grant McIntyre.

Sylva, K., Melhuish, E., Sammons, P., Siraj-Blatchford, I. and Taggart, B. (2004) *The Effective Provision of Pre-School Education (EPPE) Project: Findings from Pre-school to End of Key Stage 1.* Nottingham: DfES. Ref: SSU/FR/2004/01.

Sylva, K., Siraj-Blatchford, I. and Taggart, B. (2006) *Assessing Quality in the Early Years.* Stoke on Trent: Trentham Books Ltd.

Szreter, R. (1964) 'The origins of full-time compulsory schooling at five', *British Journal of Educational Studies* XIII, 1.

TACTYC (2007) 'Research: reception year teachers most important for primary', TACTYC newsletter October 17.

Taylor, B. J. (1980) 'Pathways to a healthy self-concept', in Yaroke, T. D. (ed.) *The Self Concept of the Young Child.* Salt Lake City: Brigham Young Press.

Taylor, P. H., Exon, G., Holley, B. (1972) *A Study of Nursery Education.* London: Evans/Methuen Educational.

TeachersTV (2006) *Early Years In Action – The Learning Environment.* Number 227. 11 January, http://www.teachers.tv/video/227 (accessed 24.1.09).

Teets, S. T. (1985) 'Modification of play behaviors of preschool children through manipulation of environmental variables', in Frost, J. L. and Sunderlin, S. (eds) *When Children Play. Proceedings of the International Conference on Play and Play Environments.* Wheaton, MD: Association for Childhood Education International, 265–71.

Thomas, G. and Thompson, G. (2004) *A Child's Place.* London: Demos/Green Alliance.

Thorne, B. (1997) 'Children and gender constructions of difference', in Gergen, M. M. and Davies, S. N. (eds) *Towards a New Psychology of Gender.* London: Routledge, 186–96.

Thorne, B. (2002) 'How to promote co-operative relationships among children', in Pollard, A (ed) *Readings for Reflective Teaching.* London: Continuum, 318–20.

Tizard, B., Philps, J., Plewis, I. (1976a) 'Play in pre-school centres – I. Play measures and their relation to age, sex and IQ', *Journal of Child Psychology and Psychiatry* 17, 251–64.

Tizard, B., Philps, J., Plewis, I. (1976b) 'Play in pre-school centres – II. Effects on play of the child's social class and of the educational orientation of the centre', *Journal of Child Psychology and Psychiatry* 17, 265–74.

Tizard, B., Philps, J., Plewis, I. (1977) 'Staff behaviour in pre-school centres', *Journal of Child Psychology and Psychiatry* 18, 21–33.

Tovey, H. (2007) *Playing Outdoors. Spaces and Places, Risk and Challenge*. Maidenhead: Open University Press.

Trevarthen, C. (1994) *How Children Learn Before School*. Lecture Text. London: British Association for Early Childhood Education, 2 November.

Ungar, M (2007) *Too Safe for their own Good: How Risk and Responsibility Help Teens Thrive*. Toronto: McClelland and Stewart.

Van Liempd, I. (2005) Making use of space: theory meets practice, *Children in Europe* 8, 16–17.

Visser, J. G. and Greenwood, I. G. (2005) 'The effects of playground games, as agents for changing playground ethos, on playground disputes', *Education* 3–13. June 27–30.

Vogele, C. (2005) 'Education', in Kerr, J., Weitkunat, R. and Moretti, M. *ABC of Behavior Change. A Guide to Successful Disease Prevention and Health Promotion*. Philadelphia: Elsevier Churchill Livingstone.

Vygostsky, L. (1967) 'Play and its role in the mental development of the child', *Soviet Psychology*, 5(3), 6–18. (Original work published 1966).

Vygotsky, L. (1978) *Mind in Society. Development of Higher Psychological Processes*. Cambridge, MA: Harvard University Press.

Waite, S. and Rea, T. (2006) *Pedagogy or Place?: Attributed Contributions of Outdoor Learning to Creative Teaching and Learning*. Paper presented at the British Educational Research Association Annual Conference University of Warwick 6–9 September 2006, http://www/leeds.ac.uk/educol/documents/162159/htm (accessed 18.10.2007).

Walden, R. and Walkerdine, V. (1986) 'Characteristics, views and relationships in the classroom', in Burton, L. (ed.) *Girls into Maths Can Go*. London: Holt, Rinehart and Winston.

Walkerdine, V. (1996) 'Girls and boys in the classroom', in Pollard, A. (ed.) *Readings for Reflective Teaching in the Primary School*. London: Cassell, 298–300.

Walkerdine, V. and Lucey, H. (1989) *Democracy in the Kitchen: Regulating Mothers and Socialising Daughters*. London: Virago.

Walsh, P. (1991) *Early Childhood Playgrounds. Planning an Outside Learning Environment*. NSW: Pademelon Press Pty Ltd.

Walsh, P. (1993) 'Fixed equipment – a time for change', *Australian Journal of Early Childhood* 18(2), 23–9.

Walsh, P. (1998) *Best Practice Guidelines in Early Childhood Environments*. Sydney: NSW Department of Community Services.

Webb, L. (1974) *Purpose and Practice in Nursery Education*. Oxford: Blackwell.

Wells, G. (1987) *The Meaning Makers. Children Learning Language and Using Language to Learn*. London: Hodder & Stoughton.

Wetton, P. (1983) 'Some observations of interest in locomotor and gross motor activity in nursery schools', *PE Review* 6(2), 124–9.

Wetton, P. (1988) *Physical Education in the Nursery and Infant School*. London: Routledge.

Wetton, P. (1998) 'Physical development in the early years', in Siraj-Blatchford, I. (ed.) *A Curriculum Development Handbook for Early Childhood Educators*. Stoke on Trent: Trentham Books Limited.

Whalley, M. (1996) 'Working as a team', in Pugh, G. (ed.) *Contemporary Issues in the Early Years* (2nd edn). London: Paul Chapman Publishing.

Whalley, M. (1997) *Working with Parents*. London: Hodder Education.

Wheeler, O. and Earl, I. (1939) *Nursery School Education and the Re-organization of the Infant School*. London: University of London Press.

Whitbread, N. (1972) *The Evolution of the Nursery-Infant School*. London: Routledge and Kegan Paul.

Whitebread, D. (2000) *The Psychology of Teaching and Learning in the Primary School*. Abingdon: Routledge.

Whitebread, D. (2008) *Play and Learning: Psychological Perspectives*. TACTYC Conference PP. 8.11.08.

Whitebread, D. and Coltman, P. (2008) *Teaching and Learning in the Early Years* (3rd edn). Abingdon: Routledge.

Whitebread, D., Pasternak, P., Sangster, C. and Coltman, P. (2007) 'Non-verbal indicators of metacognition in young children', *Iskolakultura* 11 (12), 82–91.

Whitebread, D., Anderson, H., Coltman, P., Page, C., Pasternak, D. P. and Mehta, S. (2005) 'Developing independent learning in the early years', in *Education* 3–13, March, 40–50.

Whitebread, D., Dawkins, R., Bingham, S., Aguda, A. and Hemming, K. (2008) 'Our classroom is like a little cosy house!', in Whitebread, D. and Coltman, P., *Teaching and Learning in the Early Years*. Abingdon: Routledge.

Whitehurst, J. (2001) 'How the development of high quality outside areas for reception children can promote play and personal, social and emotional learning'. Unpublished MA dissertation, University of Hertfordshire.

Whitney, I. and Smith, P. (1993) A survey of the nature and extent of bullying schools', *Educational Research* 35, (1), 3–25.

Whyte, J. (1983) *Beyond the Wendy House: Sex Role Stereotyping in Primary Schools*. York: Longmans for Schools Council.

Williams-Siegfredsen, J. (2005) *The Competent Child: Developing Children's Skills and Confidence Using The Outdoor Environment: A Danish Perspective*. Paper presented at the British Educational Research Association Annual Conference, University of Glamorgan, 14–17 September 2005, http://www.leeds.ac.uk/educol/documents/143308.htm (accessed 18.10.07).

Wood, D. (1988) *How Children Think and Learn*. Oxford: Blackwell.

Wood, D. (1998) *How Children Think and Learn: The Social Contexts of Cognitive Development* (2nd edn). Oxford: Blackwell Publishers.

Wood, E. and Attfield, J. (1996) *Play, Learning and the Early Childhood Curriculum*. London: Paul Chapman Publishing.

Wood, L. and Bennett, N. (1997) 'The rhetoric and reality of play: teachers' thinking and classroom practice', *Early Years* 17(2), 22–7.

World Health Organisation (WHO) (1981) *Global Strategy of Health for All by the Year 2000*. Geneva: WHO.

Wragg, E. C. (1993) *Class Management*. London: Routledge.

Wragg, E. C. (1997) 'Oh Boy!', *The Times Educational Supplement* 2, 16 May, 4–5.

Wragg, E. C. and Brown. G. A. (2001a) *Questioning in the Primary School* (2nd edn). Abingdon: Routledge.

Wragg, E. C. and Brown. G. A. (2001b) *Explaining in the Primary School* (2nd edn). Abingdon: Routledge.

Yerkes, R. (1982) 'A playground that extends the classroom', Report: ERIC ED239802.

Yilmaz, S. and Bulut, Z. (2007) 'Analysis of user's characteristics of three different playgrounds in districts with different socio-economical conditions', *Building and Envrionment* 42 (10): 3455–60.

Zaichkowsky, L. D., Zaichkowsky, L. B., Martinek, T. J. (1980) *Growth and Development: The Child and Physical Activity*. London: C V Mosby.

Index